Jean —
— Merry Xmas '99

Don

Unframed Originals

Books by W. S. Merwin

Recollections by
W. S. Merwin

UNFRAMED ORIGINALS

An Owl Book
Henry Holt and Company
New York

Henry Holt and Company, Inc.
Publishers since 1866
115 West 18th Street
New York, New York 10011

Henry Holt® is a registered
trademark of Henry Holt and Company, Inc.

TOMATOES *first appeared in* Grand Street;
MARY *and* THE SKYLINE *first appeared in* Antaeus;
Excerpts from HOTEL *and* LA PIA *appeared in* The New Yorker
with the titles "A House Abroad" and "Anna";
LAURIE *first appeared in* The Iowa Review.

Library of Congress Cataloging-in-Publication Data
Merwin, W. S. (William Stanley).
Unframed originals: recollections / by W. S. Merwin. — 1st Owl
book ed.
p.   cm.
"An Owl book."
1. Merwin, W. S. (William Stanley).—Childhood and youth.
2. Poets, American—20th century—Biography.   I. Title.
PS3563.E75Z476   1994
811'.54—dc20   93-43426
[B]   CIP

ISBN 0-8050-2871-4

Henry Holt books are available for special promotions and
premiums. For details contact: Director, Special Markets.

First published in hardcover in 1982 by Atheneum.

First Owl Book Edition—1994

Printed in the United States of America
All first editions are printed on acid-free paper. ∞

1 3 5 7 9 10 8 6 4 2

FOR MY SISTER RUTH

Note

The different sections of this book were written as separate pieces, at intervals over a period of several years. Each was intended to stand by itself, but each was part of the whole enterprise; they are the product of a single impulse.

The aim was not a chronological reconstruction, but a presentation of things that originally happened in sequence but now occur in the same moment in my mind, and so have become simultaneous, like flakes of snow that have fallen from different heights into the sea.

Each of the pieces is made up of reflections of other people. The one memory in which all those lives still appear is what now unites them.

Contents

Foreword to the 1994 Edition

As most children do, I suppose, I took it for granted that the things I saw around me every day had always been just as they appeared when I saw them. That was the way they were. At the same time, I learned quite early that they had come to be from a time before, when they had been different. The contradiction, after all, survives childhood and becomes part of what we continue to think of as the present. But when I tried to inquire where things and people had come from and what they had been like before, I knew then it was like trying to fly. No one else seemed to encourage the enterprise, and again and again silence closed over it. The urge to know, and the frustration that accompanied it, continued through my childhood, and when my parents died, my efforts to find out their own stories and origins had not come to much.

They had told me odds and ends, from time to time. There were little collections of old photographs that I had not seen in my parents' lifetimes. Some were pictures of people I could not identify, and whom nobody by then would ever be able to identify. There were scraps of diaries, not journals, but simply records—visits, appointments, expenditures—most of them my mother's, for she was a careful and orderly person. Indeed, she kept notes of many things as they occurred, including telephone conversations as she listened, but she did so in a shorthand that she herself had evolved, which she declared proudly was an absolute secret and would never be read by anyone else. Even so, she destroyed almost everything of the kind, including letters. Late in life, at my persistent urging, she wrote down some sparse notes about her immediate forebears, on a half-used yellow legal pad, but she stopped after a few pages.

I think I understand something about her reserve. She had been an orphan—her own plain word for the plain fact— since she had been a small child. Both parents died when she was still virtually in her infancy. Then the grandmother who brought her up in Pittsburgh for several years in respectable poverty died, too. Then her elder brother, her only brother, Morris, took care of her out of his first wages for a few years, and he also died, in his early twenties. By that time she had prepared herself to earn a living as a secretary—and she was proud of her superlative secretarial skills. They became part of her: exact and thorough and not given to divulgence. She made it clear that she preferred not to talk about her early life, and what she remembered of it I can only guess. Its faces were gone, and she did not return physically to its scenes. Once, driving in Ohio, perhaps before I was born (I remember it only because I was told about it), she had asked my father to make a side trip to see Cheshire, the town along the river which she had not seen since she had left as a small child. When my father was driving he did not like stopping at places he had not thought of himself. He took no interest in my mother's family and as I remember the story they did not even drive through the town. She said that she had wanted to see the cemetery.

My father's feelings about his own early years included a static and somewhat adorned attachment to his image of the small village on the Allegheny River where he had been born, and only a vague interest in events or characters of those years if he was asked about them. He returned at intervals to western Pennsylvania to visit his mother and two sisters, but what they shared, and what they remembered, and indeed the other living members of his family, remained to me scarcely more than distant shadows.

I have come to see that neither of my parents was really able to talk much about their pasts. How much of that inability was innate and how much had been formed by the self-protective habits they had fashioned for themselves I cannot tell. I see now something of how isolated and anxious my parents were, both of them, and at what pains they were to persuade themselves and everyone else that they were neither of those things. I think that both of them grew out of their many fears, my mother considerably before my father, but some of the habits had become their way of being, and about matters of intimate memory they never spoke freely. It is not an uncommon fate, after all. In my twenties it occurred to me that the middle class could almost be defined by its agreement to obliterate origins. But I have come to think that every social group probably encourages the alteration or ignoring of history in order to perpetuate a more acceptable image.

When I was living in Europe, in the years after I left college, the curiosity about my parents' pasts and the places they had come from acquired a new and insistent urgency, and when I came back I tried to learn more about them. By then I saw that my parents' familiar reticence about such things was not completely hostile to my wish to know, but that it was on the side of distance and forgetting, and that the picture had faded considerably from many of the pieces of the puzzle, even for them. And I realized then and later that every one of the few relatives whom I had known while I was growing up would have been startled to the point of incredulity by the very idea that I or anyone might consider them to be subjects to write about, and that they would have resisted anything so senseless. For most of them a project of that kind would have seemed plain shocking, as though they had been told that the walls of their houses had been transparent for most of their lives.

After my parents died and I had before me all the information that I was likely to have, I was struck again, of course, by its utter inadequacy. Nevertheless, there were pieces, small and few and faded though they were, and I began to look for connections among them, to see how much of the framework might still be visible. I wanted to find out, before I forgot any more myself, what I might know by then about whatever I had managed to learn.

—W. S. Merwin
January 1994

Unframed Originals

Tomatoes

WEATHERED picket fences not much higher than my knee stood around the vegetable beds, dusty but shining, and I admired them. I would have liked to have fences like that, by the house I imagined myself living in, as I would have liked to have a boat, and a horse. I thought I might be able to make fences like that, for a garden, if I were allowed to, and if I could find the right pieces of wood somewhere. I admired the bare straight walks around the outside of the fences. It would have been hard to judge the size of the garden because the paths led through the shadows of tall bushes, and beyond the bushes, and under the trees. One path at the end disappeared among the leaves and shadows. All of that was still the garden, and I could not tell how far it went. I had never seen a garden like that. I awoke to the realization that I had not known, until then, what gardens were really like. Everything that I had heard called by that name, including the narrow bits of yard outside our kitchen window at home, with its yellow irises and its hardy asters and its one rose, fell short of this, and retreated. They were all mementos of something or apologies for something, decorations or disguises. The one I was standing in was a real garden, not a corner or a border or a circle in a lawn, or a section of something else. Where it was it was the whole place. And real things to eat grew there. I had scarcely arrived there and I did not know how long I would stay, and there was nothing for me to do in that garden. The sun shone straight down into the middle of the vegetable beds and held the leaves still. It had been summer for longer than I had known.

To the left of the beds, on the other side of the path, was a low whitewashed building with one door and one window and a morning glory vine climbing a string trellis to the eaves. I admired the building too, and thought that I would like to live, alone, in a house like that. I wanted to stay in that one. As I looked at the vegetable beds in the sunlight, with the mens' voices passing over my head, I did not know how old I was.

Yes, I knew I was nine, but that did not seem to mean what it had meant a few minutes before. Maybe I was nothing but a child who could not read or write yet, or tell time, or put on my own clothes. Or maybe I was grown up, and understood more than I had suspected, and could decide things for myself. The old man who was showing me the garden asked me how old I was and I said, "Nine," but I was sorry to pass on such worthless conventional information. I expected that he would see through it and understand that it referred to nothing at all, but he seemed pleased and surprised. Rather than leave it at that, I said I was almost ten. "Good for you," he said, and nodded, and turned to nod again, approvingly, at my father, who was standing with Uncle Port, on the path to the whitewashed house. My father did not reflect the same pleasure. He was waiting.

On his face was an expression that I had not seen before. He was displeased and impatient—that much was familiar. He appeared to have grown smaller since we had come into the garden, and to be drawing back although he was standing still and wanted the old man, and everything else there, except me, to move forward. When the old man spoke, my father's stiff smile twitched politely, vaguely. The smile had nothing

4

to do, directly, with what the old man said. I could see that my father was not going to answer. And Uncle Port, of course, did not say anything. I did not need to look, to know that he was standing there with his head on one side, and another sort of smile, gentle, pained and sad. His expression would be saying that he was sorry, and that there was nothing he could do. But he was not in a hurry.

We were all wearing white, and the whites were all different. My father's clothes were starched, and gleamed. The sun shone through his white shirt with its heavier and lighter white stripes, and showed his white undershirt and his sloping pale shoulders. Port's white clothes were dimmer, thicker, older. They looked big for him. The old man's white clothes had had everything washed out of them again and again and then they had been ironed. The shadows sank into them and were at home. I was wearing creased white shorts that must not get mussed or dirty. And white buck shoes. The old man had on a straw hat.

I did not know how old I was because none of the others knew what to say to each other, or what to do next. The old man preferred to talk to me, and my father did not want him to. I could tell that he was blaming the conversation on me. He wanted the old man to go into the whitewashed building with him and Uncle Port, while I waited outside. The old man said that if I was to be kept waiting I had to be made at home. My father, cutting across what the old man said, told me to just wait right there and not touch anything and they would not be very long. But the old man persisted. "He won't do no harm," he said. And to me, with a sweep of his hand, "You help yourself to anything you please." He pointed to some tall, lush bushes with intricate curling leaves, the sunlight glittering on tiny glass spines all over their fronds and long stems, their dark shadows hiding their feet, and he asked me if I knew what those were.

"Sure he does," he insisted to my father, without waiting for me to answer. And to me he said, bending down to point,

"Them's tomatoes." He pulled aside some of the leaves. "Some of them's ripe," he said. "You can eat them right now."

"No," my father said, shaking his head. "That's alright now." And to me he repeated, "You let them alone. Don't touch anything."

"They won't bother you," the old man told me. "One time people used to believe they would kill you. Deadly poison. You believe that? Thought you'd die if you ate one." He laughed. "But we know better now. You just help yourself, if you see anything you want."

He turned toward the door of the building and I saw that he was bent over as though he was too tall for the doorway, but he was not even as tall as my father. The shadows of the morning glory spilled along the wall. My father turned and said to me, behind the old man's back, "Now remember what I said. You be a good boy." That stiff, tight look was still on his face. The corners of his mouth were drawn back and pinched. The old man took his own hat off and motioned to the others to go in, but my father said no, and asked him to go first. So the old man put his hat back on and went in. My father motioned to Port to go next. He put his hand on Port's shoulder and gave him a little push. And then he himself went in last.

Port knew what they had to talk about once they were in there. Even I knew. And I knew, in a general way, what the papers were that my father was carrying, besides the copies of his church bulletin—the bulletin several weeks old, and the church three hundred miles away. Very possibly the old man himself knew, and the matter had already been discussed with him. That seems likely. I doubt that my father had been asked to spring the subject on him for the first time. I am not even sure why he had been asked to talk to the old man about it at all, alone except for Port, at that decisive point. The garden in which the little house stood was not far from my Uncle Harry's house. Harry was my father's elder brother—twelve years his senior. The old man was their father. My grand-father.

He was then eighty-one. It was the first time that I had ever seen him, and it would be the only time. When I try to imagine his face I see nothing, and then the features of his children. I do not know that I ever saw a picture of him. And that was the whole of our conversation. By the time the talk inside the house was over, and they all came out again, my father's voice was on the way to saying goodbye. If he had been calling on a member of his congregation, he would have been about to say, "Let us join in a moment of prayer." And squeezing his eyes shut, he would have begun, "Our Heavenly Father . . ." He may even have done it on that occasion. If he did, it was brief. Both he and Port were anxious to be go-ing, and my grandfather did not try to keep them. While they had been in there he had agreed to leave the low house that had been a shed, in the garden, and to spend the rest of his life in an old men's home. He had signed the papers.

It is possible that my father had been asked to intervene in that phase of the decision because the others had not been able to persuade my grandfather to sign and go. The old man was said to be stubborn, and perhaps he was. He may also have had misgivings about signing himself away, finally, to go somewhere wholly strange and institutional, at his age, even though he had been restless and on the move for much of his life. Harry no doubt shrank from urging his father to get out, particularly if the old man was reluctant to leave.

Harry had not been the only one, after all, who had brought Pap home, to Harry's own house, to live, without any real warning to Harry's kind, gentle wife Clara. When Harry and his sister Edna (to whom Port was married) and my father had got into my father's car to go for a trip, Clara had thought they were just off to Pittsburgh to check on the old man. Their father, at that time, had been staying in an old rooming house somewhere in the city, but they were not even sure he was still there. Clara was taken completely by surprise when they turned up, late in the day, with the old man sandwiched in back, and brought him and his suitcase into the front room and dropped them off there, for good. That had been twelve years earlier, before I was born, and that was the way they had always been, all of them, as Clara would say: if they meant to do something they thought you might not agree to right away they wouldn't tell you a thing about it, they'd just do it and surprise you. One bedroom of the house was rented out then, to help with expenses—it was the depression, and besides sometimes Harry didn't make it home with his pay. Harry and Clara's two elder daughters, who had been occupying another bedroom, were moved up into the attic, and their room was given to Pap.

The arrangement never worked very well. Clara felt that the old man had been, as she said, dumped on her to take care of, with no consideration at all for her. She took particular exception to a growing number of her father-in-law's ways—such things as the everlastingly renewed stains of tobacco juice around the house on carpets and furniture. Finally Harry and Edna got the piece of land with the little house on it, and Harry fixed up the building and moved Pap in there. And there he had been ever since. Harry would walk over to see how his father was getting along, and take him things to eat, and tobacco, and maybe stop for a drink on the way over, or have a few there with the old man, or on the way back. And all those years my father had known, when I had asked him, where his father was, and he had never told me, even though we went to Harry and Clara's house to visit, when we went back to Grandma's.

Pap had grown up along the Allegheny River, near Templeton. He had been born there before the Civil War, and baptised John Denton Merwine, with an "e". He was one of three sons of Jacob Ruffner Merwine and his wife Hannah, whose maiden name and birthplace I have never known. I am ignorant too of when and where the spelling "Merwine" came in. It had been in use for at least two generations by the time Jacob was born, in 1812. According to one set of records Jacob's father was named Peter, and his mother Elizabeth Coult, and they lived and farmed in Monroe County, Pennsylvania, near Tunkhannock, where Peter's own father, also named Peter, had a farm. The father or the son—perhaps both —made sails, besides, for markets in Philadelphia and New Jersey. The elder Peter, and his wife Mary Denton, had been among the first settlers in Tunkhannock Township. The same records declare that, two generations before the elder Peter, another Jacob had come to America from France, but I find that hard to believe. I cannot conceive of the name, in any form or spelling, ever having been French. Other records exist, in plenty, of Merwins (without the "e") in New England in the eighteenth century and earlier. According to them, the name was brought there in 1635, by one Miles Merwin, from Wales.

My father's family referred to John's father as Old Jake—I do not know why, unless it was simply to distinguish him from his son, Jacob Jr., young Jake. Old Jake left the family homestead in his early twenties and went out to the Allegheny. That was in 1835. He was murdered there, at Montgomeryville, twenty-seven years later, when he was just fifty and my grandfather was six. I have heard several versions of the story.

Old Jake had been running a hotel at the time, at Templeton, and in one account he was out delivering his payroll, at night, with a horse and carriage, when he was shot and robbed. He was not the only hotel keeper in the family. His elder brother John, who had stayed at home and had become both postmaster and judge, and was known as one of the best educated men in Monroe County ("his education," according to a local record, "being largely self-acquired, and of a practical nature") turned the old homestead into a hotel that was famous in the region for more than fifty years. I have heard that my grandfather, too, ran a hotel in Templeton, but that may be nothing but the result of someone's confusing his story with his father's.

I knew none of this, even as rumors, when I was a child. I was almost thirty, and my grandfather had been dead for twelve years, before I learned that his father had been killed, and when. And I heard that from my father's cousin, Mary. Once I knew it, and spoke of it openly to my father and his sisters, they said, "Oh yes," and put it aside again. When I was growing up, my father never spoke of his own father at all, outside the immediate family, and even at home there were no casual references to him—there were virtually no references of any kind, ever. It was as though my grandfather did not exist and never had existed, or had vanished mysteriously, not only from the physical world, but from the minds of his off-spring, long before I was born. His family's lack of interest in the past, the closeness even of their gossip, its tiny scope, no doubt made it easier for them to drop him from conscious-ness, and it may be that it worked the other way around as well, and that their effacing him from their minds contributed to their indifference to what had happened to others in their past.

My father did not hear questions he did not want to hear. It was a trait that he and the rest of the family were said to have inherited from my grandmother, although they laughed about it and called it Merwin behavior. Ascribing its origin to her (and it was quite true that with her it was remarkably obvious and pervasive, and had become set with age and matriarchy and a deepening physical deafness) justified it and permitted them to take pride in its incorrigibility: it was a family trait. And my grandmother alone, for them, had come to signify the family. Even the name, in their use of it, no longer referred to their father.

I do not remember when it first occurred to me that there must have been such a person at one time, but once I con-ceived of my father having a father, once I knew of my grandfather's existence, my wish to know about him persisted, along with other unanswered questions, and it stepped into the open after I started school. Many of the pupils were Irish or Italian, and most of the teachers, it seems to me now, were Irish. They tended to assume that everyone came from large, closely tangled families. A number of the other children's grandparents, and even some of their great-grandparents, were living right there at home, features of their descendants' daily comings and goings. I did not go so far as to envy those classmates—at least not often or consistently—but I was curious, puzzled. Their lives were as remote as the lives of children in books, who had fishing poles and straw hats, and went barefoot or wore patent leather shoes.

My mother's parents had both died when she was a small child. She had no immediate relatives at all. It was a fact that she had to explain to people, periodically, but I had come to take it for granted that it was a perfectly natural way for things to be. I knew my father's mother, indeed, but she lived far away where everything was different, and I seldom saw her. She was over seventy when I was born, and I never felt close to her. But at least I knew who she was, both through my own experience and my father's and aunts' reverential view of her. On the other hand, if I asked about my grandfather, my father did not hear. Or if I repeated the question until he heard, he would say, "Never mind," or even, "Never mind, now." The "now" was purely for emphasis and warning. It meant that the subject was to be considered closed— never having been opened—, and that any more questions would be considered disobedient behavior, and dealt with accordingly. So the matter was a secret, and there was no suggestion that it would ever be anything else. Both my parents, in their markedly different ways, were secretive. There was small likelihood of getting either of them to divulge anything they did not want known. I tried asking my mother about my father's father. My mother told me that I should ask my father. But her tone lacked the vaguely ominous and long-suffering note of my father's rare responses to the questions. Instead, it revealed a measure of scorn for the whole subject, a touch of mockery. Not information, but a different perspective. With regard to her own lack of relatives, her manner suggested that having a limited number of kinfolk was no disadvantage, and that in fact large families were unkempt and, if not actually disreputable, nothing to be proud of.

When I did, at last, meet my father's father, and stood in the garden with him, in the sunlight, among the bright reflections of the leaves, everything was still, and it seemed clear to me that the old man had been living there for a long time. That he had, in fact, been living there all the time, and I had never known. I could tell that from standing there in the garden, and it was so. Then he was gone, and everyone seemed to accept that as though it too had always been so, and the only grandparent had always been Grandma.

During the years when my sister and I were small children we lived in a manse at the corner of New York Avenue and 4th Street, in Union City, New Jersey, on the Palisades above Hoboken, and from time to time, on occasions that followed no pattern I could discern but were simply announced and almost immediately happened, we would go on visits "home to Grandma," as my father said. To me, Grandma was not the obvious focus or lure of those expeditions, but she was their official destination and their justification. My father told me that she loved me, and the statement conveyed an image of shapeless faded cotton print dresses, baggy gray cardigan sweaters, loose skin on wrists and fingers, and a worn Bible with scuffed gilt-edged pages. I accepted his assurance with a feeling scarcely more intimate or distinct than that with which I received the repeated assertion that Jesus loved me. He told my sister and me how happy Grandma would be to see us, and it may have been so. He told me that I loved her, and that too I accepted as a fact, a contribution to the meaning of the word. It did not seem necessary or important for that word to refer to an emotion, a feeling, and for the emotion to be my own, one that I could recognize. Instead, it alluded, apparently, to one of many workings of the grown-up world which I was too young to understand, but which would become intelligible, and indeed obvious to me, some day. In the meantime it was simply so and not to be questioned.

When I was small it seemed to me that the Union City manse had been the family home forever, but in fact my parents had moved there only a few months before I was born, when my mother's pregnancy was well advanced. Up until that time, when they had been living in Pittsburgh, to begin with, and then during the first years of my father's ministry at country churches in Armstrong County, near where he had grown up, it was a relatively easy matter for him to drop in on "Mumma" frequently—the young preacher, the son who had been to college and now drove a car. Eventually his own car. It was a myth, that car, by the time I was old enough to listen to what was said about it. The Ford. There may have been more than one of them, in that antediluvian time, but they blended into a single archetype in the telling. For my father, everything to do with driving and with his cars had acquired an aura which shone from all parts of the subject, and was his own mysterious possession. He had learned to drive in Kittanning, the town on the Allegheny to which his mother had moved the children—breaking definitively with my grandfather—when my father was eleven. My father's driving teacher was an old friend, a plump, merry woman of his own age named Bernie—Bernice. His close, affectionate relation with her comfortably-off family (established in local business and politics, with a white frame house under old shade trees, on a brick-paved side street—and with cars) went back to his early adolescence. He described with unfailing delight Bernie and himself at the wheel, the car hers or her family's. Again and again they launched themselves on the long hill outside Kittanning, which had been steeper in those days, of course, and prayed for the brakes to hold when they were going downhill, and for the motor not to stall when they were on the way up. Not many people had licenses, then. Bernie had had hers for a year or so. His own license, when he got it, enabled him to earn a salary as chauffeur for a Presbyterian minister, while enrolled as a divinity student at Western Seminary. No doubt he found occasion, before long, to call triumphantly at his mother's house in Kittanning, driving Dr. Shelton's big car.

My father's driving—he spoke of it as though it were something he could point to—was a treasure he cherished all his life. From the start it was a proof, to him, of his own exceptional ability and what it could achieve, a sign that he had made good and not disappointed his Mumma's hopes, or his own. My grandfather could not drive a car. He could drive a team, and was said to have had a river pilot's license—but what did those matter in the world that my father had entered in college and the clergy? Very possibly his brothers did not drive at that time either, though they were older than he was. So it set him apart, and permitted a freedom of movement which, in his case, could be deployed in such a way as to suggest special responsibilities. Even after driving had become all that is most ordinary he remained proud of his own as something distinctive, and was prompt to refer to the number of years he had driven, how early he had obtained his license, and—until he was in his sixties—to the fact that he had never had even a minor accident. "Not a scratch," he said, though it was not literally true. Yet he never learned to shift into second without grinding the gears, although he winced, clucked his tongue, shook his head, if he heard someone else do it. Sometimes his gear-crashing was blamed, by an elliptical process, on the Ford, or the car he had learned on, and the peculiarities of their gear systems. As far as I can remember from early allusions, his first car had been a hand-me-down, passed on because neither the car nor the former owner had much to lose by the transfer, and because the machine would be suitable for a novice to practice with. And then, I think, came The Ford, the first real car. In my mind it is green, with a rumble seat, but I never saw it, and it is possible that the car acquired that color in my mind from nothing except the fact that my father bought it from a doctor friend in Greenville, who warned him that it was no car for a preacher because it ran half on gas and half on cuss. It started reluctantly, by all accounts, in response to a handcrank in front. The fuel line worked by gravity, so the only way for it to climb a hill was in reverse. It stalled in the rain, or in long puddles, and had to be cranked again in cloudbursts until it shook itself. It served my father and mother, in this way, for a couple of years, on the rutted roads of western Pennsylvania.

Then and later, all through my childhood, whatever car they had or we had was indisputably my father's. At some time in their first years together he had started to teach my mother to drive. It must have been early in their courtship, or their marriage—an exceptional, romantic gesture. And he must have felt some ambivalence about it even when it was suggested. My mother maintained (it was a word she used often) that he had shown no patience at all, and perhaps in an attempt to ease the situation by generalizing it, she came to express the opinion that no husband or wife should try to teach the other to drive. The lessons came to grief quickly. I do not know what car they were driving—a borrowed one, or the Ford soon after they got it. But my mother had failed to change gears correctly on a hill, and then had not used the brakes promptly enough, nor steered accurately enough, and the automobile, which fortunately was not going very fast, had bumped the entrance to a narrow iron bridge, and injured a front fender. The curriculum ended at that spot. My mother refused to drive further, and she stuck to the decision, to which she had been brought, she said, by my father's behavior on that occasion: his annoyance at the accident and the harm done to the car. The issue became a fixation in their lives, one that they used to air the multiplying disappointments and resentments that arose between them. In the thirties my father made fun of women drivers, and my mother would remind him that he had been taught to drive by a woman—a round which neither pursued. My mother arrived at other refusals, and compared them to her refusal to drive. "It would be just like the car," she said. "If anything happened, I would never hear the last of it." She said it again when, twenty years after the accident, in Scranton, at the time when my father bought the new Olds (from a man named Burnie) he urged her to take driving lessons and get a license. And she did, finally. First Burnie himself came, a rotund man wearing his garage coveralls, and fetched her away for driving instruction —out of sight of the house. And after Burnie, a professional instructor, in a brown hat and a gabardine. And she took her test and got her license, and still would not drive the car. The license was allowed to expire. My father cited the story as proof of his own desire to remove the problem, and of her clinging, instead, to her grievance. She insisted that she would have no peace if she drove that car. Every little thing would be her fault. He went away on a trip and left her the keys and the tank of the car full of gas, in the garage, and she never took it out once while he was gone. She said he left her the keys only because he knew she would not use them, and that he never really wanted her to drive. No doubt they were both right. It was not until another whole decade had gone by, and they were in their fifties, and my mother had a job of her own in the Kittanning court house, that she renewed her license—and bought a car of her own, which she was very particular not to let him drive, citing his way of changing gears as one of her reasons. By then, if he ever spoke of women drivers, it was with a certain amusement at the joke itself, a touch of nostalgia at being reminded of a rather silly period piece. And she could give up—partly because she seldom rode in his car, with him driving—her sharp intakes of breath when he crashed his gears or braked too suddenly or turned without signalling. She could adopt an attitude of resignation, expressed with raised eyebrows, toward his driving as a whole, to which he no longer drew attention.

But back at the end of their twenties, in the months when my mother was pregnant with me, the First Presbyterian Church of Union City, New Jersey, extended the call—as it was phrased—to my father, and he was happy to accept. They moved. A new place, within sight of Manhattan. In a new state, where people pronounced their words differently. A new church, a city church, and in comparison with the former ones, a rather large one. A new house, new to them at any rate, considerably bigger than any they had lived in. A child on the way, as part of their new life. The pregnancy dated from the beginning of the year. In keeping with the turn of the moment, The Ford was replaced with a new car, The Buick. It represented distance already traversed. And a boast of arrival.

My father remained proud of The Buick for several years, its make, model, everything about it. It is true that I do not remember ever seeing another one just like it. Neither a sedan nor a coupe; a two-door, with a deep back seat, a large hump of luggage compartment on the rear, and the spare tire bolted on a rack behind that. The middle section stood up like a deck house or a top hat, and was covered with a textured black patent leather. A broad visor extending from the front of it shaded the windshield. The body of the car, from the windowsills down, was a lustrous blue, a twilit sky color. It looked as though you could see far into it, as into water, and my father, and a series of men from the church ritually, indeed reverently, washed and Simonized it. My father pronounced the word Simonize as though it were a spell. When new license plates arrived he called me into his study for the ceremony of removing them from their waxed paper and holding them up with a little "Hm" of pleasure. The rear plate was fastened behind the spare tire, under a small black oval box from which the glass corneas of three lights protruded, one white, one green, and one amber. Each glass was fluted on the inside, like the reverse of an orange squeezer, so that looking at them one saw what appeared to be the undersides of three flowers with precise narrow petals. Only the white light worked, by the time I was old enough to be interested, but I considered all three of them, and the red tail lights —particularly when seen in the dark, with the smoke of the exhaust swirling past them—to be objects of urgent but inexplicable beauty.

Besides, there were the wooden spoke wheels, the spokes enamelled the same lucent blue as the body, with fine black lines along their centers. And running boards on which I yearned to ride. I was never completely content with the plain, almost flat radiator cap with indentations around it for grasping it, once I had seen caps adorned with thermometers standing in metal rings. It made no difference to me that my father shook his head and pursed his lips at the thermometers, and said they worked only for a short time and then were no use. I was not interested in what they were supposed to do.

The Buick's importance extended to its housing. It had to itself the whole ground floor of a real (small) barn that walled off half of the back yard: a two story structure with hay-loft doors upstairs above the main ones. The building must have been the same age as the manse. Both of them harked back to the 1870's or '80's at least, the time of horses and carriages. It was obvious that the barn had had other lives that had been concealed but were there in it still. For a while, I learned—I no longer remember from whom—it had been used as a warehouse for hides, which had been hoisted from wagons in bales, by means of the pulley that was still there, up under the peak outside the hayloft doors. For us—for me, and later for my sister—the whole building was absolutely forbidden ground, and only once did I ever see what was on the upper floor. My father, one day, in an expansive mood, allowed me in beside the car, where the walls were hung with rakes and shovels and chains and there were shelves sagging with paint cans. On the far side a ladder went straight up to a hole in the ceiling. He held me up, with my head above the level of the upper floor, so that I could peer around in the cardboard light. There was nothing there but bulges. When he lifted me down he told me that I must never go up there, for any reason. In time that upper story was populated with wasps, and with assorted people and creatures of my invention, many of whom did not even suspect each other's existence. When my father was about to take the car out, the barn was called the garage. He would open its doors, and then open the gates of the fence along New York Avenue and back the car out onto the white-pebbled driveway, and whoever was going with him would get in there.

For those trips "back home"—which was another of my father's ways of referring to the periodic journeys across New Jersey and Pennsylvania to New Kensington, where my grandmother had moved after he left for college, and where he had never lived—he believed in getting an early start. By one route the distance, according to the Buick's odometer, was 444 miles. He had made it more than once in a single day, which he and his listeners considered a wonderful achievement. It allowed him, at any rate, to declare that he *could* do it in a day, though it meant leaving early and arriving late at night. Most of the trips on which he managed to do it were ones that he took by himself; usually, when the family was along, we broke the journey somewhere on the way. But whatever the plan, or absence of plan, he—who ordinarily did not like early rising—wanted to be on the road, if possible, by four o'clock in the morning. You made your best time, he repeated, during the hours before daylight. So we got up in the hollow dark, my mother cooperating with the arrangements, but bustling and clucking her tongue at the proceedings as she went, because getting up so early violated the children's sleep. Her pursed lips and her impatience with the last minute packings and closings expressed a deepening reluctance concerning those trips altogether, but I did not understand that, at the beginning. My father assumed full authority for the expeditions, and ignored, or pretended to ignore, her lack of enthusiasm. "The darkest hour," he would say to me, eyebrows and finger raised, "is just before the dawn." As we got ready, and floated out of room after room—bedrooms, bathroom, dining room ("the children have to have their breakfast if they're going to be up that long")—the light in the house looked sallow and unlikely, and the smell of wallpaper followed us and then abruptly was gone, replaced by the startling yet elusive scent of what my mother called the night air, which had its dangers. There were no cars at all, at that hour, and the silent darkness was freighted with that odor speaking of the earth. Our footsteps echoed on the gravel walk. The hinges of the back area-way door squeaked behind us. The street car wires hummed above the avenue. The garage doors grated open. The Buick started up, waking huge echoes, and the tail lights moved toward us with the smoke rising around them. My mother spoke to us, and we answered, in whispers, and we climbed in onto the stiff velvet upholstery with its own dusty night smell. In the light of the street lamp its inky blue looked black.

Now for years the trips have run together into a few scarcely distinguishable variations. As a child I could not see that they were steps in a progression, and that their quest for continuity betrayed change. I supposed that the decision leading to each of those early starts—never quite as early as my father had hoped they would be—arose from a clear and identically formed impulse, as definite and indisputable as a day on a calendar. Even my parents' different, and diverging, attitudes toward those journeys and visits seemed to me to be expressions of a single course, two sightings of the same destination. But the returns to Pennsylvania may have revealed, more than anything else, distances. And added to them.

From the beginning of her acquaintance with my father's family, my mother had felt that its women—my grandmother and my aunts who had remained her satellites—had been unwelcoming to her, had received her as an outsider, and preferred to keep things that way. She was probably right, and it would not have made much difference to her to consider that their behavior was only in a limited sense personal; no doubt they would have done as little to make anyone my father married feel at home. As I could see later, they were not remarkably open or flexible or thoughtful, and my mother's tastes and admirations, and most of her interests, were alien to theirs. They were habitually suspicious of anything or anybody from outside. And for her part, coming into a closed family circle made her particularly conscious of having no parents, herself, and no close relatives except her brother Morris, who died soon after she was married. Her own lack of kin must have made their minute ingrown sanctum, with my grandmother at its center, seem particularly exclusive. If she was withdrawn they found her snooty. And in their eyes, of course, my father remained their possession—and they too were right. He was the youngest son, and his achievements and distinctions, real or imagined, were adjuncts to their own carefully hedged self-esteem. Their adulation, dependable and uncritical, helped to nourish and restore a view of himself which my father clung to. Before he and my mother had moved east to Union City, and so before I was born, it was possible for him to drop in on them, surprising them; but once he and my mother lived in New Jersey, a visit was an occasion. He came alone less often, and if things were different, they knew why.

The atmosphere of those visits apparently improved for a while soon after I was born. There was a baby for them all to attend to, and my mother was in charge. She was meticulous and protective, and very sure of what was needed; but they, for their part, were zealously strict in their notions of what was proper, and they respected her suddenly revealed unhesitating authority. Besides, my grandmother was doubtless beyond caring much about the details of child care. She was old, and had reared seven children of her own. The process appeared to have used up most of her interest in the subject.

Unless children made noise or otherwise violated her strait views of what was good conduct she appeared to take only a remote and vague interest in them. Her relation with them— with us—was largely indirect: she spoke to someone else about them. The role of the matriarch had grown up, had been built up, around her, gradually replacing some earlier insulation, and she accepted it absolutely. My two aunts, Alma and Edna, had no children of their own. I was a toy. During my first two years, before my sister was born, we stayed longer, on some of those visits to New Kensington, than I remember us ever doing later—a matter of weeks, sometimes. I was taken along, swathed in baby things, to the houses of my parents' old friends in that region. Occasionally my mother consented to entrust me to Aunt Edna's care for a few minutes at a time. When I was almost two my father's health was not good; my mother was pregnant again; there were other demands upon my parents that called them away. By then I could be left with Eddie and her husband, Port, for slightly longer periods, and when I was alone with them they tended to spoil me. I have an impression—formed mostly of details long forgotten or subsumed in others—of the intervals with Eddie and Port as a halcyon age, and my fondness for the smells and sounds of that drab, smoky, grating town comes from those days.

My grandmother lived at 1154 Stanton Avenue, New Kensington, in what I now realize was a small house, the ground floor yellow brick, the upper story white-painted frame. Her daughter, my Aunt Eddie, and Uncle Port, lived next door at 1152, in a house that was virtually its twin, except that Eddie's front porch was enclosed in windows, and my Grandma's was open, with a big dark green porch swing at the end. The swing was not to be sat on, unless a grown-up came first and dusted it off; otherwise the soot got on one's clothes and hands and legs. My Grandma's house, inside, was the darker of the two, and it felt quieter. A black marble and ormulu clock ticked before a mirror, on the mantelpiece. Both houses faced west onto tiny patches of grass set between clipped privet hedges. At the end the grass fell away abruptly on a steep bank. Each house had a cement walk out in front, and a flight of cement steps down to the sidewalk. Beyond that there was another small bank, and at intervals a few more cement steps led down to the street—a detail that pleased me, invited me: it conveyed a remote suggestion of living in castles, with ramps and battlements. The street was not paved in those years, as I recall, but was oiled and strewn with small pebbles, and there were deep cracks and holes. It was just wide enough for two cars, but there were seldom two at once moving along it. They appeared rarely, picking their way slowly along, and they almost never parked on the street. On the far side the bank fell away again, a real drop, half as high as the house, to the railroad tracks. There was a whole broad current of them, running past the front doors of the houses, glinting and ringing. It seemed to me that the sound of them was present all the time, at those two houses. The roar and shriek of trains rose out of it and faded back into it again, echoing, as did the puffing and chugging, clanging, thumping, bell ringing and hissing of the short engines from the switching yard that fanned out, a half block to the north. When the wheels had gone the sound was still there, a clear impersonal note travelling from the springs and concerns of the outermost world, neither menacing nor addressing nor pausing, completely free of the injunctions and opinions of the family, and always there. Other sounds spoke of the actual houses. The cement walks between them echoed like slapped inner tubes, when someone's footsteps passed through. The nails of the rat terriers kept in both cellars clicked and rattled like rice on the wood and linoleum of the cellar stairs and on the cement around the furnaces. But the sound of the tracks and the thunder of trains were the ones that stamped the place and claimed it continuously, and in coming to know them close at hand I was hearing a note that led back through my grandparents' lives to the beginning, and before.

My grandmother came from farther north, along those tracks. As long as she was alive I never knew where she had been born and brought up, nor anything about her parents. I did not at any point feel intimate enough with her to ask her anything about herself and—at least by the time I knew her—she tended, as a matter of habit, to turn aside questions that were put to her, and to suspect the motives of anyone who questioned her. Whether that trait was inborn and inherent, or a commonplace of her background, I can only guess—and I imagine it was both. Some of it she, and the life they shared, passed on to her children. When I asked my father about her parents and where she had grown up, he seemed not to know, or to have forgotten; his manner offered little hope that he would remember. My grandmother's maiden name was Anderson, "from up around Clarion there." The Andersons had family reunions every so often, my father told me once as we passed such a gathering—men in white shirts, women in summer dresses, standing around trestle tables under big trees, outside an unpainted farmhouse—and he had been invited but had gone only once or so, and had not found much of interest there.

He did tell me that his mother's father, whom they had called Grandpap Anderson, had had a donkey he used when he worked on the roads, hauling and setting out crushed stone and gravel, to pay his taxes, and keeping track of the hours worked in a tattered notebook. My father showed me the notebook, held it up rather as a magician holds up a pack of cards. In time the notebook itself passed into my hands and a closer inspection evoked a different image, less bucolic but more likely, perhaps representing a later stage in Grandpap Anderson's—and the region's—life. The man with his donkey, tapping stones into the loosened surface of the road, has become, by 1897, the date on the cover, "E. Anderson, Sup.,"—I suppose the "Sup." is short for "Superintendent." S. Anderson by then must have been around seventy. On the cover darkened like wallpaper in an old house it says, "Always

Bring This Book." Inside, in fine copper-plate penmanship, are accounts for the householders of an unnamed community which must be Templeton, totalling, for that year ("Less a/c for J. D. Paul") $206.99. The tax was 6 Mills. Registration was in May. Among the accounts on page ten are two in the name of Zellafrow—one N.R.'s to the amount of $4.25, and beneath, that of John, for the amount of $.45. Thirty five years after the murder, and the birth of the rumors. On the last page of the book, in another hand, unsteady, uneducated, in pencil:

> "For 1904 W Sumers Grane
> 24 October Reedy Mill
> Sumer 8   5 Bushels Wheat
>   10 Bushels Buckewheat
> _____
>   to mill
> 25th   10 Bushels Buckwheat
> 25th   8 for Anderson"

Someone else was keeping the records by then. Under the last entry there is a child's drawing of a man in a hat, and a house with a smoking chimney. Three years later, in mid-summer, Samuel Anderson died. He had been born in Templeton. If my own father ever knew him—which he almost certainly did, since at the time of his grandfather's death he was eight years old and living only a few miles away—he seemed to retain, and certainly he conveyed, no clear image of the man. And as for his mother's remoter forebears and where they came from, I know nothing at all.

My father told me one legend of my grandmother's. Some antecedent of hers supposedly had been eaten by wolves, in a hunting lodge in the woods, in a blizzard, somewhere out in Ohio (pronounced "Ahýa".) The details were vague or missing—who it was, when it happened, just where. But years ago it was thought to be a good story and was repeated occasionally. I have not believed it for a long time. To me it seems interesting only as an isolated index of the fantasies and self-justifications of the unknown minds that produced it, accepted it, and passed it on.

It was only after my father himself was dead that I found my grandmother's dilapidated thistle-blue autograph book from the time of her youth in the 1870's and '80's. "My love for you shall never fail As long as pussy has a tail By Maggie E. Bechtel," in purple crayon. Inspirational poems, "I know God's in His heaven," "Thoughtlessness," "The Marines' Hymn," sent by my Uncle Sam during the first World War. In pencil, in a margin, "Sam gave me this long a goe." A dried pansy between the pages. And obituary notices, in no discernible order—some of the crumbling bits of newspaper pasted on top of the pencilled dates, eclipsing them. "There was a band of angels that wasn't quite complete, so God took Mother Gifford, to fill the vacant seat." Many of those born in the river settlements had moved into Kittanning and Ford City, and died in town. And from the book I learned a few of the dessicated facts that make their way into such places. My grandmother's mother had been born in Templeton, date unspecified. Apparently her name before her marriage had been Elizabeth Bechtel. One of the pencilled notices in the autograph book reads:

> "Arvill
> In the days of Solm reflections
> in the Hours of Social glee
> Keep me in thy Recollections
> for I often think of thee
> —Your Aunt
> (illegible) M. E. Bechtel"

I suppose the name was originally German.

There is no obituary notice for Samuel Anderson, and there are several for his wife Elizabeth, whatever that may indicate. She died on July 22, 1904, ten months to the day after her husband's death. They had baptised my grandmother, born at

Maple Furnace, Pa., August 8, 1854, Arvilla. When she was alive I was never certain whether she had brothers or sisters, though my father referred absently to relatives with unfamiliar surnames. In fact, Arvilla had been one of five children, all the rest of whom, at different times, had moved out to California.

Templeton is a hamlet strung out along the railroad tracks on the east bank of the Allegheny River, some sixty miles northeast of Pittsburgh. It may have been larger in the 1850's, when my grandparents were born, and around the time of the Civil War, when they were children, than it is now. Most of the settlements on that winding stretch of the Allegheny—Wattersonville, Redbank Furnace, Cosmus, Rimer, Hooks, Gray's Eddy, Mahoning, Mosgrove, Gosford—have probably shrunk in the past hundred years and more. The river, in the middle of the 19th century, was the main artery of transportation and the central earthly presence in the minds of those who lived near it. I imagine that those river hamlets, up until the first World War, still bore a general resemblance to Mark Twain's Hannibal. The broad river dominated the mental geography of the region's inhabitants even after the advent of the Ford. Among many of those who had been born there in the 19th century and had not moved away nor learned to drive, it continued to do so after the Army Engineers had thrown their dams across its current, and the days of river traffic were effectively over. Not only my grandmother, but my Aunt Mary in the following generation assumed that one envisaged any place in the region in relation to the river.

At the time when my grandparents were born, the railroads were new-fangled. It was a number of years before the rails came down the river valleys, around the time of the Civil War. The various lines through the region—the Buffalo, Rochester, and Pittsburgh Railroad along Little Buffalo Run, Patterson Creek, and Long Run; the few miles of the Winfield Railroad, from West Winfield to the Allegheny, along Rough Run and Buffalo Creek; the Low Grade Division of the

Pennsylvania Railroad, along Redbank Creek; and the main line, the Buffalo and Allegheny Valley Division of the Pennsylvania Railroad, along the east bank of the river—all followed the river and its tributaries. The river settlements through that section are on the east side of the water, which may have had to do, in the first place, with currents and boat landings. The talk of the coming of the trains, the requisitioning of land for them, the cutting of the woods, the grading of the slopes and building of the roadbeds, the laying of the tracks, were a long progression in the valley, impetus and form of irreversible changes, but it was still the river valley, enduring the general eager theft and defacement that characterized the building of the American railroads. The conflict between the older water transport and the new rail companies had begun with the inception of the railroads themselves, and it figured in the daily talk of the era. It must have been a matter of common knowledge when the railroads bought up, one by one, the dams that maintained the levels of the doomed canal system, and let them fall into ruin. On one page of my grandmother's commonplace book is the date of the Johnstown Flood, caused by the collapse of one of those dams. It was one of the spectacular catastrophes of her lifetime, a date that she was unlikely to forget as long as it meant anything to her, and she may have written the bare cipher on that page less as a simple reminder than as a somewhat incredulous mark of her own presence, like initials on the bark of a tree. The flood happened when my grandmother was thirty-five, a mother of three children. Rumors reached her of people seeing bodies floating in the river far below Johnstown. Some said they had seen them passing under the bridges at Pittsburgh, and down the Ohio. There were people who went to Pittsburgh just to look. As an old woman my Grandma spoke of the bodies as though she had seen them herself, floating down the Allegheny past Rimerton.

The right-of-way there and in Templeton runs close to the

river, and many of the houses, which must have been built
at about the time when the rails were laid, are set between
the edge of the bank that drops steeply to the water, and the
tracks. They face the railroad line: long, low front porches,
a few board steps up from the ground. I do not know what
Samuel Anderson did for a living in Templeton; he may have
been a tax overseer for years before the notebook that ends
with a child's drawing, but the book itself does not look like
the record of a full-time public official. As for my grandfather's father, Old Jacob's hotel was probably no larger than
most of the other frame houses lined up along the slope, with
their chicken coops and vegetable gardens and outhouses in
back of them. Everyone in the place knew everyone else
pretty well. Arvilla was two years older than my grandfather,
and had known him since he was a baby. She was eight when
his father was murdered.

Some time not long after that, Old Jake's widow, Hannah,
decided that she could not manage to bring up the three boys
herself, and she farmed out Jim, aged seven, with the Heinz
family at Widnoon. John, my grandfather, went to the Rimer
family, up at Rimer or Rimerton. One of the obituary notices
pasted across its date in my grandmother's commonplace book
is that of Annie A. Rimer, who may have been John's foster
mother. Neither the hamlet of Rimer, as my Aunt Mary referred to it, or Rimerton, as my father, who was born there,
called it, nor Widnoon up on the hill, where some of them
went to school and are buried, was more than five or six miles
from Templeton. It was all in the neighborhood. And when
Mr. Heinz began delivering his wife's locally celebrated chili
sauce from door to door in his wheelbarrow—as the legend
goes, at any rate—it was only a year or two before he had
to take a wagon and go farther afield, or get somebody else
to go for him. All the way to Templeton, before long. Jim
left the Heinzes in 1871, when he was sixteen, to go to work
in a furnace, perhaps at Mahoning, for a dollar a day. In his

early thirties he moved, with the beginning of the exodus from the river settlements to the industrial towns. He went down-river to Kittanning, where he ran a barber shop, and in later years worked as a night watchman. Young Jacob, whom Hannah, it appears, kept with her and brought up at home, later had something to do, my father told me, with the barge traffic on the river, and for a while was a policeman.

But of John, my grandfather, and the Rimers, at that time, I know nothing at all. I have heard from several members of the family that John had a river pilot's license, but no details about when and how he acquired it or used it. He seems to have worked in various capacities, up and down the river, and to have known the waterway at least as far as Pittsburgh. My father's family legend about the Heinzes has it that as they grew more successful in selling an increasing assortment of bottled vegetables, their sons set up an office in Pittsburgh and distributed the produce from there. Eventually they began to urge their parents to move the whole enterprise to the city. The elders were reluctant to leave, suspicious of the Babylon down-river, and they held out, preferring the world they knew. At some point they said they would go only if they could take their own house, the actual building up on the hill, six hundred and fifty feet above the river, along with them. They may have supposed that putting such a condition upon their moving would rule out the idea once and for all. But arrangements were made for uprooting the farmhouse from the site on which it had been reared, and the shade of its trees, and its garden, and edging it on rollers down the narrow, rutted, steep road, several miles to Gray's Eddy, or more probably to Rimerton, and sliding it onto a barge. The operation would have been complicated by the final grade down to the river. By the time I first saw Rimerton, the boat landings had gone from that part of the shore, but my father told me of seeing a team of beautiful horses, when he was a child, come down the road to cross the water on a flatboat, and on the way down the brake of the wagon failed, and the wagon rushed ahead, out of control, pushing the horses ahead of it onto the landing and the wharf, and off the end into the river, where they drowned before they could be cut loose from the harness. He remembered them being dragged out by other teams, and how he cried, and he showed me the spot where they had been buried—at least he thought it was the place. It is one of the handful of clear images of that time that he conveyed to me, something that had continued to impress him. And they had brought a house down that road, on rollers? So the story goes, and my father said that his uncle, young Jake, had something to do with providing the barge, and with the loading, and that my grandfather piloted the house down to Pittsburgh, where I was told it still sat unassimilated among the red brick mill buildings of the latter-day Heinz plant. If it happened like that at all, I imagine it was in the 1880's, in the decade after my grandparents' marriage. I know nothing else of that period of their lives except the dates when their first children were born.

They lived in Rimerton, perhaps from the time they were married, and I assume they called it that, since their children did. They ran a store in the house, and my grandmother took in sewing and did millinery work. I have heard that my grandfather actually owned a house in the village at one time—whether bequeathed to him by the Rimers or bought with earnings, or indeed whether he owned one at all, I am not sure. Nor do I know anything of his habits, his appearance, how much of the time he was away working on the river. And of my grandmother there are no pictures from that far back. In the oldest one I have seen she is already a woman in her sixties, heavy set, heavy jawed, heavy lidded—the heavy eyelids she passed on to several of her children—with gray hair; but still, in that picture, she looks startlingly young to me, since I never saw her until some years later.

No doubt her religion, which was to become the principal

concern and focus of her life, was important to her from early childhood in Maple Furnace and Templeton, during the years of the Civil War. It is not easy to see, through the features of a woman past seventy, the child far behind them, but I find it hard to imagine her except as a very serious little girl, and the form of her religion—what my father referred to as "her church," "her Bible," emphasizing the pronoun—must have set early and changed little over the decades except to grow more obdurate. But she was born into it, or into something very like it. An unquestioning and vehement fundamentalism, a literal insistence upon the letter of the Word of God —taking the King James version for the original. A fierce self-righteousness and a view of the world in the light of an imminent Last Judgment—they were all around her as she was growing up. They were thundered from the pulpit in voices emulating the already legendary travelling evangelists of the days of her parents' youth. And they served her, as they served all of the faithful, in making a day-by-day sorting without appeal of the sheep from the goats, the saints from the dwellers in outer darkness in Templeton. But even among neighbors who had grown up to the beat of that same relentless piety and had accepted it as their own special salvation she was remarkable, and admired for the unbending force of her conviction and the rigor of its application to decisions and events and people. She was a Methodist, as it happened, no doubt following the affiliation of her parents, and the sect that was represented most pertinently—it may have boasted the only church—in Templeton. And the Methodists in particular, among the denominations in the river settlements, harked back directly to the itinerant Wesleyan preachers who had whipped up the Fear of the Lord there within the memory of the middle-aged. The fire of the earlier years had subsided—by comparison, at least—to a scripture-quoting pietism, a pursing of lips and a willing suspicion, a straight and narrow Grundyism. It had soured. In that faith she had brought up her children. Before my father could read, she taught him:

It is a sin
To steal a pin
And how much greater
To steal a tater.

She made "Be sure your sins will find you out" into a household motto—"sins" meaning, above all, lies or theft. During
my father's childhood the family was poor much of the time;
sometimes the children had no shoes, and there was not
enough to eat. One summer day when he was four or five my
father picked a few ears of corn from a field along the lane,
up the river, and brought them home in his wagon, and his
mother asked where they came from and how he had come
by them, and when he told her she scolded him severely and
made him take them back and apologize to the owner, and
pay for them. It may have been perfectly usual and normal
behavior on her part. It had the effect she intended it to have:
he remembered it, with mortification, for the rest of his life.
By the time I knew her, her eyeglass case, her sewing, and her
Bible were always in her lap or within reach of her rocker,
and some of the psalms, as she quoted them, referred to a
startling distance, but by then the world around her had
grown dubious and evanescent. She was still contemptuous—
as were her daughters—of those who maintained that we were
descended from monkeys, and there were usually several
tracts tucked into her Bible announcing, with apposite chapter
and verse, what could be expected in the life to come. She was
never altogether reconciled to my father's slipping away into
Presbyterianism, even though the Presbyterian Church led
him to college and to his ordination as a minister. She hoped
it would be alright—meaning that she hoped it would be overlooked.

Her politics were as inflexible as her religion. Indeed there
was probably no clear division between them. Both were as-
pects of the same viewpoint and temperament, both had been
formed by the same circumstances and at the same time. She

would no more have voted for a Democrat than she would have stolen a wallet or gone to Mass. Somewhere in her heedless loyalty there remained an impression from her youth of the Republican party as the party of Lincoln. It was also, in the poverty of the river settlements, the party of respectability and therefore both of social aspiration and conservatism. Her scorn of "Dixie" (pronounced "Dixeh") had its origin in her childhood not so many miles north of the Mason-Dixon Line, and the talk of the Civil War and of friends who had helped runaway slaves escape to Canada, but it was certainly emphasized in later years by the solidly Democratic allegiance of the South. But since her Republicanism was not hampered by reason, she did not hesitate to make stern comments on the Carnegies and Mellons, the rich who avoided paying the poor an honest wage; and she spoke, or my father did, of early meetings held by labor organizers—John L. Lewis among them —in her cellar. I am not sure whether that would have been the cellar in Rimerton, or the one later, in Kittanning, but I imagine it was the former; and I suspect, if only on grounds of likelihood, that my grandfather, whose politics may have been less impacted and more pragmatic than hers, may have had something to do with any such gatherings.

And the children—Harry is the first of them for whom we have a certain date. He was born in 1884. But there was one daughter, Bertha, about whom there was always some unresolved mystery. The other daughters spoke of her as being different, and called her a gypsy because she wore flashy jewelry and was said to have a good time. They never had much to do with her. She may have been born before Harry. In any event, from 1884 until the end of the century the babies continued to arrive every two or three years until there were seven all told. After Harry came Alma, then Vince, Edna, Samuel, William (my father) and Dewey. Dewey (pronounced "Dyeweh"), born the year of the Admiral's "Damn The Torpedoes, Full Speed Ahead" attack on Manila Bay, lived only a few years and died of some childhood disease such as scarlet fever, leaving behind him a tiny rocking chair that remained in the family for five decades and more. It was always referred to as Dewey's chair, and any mention of it had the faculty—at least in my own experience— of making a whole room of the Rimerton house appear around its image: an upstairs back bedroom full of afternoon sunlight, with a plank floor, rag rugs, a bed covered with patchwork, a picture of Jesus, a few tan faded photographs in heavy frames, a smell of dry wood, a single window propped open looking out in late summer over the dusty vegetable patch going to seed, the parched outbuildings, and the glare of the river on which the green shadow grows from the far bank.

In large families there are bound to be marked differences in age among some of the children. Harry was at least twelve years older than Dewey. And after Dewey was born the household stayed on at Rimerton for another decade and more, while the marriage pulled apart and the family ties loosened— some of them.

Nobody has spoken of those years except by way of head-shaking and sighs and reprobation of my grandfather's drinking. Perhaps none of the family could have described clearly much of the progress of that dissolution. My grandfather's absences while he worked on the river, or for whatever reason, grew more frequent and longer until he was away much of the time, and often no one at home knew where he was. When he showed up, my father said, he was usually drunk, and frightened them. Sometimes he had no money and his clothes were a disgrace. Sometimes he brought what seemed like a lot of money, acquired heaven knew how, and the household stocked up on food despite Grandma's misgivings, or he brought the staples himself: hams and flour and corn meal and dried beans. Sometimes he took to outlandish behavior: once he swept up all the homemade bread and hid it. Another time he flourished a pistol and shot the bucket at the pump full of holes, laughing, and then sent Edna or Alma to pump the bucket full of water, shouting "Fill it up! Fill it up!" Everyone thought he was serious, with that pistol, and later when they may have doubted that, they insisted on it; the story was beyond changing. On the other side, my grandmother's militant respectability stiffened. She took in more millinery work to feed the family, and she read the psalms, with her thimble on her finger.

It was late in my childhood before I began to guess that although the canonization of my grandmother was a matter of general accord and was taken for granted—it represented, in itself, the family bond—subscription to her particular judgments varied considerably, in practice. The differences acquired a geography once the children were old enough to leave home. Vince finally settled in Canton, Ohio, and seldom came back. A niece remembered his good nature and his humor. Sam had had problems of his own with his mother's determinations. He was three years older than my father, but for some reason my grandmother liked to dress them as twins when they went out, and usually in sailor suits; she continued to do so when they were both adolescents, living in Kittanning. The three years' difference in age made the charade particularly galling for Sam. People in town stared openly at this duo out of a side show. In my father's account, one woman who looked long and hard at them as they walked past, and then stopped and turned round (Sam turned too, to check) to look back, and stood still, mouth open, gazing at them, finally undid Sam, who drew himself up, walked back, and said, "Lady, if I'm wearing something that belongs to you, I'll take it off right here and give it to you." From then on he refused to dress in that fashion. He had scarcely reached enlistment age when he disappeared, and eventually word came that he had joined the Marines. He was sent to France soon after the United States entered the first World War, and was wounded—a bayonet from under the chin into the hard palate—and sent home. He too settled in Ohio, near Bowling Green, to farm.

And Bertha married and left. For a time she remained in the

region, but they saw little of her. Eventually she and her son, whose health was poor, moved out to the southwest. The other daughters spoke of Birdie with a certain disdain, as though she were scarcely one of the family at all. They considered her gaudy and flighty—but others in the family remembered her as pleasant, affable, merry, and generous.

The elder daughters, Alma and Edna, married but continued to maintain the tight inner circle with their Mumma at the center and my father as their hero. The others may not have been quite so implacable in their attitude toward my grandfather, but apparently after growing up and moving away from Mumma nobody saw much of him—with the possible exception of Harry. In the family sanctum around my grandmother my father's role was actually enhanced by the form of his leaving home: in spite of his scant schooling he managed, at sixteen, to obtain, through someone in a Presbyterian Church in Kittanning, a scholarship to Maryville College in Tennessee. In due course the college itself was also canonized, though I do not believe my father ever returned there after his student years, and he did not receive a degree. But he was the son who was away in College, and they were proud of him, and he wrote home telling of the difficulty of the studies, his phrases punctuated with Bible references giving book, chapter and verse—a style which marked his letters all his life. Both for him and for his mother and his elder sisters, his going to college represented a further separation, and a particularly significant one, from his father: a sign that he, and they, could do well, and better than John D. had ever done, without him. It was a proof—had any been needed—of their superiority to John D. and all that he represented to them. And of course the proof, and the separation, were further magnified when, after a spell in the Navy during the war, my father became a theological student, and Dr. Shelton's dressy chauffeur, and a minister. Through all those years, where was my grandfather? My father said that once, perhaps when he himself was at Western Seminary in Pittsburgh, he had traced his father to lodgings in a rundown neighborhood in the city, and had found him living in a single room, kept very tidy and clean, with the few belongings neatly arranged, and my grandfather himself clean and dressed in freshly laundered summer clothes. The cleanness was what had particularly impressed my father. They had found little to say to each other.

So when we went home to see Grandma, from Union City, we went to visit the sanctum. Besides the two houses down on Stanton Avenue by the tracks, there was Alma's. In those years she lived in a frame house a few blocks up the hill. Many years earlier, long before I was born, she had married Ralph Spence: thin, slow, aquiline, self-effacing, seldom out from under his hat. He worked at the Alcoa Aluminum plant, as a foreman in charge of keeping the premises painted. It may have been from Ralph that my father picked up his high regard for the protective virtues of aluminum paint, which led to his periodic campaigns to paint miscellaneous objects around the house, from tools to paperweights, aluminum. I was startled, after Alma died, past ninety, to see a photograph of her and Vince and Harry as small children, some time well before the turn of the century, which shows her face, though already sly, tilted, and watchful, yet with a softness, an openness, a prettiness in the features, all of which had long vanished by the time I knew her. Only a few years after that picture was taken, or perhaps even at the time, she was said to be able to go down into the cellar and grab a rat, with her bare hands, out of the cellar wall, and then the real sport was to plunge it into kerosene and set a match to it, and let it loose at the edge of a field. Did those things really happen, or did the children make them up afterwards out of remembered fantasies? Either way they indicated what her character was thought to be. She had been brought up in circumstances where a penny was important, and she had become tight-fisted for choice, and was convinced that the whole world was conspiring to steal what she possessed. My mother said

Alma still had three cents out of the first nickel Spence ever earned. They called her Dutch, behind her back, though she knew it; it was, or it became, an adjective meaning stingy. When she went out she carried her black patent leather purse clamped under her arm, and she never set it down even when visiting another member of the family. All through my childhood I thought she looked an old pumpkin, days after Hallowe'en: the graying orange skin, the shrivelling mouth and cheeks.

She treated Spence more or less as a lazy hired man. Both she and her younger sister Edna behaved with the evident implication that they had married beneath them, and that their roles in their marriages involved a daily wordless charity—an attitude that exasperated my mother, who was sorry (as were many others) for Ralph, and felt real affection for Edna's husband, Port. In later days it seemed remarkable to us that Alma had married anyone at all and when the subject arose we arrived again and again at the conclusion that she must have waylaid Ralph and dragged him to the altar. In Edna's case it was hard to guess how she had come to marry Port in particular, considering the assortment of ethnic prejudices that were treasured in the family, by those sisters especially, and his Christian name, Alonzo, with its hint of Mediterranean antecedents. (But closer to hand there is a Porter, from Mahoning, among the obituary notices in my grandmother's commonplace book, though with no date of death and no indication of what the relationship may have been.) His complexion, besides, was remarkably swarthy for that circle. Edna herself had been fair, and she went gray at an early age. There was something asymmetrical about her mouth, her face, her body, her walk—and whatever they did. With age her shoulders rounded and rose to one side in a hump, and she looked up as though from beneath it, a turtle gesture, revealing her high cheek-bones and her trembling, distracted smile. She had a slight lisp and a deep, rasping, but pleasant voice.

The three houses were referred to by the names of the

women of the family: Grandma's, Aunt Eddie's, Aunt Alma's. When we went on visits it was Aunt Eddie's that we
were, in fact, heading for. My father drove according to a
private principle that evolved, emerged, set, over the years,
until it became so obtrusive that my mother refused to travel
with him any longer. On the road he was anxious to make
time. Detours distressed him and he took them personally.
They were proofs of corruption and deliberate malevolence.
He said they disgusted him. He did not speed, though he drove
faster than my mother said she would have preferred, especially when he was trying to catch up, after delays. He was
reluctant to stop, unless the stops had been agreed upon in
advance and so could count as minor destinations. There were
several traditional places where we might break our western
journeys. Ridgewood, New Jersey, where my mother's
cousin Betty lived with her husband Calvin Jones—a Firestone
salesman and a pillar of the Dutch Reformed Church, which
my father said was alright even though it was not Presbyterian
—and their two sons who were several years older than I was.
But if we were on a trip, even if we stopped we would not
stay long, and my father would inaugurate the visit by saying
so. Then there was the Cochran House at Newton, where we
might stop for a meal if we got there at the right time. But
as soon as my father stopped anywhere he was anxious to be
on the way again. He loved to drop in on friends of former
days, either unannounced or as the immediate sequel to a telephone call made a few miles from their door—to surprise
them. The habit embarrassed my mother, who pointed out
repeatedly how inconsiderate it was, but my father listened
to her objections, if he listened at all, only to sigh and press
on, perhaps a little faster. And once he had sat down in the
friends' chairs, if he allowed himself to be persuaded to stay
for supper and the night he would insist that we must all get
up at four, for an early start, which meant that the rest of the
household must get up too. Oh no, please don't. Oh yes of
course, you have to have breakfast. The early departures were

spoken of as one of the many mysterious necessities of the ministry.

My mother occasionally made stipulations in advance about stopping at specified points of interest. She took pictures, and notes in shorthand, at such places. But often she failed to get her wish. We would be too late to stop, or there would be someone else whom my father had discovered he should visit, and surprise, instead. We never turned aside at Caverns advertised with Indian Heads, or at other Natural Wonders; there wasn't time, and they weren't worth it. Both parents agreed on that. But once we visited a sauerkraut factory and peered over the edge of an enormous wooden vat to see a man in rubber boots down in there, walking rapidly in circles, counterclockwise, and flinging handfuls of rock salt before him in wide arcs as he went. We were informed that it was dangerous for him to be down there too long. The fumes from the sauerkraut might overpower him and he might lose consciousness and would die if there was not someone always keeping an eye on him. They gave us a free can of sauerkraut as we left, and it lasted on the shelf among the canned goods for some time, as a souvenir.

In spite of the early starts and the precipitate nature of the visits, it was often late when we approached New Kensington, and usually we had to stop at least once, in dark towns, to telephone Aunt Eddie and tell her not to worry, we were alright, there had just been detours and delays, one thing after another. And by the time we reached the familiar turnings the streets would be silent, no cars but our own rolling under the faithful streetlights, no one in sight on the sidewalks, and the glinting windows of the houses reflecting the measureless night. We would trundle slowly along Stanton Avenue, which in that light appeared to be the back of somewhere, running along the edge of the space where the tracks gleamed and echoed. We skirted potholes and peered out to see whether there was a light still on at Aunt Eddie's, and there would be one, under a pink hemisphere shade, downstairs in the living room, or out on the glassed front porch. A forty watt bulb. We would ease to a stop by the cement steps up to the sidewalk, and open the car doors as stealthily as possible. The night air smelled sweet to me—a different sweetness from the air of the small hours in Union City. Suddenly the scent of soft coal smoke and petunias, that lingered above the cement walks cool with the dew, came back to me rich with a knowledge that was rightly mine but that I could not grasp. I was happy to be there, and happy to think that I would soon be in bed asleep. I stood on the sidewalk and looked up, a little giddy from the hours of travelling, and breathed the night. The less lights there were the higher the black sky was, behind the stars. A hand drew back a curtain at the window onto the porch, and waved and was gone. A moment later the glass door between the hall and the porch opened, reflections of the pink lampshade glittering in the bevels of the panes. The flashes looked bright enough to wake the whole street. The knob receded only a few inches, and Aunt Eddie popped through, tiptoeing in bedroom slippers, her face sagging, her head swathed in nets and a wrapper which did not hide the flat metal clips clamping the curls of her permanent. She was in her bathrobe, because it was that hour, and as she came she held her finger to her lips, watching us with a smile that made us all conspirators. The outer lock, when it turned, made more noise than we had made in getting out of the car. Aunt Eddie opened the front door a little and greeted us in a whisper. Port appeared behind her in his dark bathrobe, and he and my father whispered and brought in from the car what was needed for going to bed. Once the street door and the inner door were closed and bolted behind us we could stop whispering and talk in low voices, as though we were telling secrets, while the children were put to bed. The stained glass window was still there at the turn of the varnished stairs, in a whitish gray standing sleep of its own, and on the sill in front of it, in a pot, a dark plant which never grew at all.

In the early years, when Grandma lived next door, we almost never saw her until some time the next morning. But after her house had been sold and she had moved in with Port and Eddie she might wake when we arrived, and call out as we came up the stairs, and we would be led in to the side of the big bed, to greet her. Once when I had come without my sister I was taken in and she had not remembered who was coming, or had not been told, and was lying asleep, and sat up and asked who I was. When they told her she said, "Well, Peg O' My Heart!" And just then she seemed young and warm and affectionate. But whether we greeted her or not, a moment later I would be lying under a patchwork she had made, in the bedroom over the back porch roof, with the light still coming in from the hall, and the voices whispering again. The sheets felt rough. My mother told me they were made of linen. Once as I was falling asleep I found a darned spot in the upper one and lay there feeling sorry for Aunt Eddie and Uncle Port, who I imagined must be very poor.

What did we do there, my sister and I? Almost nothing, which was what was demanded of us. At home our lives were surrounded by injunctions. On visits there were more of them. The dogs must not be touched. But there was not much temptation to do that. They barked and snapped when they were let out of their cellars, and Port was the only one who ever played with them, teaching them to jump through the hoop he formed by clasping his hands. Out back in a section of the garage that had been walled off to make a coal bin, visible through a gray lattice, was a giant snapping turtle which I was told could bite a broomstick in two. We must not go close enough to touch the lattice. Besides, it was covered with coal dust. The houses had a sweetish plaster smell that varied from room to room and from object to object but still was recognizable in all of them. There were artificial flowers in vases—petals and leaves made of celluloid and a kind of beadwork, and some of the waxy variety that I knew from cemeteries.

And Grandma sat up in her room over the living room, in her rocker by the window facing west out over the tracks to the viaduct where it sloped down to street level on the far side, and the heads and shoulders of cars could be seen passing up and down, unheard. Beyond the viaduct, on a rooftop, a billboard held up a huge picture of the sun. Through the struts of the sign one could see the line of hills across the river. Down in the living room we could hear the rocker move, and someone might call out "Is everything alright, Grandma?" and then, since usually there was no answer, go up and see. Grandma was stitching at her quilts, crocheting, reading her Bible, gazing out of the window. She was not to be disturbed, and we did not intrude on her. She came down to meals in the dark dining room and sat under the apricot-pink Tiffany lampshade; the chain from the bulb ended in a thumb-sized owl with ruby eyes. Grandma sat at the oak table and drifted in and out of the talk, one elbow by her plate, a hand in the air that occasionally waved as she grew older. "What are you waving at, Mumma?" Eddie would ask her, and first Grandma would not hear the question, and then she would laugh and say, "Oh."

We went out paying calls with our parents. We had to go up and see Aunt Alma—that was the way it was put, from the moment we arrived at Aunt Eddie's. And sit in Aunt Alma's kitchen or out on the porch glider, while the grownups talked of things and people we knew nothing about and never would. There were days when my father left with the car on ministerial affairs, and on visits of his own. My mother remarked of those three houses that there was not a book in any of them. And nobody came to call. Port had many friends at work and at the Lion's Club, and at every corner downtown. Spence belonged to the Masons and perhaps to a lodge or two. But nobody came home with them or stopped by for them there. Except for a Mr. Huff, a brush salesman with whom Edna and Port had made friends, who they said had studied for the ministry but had not had enough money to continue, and so had become a brush salesman instead. When Mr. Huff came to see them he opened his suitcase of samples on the kitchen floor, as a display of his life since he had seen them last, and after the brushes and their merits had been discussed he would stay for a meal. When he had left they would talk about what a fine man he was and how they hoped his luck would improve.

Occasionally, even in the early years, I found myself left in Port's care, and it was like being unexpectedly set free. He might take me downtown, as though he were gathering me up and wafting me to another country. Once out of sight of the house we would slip down the bank on a narrow path and walk rapidly along the tracks—something so unthinkable that it made me laugh with the sheer wildness of it. Iseley's sold towering ice cream cones for a nickel. My mother ruled categorically against them: if they were that big, heaven knew what was in them. But Port would get me one, and tell me to hurry up with it and he'd get me another. We sat high up in the shoe shine stalls with our feet on irons that looked like horse heads, and had our shoes shined, and Port talked with friends—everyone seemed to know him. Back home, we sat on the front steps and he played with the dogs and I watched the trains.

They were a wonder to me, like a fire or a body of water. In the earliest visits to New Kensington I had been carefully herded back from the top of the bank and the steps down to the sidewalk. But Port, above all, told me even then that I was not afraid of the trains when they thundered and screamed and clattered past only a few feet away from the front bank, so that I could feel the ground shudder and see the panes shiver in the windows, and if I was in the kitchen I could hear the glasses and plates and utensils clink and sing. When I was a baby, Port would hold me up and lift my hand to wave to the engineer, who might be somebody Port knew, and in those days I laughed at the roar as at the touch of cold water, and he would put an engineer's hat on my head, backwards, and call me the Toughest Guy in New Kensington. Later I was allowed to go by myself as far as the top step, and sit there to watch the trains and count the cars. I could hear the trains coming from far enough away for my heart to beat faster as I waited for them to rush and be there in front of me. A half block to the north the yellow cement viaduct crossed the tracks. When a locomotive streaked under the blackened center of the span the plume of white smoke was abruptly chopped across, and when it emerged on the near side the smoke shot straight up again, hiding the heads of the pedestrians, who never seemed to change their pace, and the car roofs gliding soundlessly across. As the trains passed, the whole street rattled and echoed; and then when they were gone, and the rear platform of the caboose, with its pair of red lamps, was clicking away along the narrowing tracks, a hush returned suddenly, a stillness in which every sound was small and moved slowly as though in water, especially the bells of the engines in the switching yard beyond the viaduct, and the puffing and hissing and chugging from there, and the clang of freight car bumpers striking as the cars were coupled together.

Sometimes Aunt Eddie told us that Harry and his family might be over to visit while we were there, and she would say again how much she liked Harry and Clara's daughters, their "girls", all of whom had boys' names. I do not remember them ever coming to Stanton Avenue during our own visits there, but we would go and call on them. They lived not far away—not nearly as far as we did. They were right across the river at Natrona Heights. From downtown New Kensington you could take a street car. Harry was a plumber and contractor, and his relation to Grandma's closed world was, from his sisters' point of view, somewhat ambiguous. He had moved away, but not so definitively, nor so far, as Vince or Sam or Birdie. He and Clara and the girls did come and visit Grandma fairly regularly, particularly on holidays. On the other hand, Harry's life was not tied to his mother's. He made no pretense of being accountable to her, and he did not emulate her fundamentalist religious zeal. No doubt Grandma and his sisters still inquired about when he had last been to church, and no doubt he answered evasively if at all. It was no wonder to them that there were other indications that he had fallen away from his Redeemer. They shook their heads and clucked their tongues and dropped their voices to admit that Harry too had been known—the voices dropped still lower—to drink, and poor Clara had had her problems. His sisters claimed that they had smelled it on his breath, and there were times—more shaking of heads, by way of finishing the sentence. To some unmeasured degree he had let them down. He might even have been capable of voting for a Democrat. I was glad to go to their house; my mother and Clara liked each other. But there was always a stiffness, an estrangement infusing our being there, some unease emanating from the fact that we came from the sanctum and its well known disapprovals, and from my father's reservations and all that had remained unspoken for years between him and his elder brother who had grown up to be one of the men on the block, while my father clambered toward the pulpit and then looked out from there.

From the tiny slow-moving vortex around Grandma, Harry and Clara and their family a streetcar ride away appeared as an outpost. Beyond them, even the rest of the family grew remote and receded toward the rest of the world. I had glimpses of how attenuated many of the relationships had become. One day when I was in the car with my father he pointed to a boy with curly red hair, on a street corner, and said, "I think that's your cousin so-and-so." But when I wanted to stop at once and meet the boy, my father said no, he wasn't sure, we'd do it another time. I saw that the family had branches that I knew nothing about, and I recognized as lip service my father's repetition that we must go and look them up one of these days.

Yet we did make one historic trek into the family distances.

Once in particular my father took only me with him when he went to Grandma's. It was after we had moved from Union City back to Pennsylvania, to Scranton. We had not been there long before the Buick, which had been giving my father more and more trouble, breaking down far from home and mechanics, at unforgiveably ill-chosen moments, was replaced suddenly by the Olds: new, egg-shell gray, with long streamlined front fenders that housed the headlights and flowed on to an elegant humped shape introduced that year. A bargain at $815.

The move to Scranton had served to emphasize emerging disaffinities between my parents. The issue of cars and driving had revived. When my father left my mother and sister at a summer cottage by a lake, and took me with him on that trip, it was surely after a discussion in which my mother said she would rather stay behind anyway, and reminded him that she was used to being left without a car. And his taking me with him, away from the lake, was a move to repossess himself of me. He blamed her, rather than any behavior of his own, for turning the children against him. The fear that we were growing away from him had been gathering in him for years and was both effect and cause of some of his angry and capriciously punitive behavior toward us and toward me in particular. Another of his responses to it, for some time, had taken the form of calling me into his study at home, where I would stand in front of the desk, uncomfortable, hot, wondering what I had done wrong now, and he would tell me to shut the door behind me. Then he would fish in the lower recesses of his desk for a moment, shut a drawer and sigh, and tell me that we just were not spending enough time together, he and I, and that he was sorry it was happening but he could not help it right now because he was so busy and had so much on his mind. But these were precious years that would not come again. He would tell me then how hard things had been for him when he was a boy, and how fortunate we were, we children, and how much easier life was for us, with our yard to play in. And he said how important it was for me to study hard and do well at school. And how he wished we could move before long and have a big place in the country with room, where children could run, and with shade trees, and a dog, just an ordinary dog, and maybe even a horse. I reminded him, out of loyalty, that we did have a dog. And he said we would do more things together. Then he would start telling me about insurance, how I would come to realize its importance when I was older, and how we were going without some things now so that we children and our mother would be taken care of if anything were to happen to him—which meant if he were to die. I would feel like crying, and he would come and put an arm around me and tell me that I must be a good boy. And then he might show me something out of his desk, such as the pocket knife which he said was the one thing he had that had belonged to his father, the one thing that his father had given him. Talking as though his father were dead. Or he would tell me something which ordinarily would not have been mentioned, and caution me not to say anything about it, to anybody. It was on one such occasion that he told me most of the little I learned about my grandfather. And then he might give me something, such as a card printed with the Ten Commandments, the names of the Books of the Bible, the Apostles' Creed and the Lord's Prayer, and pat me and say that he would try to find more time to be together, and we would be pals, and I would nod, and go, feeling grief inextricably tangled with my own unexpected and unconvincing goodness, and shutting the door behind me.

And when he decided to take me with him, alone, back to Grandma's, in the new car, the trip was presented, to me, as one of the often-postponed things that he always wanted us to do together and usually did not have time for. He contributed to the announcement and the preparations an air, more than half serious, of a male conspiracy against the women of the family. We men together. "Women," he repeated: "you can't live with them and you can't live without them." It was an attempt to conceal his own uneasiness at the decision, and at the prospect of being alone together, and at the necessity of putting a good resolution into action—the resolution having to do with the oft-projected camaraderie between us. Once we were actually on the road he became morose and preoccupied again, and as irritable as ever. Even as an old man he remembered and reproached himself for the severity of his wrath when I stepped out of the car, once, where he had parked it, into a mud puddle, in my new white buck shoes with elaborately perforated wing tips. The oppressiveness of his behavior to me was so obvious that in New Kensington Edna and even Alma were stirred to take my part and remonstrate with him. He was more affable when there were people present to whom he could show me off before proceeding to discuss matters of real moment which did not concern me; I was not to "butt in" on those parts of the conversation, which to him were the conversation itself. It seemed to him then, probably, that many things, even most things that he considered his, were slipping from him. And that must have had something to do with his idea of going, in the new car, to visit the rest of Grandma's children, his brothers and his other sister, and of taking Grandma and Alma and Eddie and me along.

But in fact I do not know what was in his mind, nor how long he had been planning that further family trip. He may have been brooding on it for some time without saying anything about it. He may have had it all decided when he proposed to take me with him, alone, to New Kensington, and still not have spoken of it to my mother, who would only have sniffed at the mention of such an excursion. On the other hand, for all his insistence upon fixed destinations and making time, he abhorred being what he called tied down by having to be somewhere, and the whole journey, complete with his mother and sisters, and me, to see far-flung relatives, may have arisen from a moment's impulse after we got to New Kensington: a response to a wistful phrase of Grandma's, or to some new remark about the car.

Grandma was well into her eighties by then, but he planned an early start so that we could make good time, because there was a long way to go. The three ladies wore high shiny black straw hats with narrow brims, and long coats although it was summer, and held their black patent leather purses clamped under their arms, as we assembled in the dark air, hours before dawn, and shuffled, whispering, down the walk and the front steps, holding Grandma by the arms, and settled into the car, and were off. No one had been warned that we were coming.

We stopped first, early in the day, to see Birdie. I could not understand why they spoke of her, and everything about her, as though she were an unfortunate, and somewhat ridiculous. But I cannot be sure now how much of her I remember and how much I have dreamed. When I came to think back to her she seemed to have been quite happy, in a house that opened right off the asphalt of a back street, with no sidewalk, past the doorsill. The tiny front room was full of sunlight, and there was a canary singing in a cage. Birdie was a well covered, smiling, welcoming woman in a bright yellow wrapper, wearing big, dangling earrings. Her son Billy, a quiet, thin young man, had painted the pictures on the walls: copies of Christ Praying in the Garden of Gethsemane, of a head of Christ as a young man, of a scene in which a young girl was listening to a bird in a tree—pictures that I recognized because we too had reproductions of them at home, but these were real artist's oil paintings, and I was impressed, and felt that I would like to learn to paint like that. We were told that her son was going to be, or perhaps already was, a commercial artist. Birdie wanted us to stay and eat, but my father and Alma and Edna agreed that we had to be on our way, and we started off again and drove to Canton, Ohio.

There my father inquired about the address until we

reached an old red brick industrial building where Vince worked in an office. My father went in to look for him and brought him out to the car to talk to us, and Vince stood there in his shirt sleeves, with garters above the elbows. The rest of us waited in the car. Vince bent down and talked through the window. It was lunch time, and he suggested that we have lunch together, but we had to get on our way, because it was so far. I believe we stopped somewhere else for lunch, after all. Of Vince himself I remember almost nothing except a resemblance to Uncle Harry, and his white shirt fluttering in the breeze, outside the car window, on the street.

From Canton we headed for the farmland near Bowling Green to look for Sam. We had a rural address that sounded definite and authoritative at a distance of several hundred miles, but began to dissolve as we drew nearer to the region it referred to. There was no indication of how to approach the place, where it was near, a landmark or a road with a name that people might know. The afternoon was well advanced before we came near enough to be rolling along dirt lanes past cornfields, stopping to ask. The trail faded. Nobody seemed to know Sam Merwin and where he lived, and we were not sure where we were, and it kept getting late, and cloudy, and chilly, and Grandma was anxious and asked where we were, among the flat green fields. Someone finally remembered and directed us, and we arrived at the uncut grass and the house like a box, not old but worn, standing by itself, where no one was expecting us.

It was a small building, looking temporary and thin, with a covered space to one side that I learned was called a breezeway, which everyone agreed would be very cold in the winter. Sam was there, and he said yes it got very cold there, and his wife came to the door behind him, plump and smiling, and their children were inside as we filed in. They stood still, by the beds, and looked surprised. Sam's mouth was puckered, without teeth. He said he never thought to see us, and his wife agreed, laughing. We sat down, as they said to do, on the few chairs and on the beds. They talked about what Sam had been doing. He said he was on relief some of the time, and that he had the whole place for two dollars a month. He said "dawlers", like my aunts, and they nodded. It sounded to me as though the rent was a good arrangement, and Sam said he had been lucky to get the place, but he kept repeating that it was just for the time being. I thought they might be poor, and the thought depressed me, with us sitting there and asking questions. I felt that we were embarrassing them, looking at their poverty when they had not been expecting it. I knew that my mother was right, and that we should not have turned up without warning. I do not know how long it had been since Sam had seen his mother—he was then forty-five—or whether she had ever set eyes on his children. They remained silent, staring at the woman they had been told was their Grandma, and at their aunts and uncle and cousin, across the great gulf that had just been set in front of them. And their elders did the same, not knowing what to ask each other, and their questions not making things any better, though Sam and his wife kept saying they were glad to see us and what a surprise it was. They all talked this way and that, for a while, about some things that had happened to them, and who had had children and accidents and sicknesses, and had died, in all the years since anybody from New Kensington had last conversed with Sam or heard much from him. None of the subjects went on very long. Each came to an end as though nobody else was listening. And then my father stood up and said we must be going, and Sam spoke with admiration of the new car. Maybe my father suggested that we might all have a word of prayer, and stood there and squeezed his eyes shut and pronounced it, or maybe he let it go that time. I forget. We went out through the broken things lying in the high grass, and got into the car and left, and drove all the way back to New Kensington by the shortest route, but there were detours and we got lost, and everyone was very tired and no one talked much, and we got back very late, amazed at how far we had driven in one day.

I never saw Birdie or her son again, or Vince. And three years later Sam was killed by a car, on the road north of Bowling Green. He opened a taxi door and was pitched out onto the road and struck by the machine just behind, and died of a fractured skull.

Neither my father, nor his sisters, nor Grandma, said much afterwards about the trip to Ohio, except to repeat how many miles we had driven, in how many hours. It did not occur to me that Edna's or Alma's or Grandma's moods varied at all, and I was accustomed to assessing my father's emotional states practically—in terms of their probable effect on me. I could not have guessed how any of them felt about that round of visits, in the days that followed, and they may not have known, themselves. Nobody talked about where we had been, except to say that the people we had seen were alright. Birdie was alright, and Vince was alright. And Sam was alright.

And for the same reasons I can only guess what my father may have felt when, a few days after that trip, he and Uncle Port and I got into the new car to drive over to Uncle Harry's so that my father could talk to his father about going into a home. It was not until after we were on our way that I was told where we were going, and that I was being taken along so that I would have a chance to meet my grandfather. As for the institution itself, my father said that he had been to see what it was like, and that he was sure his father would like it there: the old man would be able to make friends, and walk out of doors, on the grounds.

At the far side of the New Kensington bridge I looked, as always, at the black scoreboard with the white skull and crossbones on it, and the number that stood for how many people had been killed in car accidents at that intersection, so far. The number had not changed since we had left for Ohio, in the dark, and I had read it by the beam of the headlights. As we drove, the backs of the two heads in the front

seat turned, and nodded, and my father and Uncle Port discussed the possibility of taking my grandfather some chewing
tobacco, and spent some time deciding which brand he would
prefer. Hearing them talk about buying chewing tobacco was
like watching them try on costumes. They worked at recall-
ing what kind they had ever seen him chew, what cans he had
kept it in, what packages they had watched him take it out of,
and the names sounded foreign as they repeated them. And
yet I had seen advertisements for those different brands of
chewing tobacco covering the sides of barns all the way across
Pennsylvania, and when I had read them aloud the first time
my father had shaken his head and I had not done it again.
Mail Pouch. Chew Mail Pouch. Red Man. With a Red Man's
head, in red. Beech Nut. I hoped they would get him Red
Man. As the names were discussed the barns reappeared, the
wooden houses near them, the hayfields and hills, as they
would do again and again, over many years. Turns in the
road, fences, trees, signs by day or night, light on boards and
grass and animals rose distinct and still. And the drive to
Uncle Harry's remains clear, and the store where we stopped
and they went in for tobacco.

There was an ice cream sign in an iron frame out on the
sidewalk, like the recruiting posters in front of the Post Office. They bought Beech Nut. I can see the glint of Uncle
Harry's front door. But the face we were going to see, my
grandfather's, does not appear. I look up in the sunlight to the
straw hat and I see the shadow of the brim, but not what the
shadow is falling on.

Years after my grandfather died, and after my parents too
had died, I wrote and asked my sister whether she had any
information about him or had ever seen a picture of him, and
she sent me a post card with a sepia print of a carefully—even
elegantly—dressed man, perhaps in his thirties, with a neat
moustache—a picture taken, probably, in the 1880's. In the
letter that came with it she asked, "Could this be our grandfather? And if so, why on a post card?"

Mary

O NCE I imagined, with no way of saying it, that my parents, and everyone of their age, kept somewhere among them the whole of the past. They possessed it, and could converse with it at first hand. There were people who existed in another room, which I could not be shown because I was too young. My elders did not talk to me about all this, but they referred to it among themselves. It would belong to me in due course, and sooner if I behaved.

In the meantime, I was convinced that I knew less about my family, and my parents' famiiles, than it was usual to know. It was an ignorance that my parents evidently approved of and abetted. It belonged among the things I should be proud of. Yet I believed that I should know the colors in the sepia photographs when I saw them. More than once I have dreamed of going home past a harbor, in the first moments of a happy reunion, after long waiting, and noticing fondly the familiar glassy darkness of the water in which the boats were moored, and feeling certain that I should know the names of all those hulls, though the sterns were blank, and I was aware that the boats were not the ones I had seen long before.

My father referred to his family as "the family," and he

called us "our family." His family was related to our family, but lived far away. Or we lived far away. In the beginning, my father described, as a remarkable feat, how he had driven back to his family and made it in one day, starting long before it was light and arriving in the small hours, the mention of which made listeners cover their mouths. When he told it I saw his family all waiting in one place, looking east, some in doorways, with arms folded, some watching at windows until he got there.

Mary was not among them. She was one of the family, a real relative, my father's cousin, but she lived with us, off and on. Though it was always said of her that when she went back home, away from us, she sighed with relief as she crossed the Delaware into Pennsylvania, and said that now she was back in God's country again. Aunty Mary, she was called, when she was with us. It would not have been respectful for the children to call her Cousin Mary, though that would have been more correct. Sometimes it was said that she was living with us, and sometimes that she was staying with us. She may have been there when I was born.

There at the house—not at the hospital, across the river in New York City. She was living with us two years later, when my sister was born, in the same hospital. When my father said that Mary was a good soul, he sometimes repeated, as an illustration, his story of bringing my sister, bundled in blankets, home from the hospital, carrying her up the long, brown flight of front steps, tossing her (he said) onto the bed, with Mary watching. And saying, "Well, I guess she'll do, but she'll never be the boy her brother is." To tease Mary, who took it—as she took whatever came her way—with unhesitating seriousness. And according to him she said, "You wait. She'll be rubbing your old back when he's out with the girls." It is possible that I was standing there, but all I am sure of is the story, at which people were expected to laugh.

She must have kept going out to the vestibule—two walls, two doors, a rubbery smell, and an echo—and putting her face against the outer door, to peer down through the jungle of fruit and flowers, ferns, and straight lines etched into the frosted glass. (Later, though it was forbidden, whenever I could I would touch those flowers—the same places she must then have looked through: there was something about them that I could never quite believe nor quite disbelieve.) The round black-rimmed spectacles clung loosely to her long, indefinite nose. Each time she went out to look, clumping through the dark hall without hearing herself—heavy shoes, cotton stockings worn loose—she did so with the extra ungainliness of a strange action. Hurrying to answer the door, when she was sure nobody had rung. She was fated to spend most of her life alone in houses, and she did it in a manner to which she seemed to have been born. It was a manner that she shared with others of my father's family, a variation on a theme—like the shapes of their hands. She seldom looked out of doors or appeared at windows in the normal round of the days. Incessant unseen cleaning, cleaning. She wore her glasses, which may have been the originals, low, and generally stared over the tops of them. That ruins your eyes, my mother taught, to suppress emulation. They were given to sitting a bit crooked, besides, and they were made up partly of tape and string. You would think Mary would go and get fitted, but nobody could ever tell her anything. She kept the case in the torn clean pocket of her apron, along with string, keys, and clothespins. She waited, then, crowded up into the coats hung in the iron clothes-stand, her damp left hand on the brass doorknob embossed with a vine thin as a vein. She was hard of hearing. Most days she had cotton in her ears. Those were the very days when she insisted that she had a cold but could really hear everything. Surely she would have taken the cotton out, on that occasion, and put it down somewhere, just the same, but it was better in the long run to keep an eye open.

When the car stopped she probably fumbled with the rattling door and finally yanked it open and stood holding it, while my father, carrying a pale blur, came in at the gate and up the flight of front steps. He looked down at each step. She may even have smiled. October. Beside the brown banister the catalpa leaves had turned their true elephant color. Somebody from the church must have been driving. It was always hard for Mary to say hello. Some of it I know because she never changed.

Around Mary there was always a breath of winter—not cold, exactly, but a muffled, hueless presence, a waiting vapor. I became aware of that bleak atmosphere, first, at the head of the inside stairs, in the hall by the bathroom door, and then all through the house, above radiators and behind doors, when my mother was in the hospital and only Mary was there to mind me. I was alone then in the house in which Mary was alone. She did not hear me. I was a recurring surprise to her. My father had told me to obey her, as he left. He had to be out much of the time—down at the church rehearsing his sermon; making calls on members of the congregation; at meetings of elders, deacons, trustees; installations of officers. When my mother was at home he had one voice, and when only Mary was there, he had another. He seldom addressed himself to me; maybe I embarrassed him. He asked about me, above me. Then it seemed that I was the one who was hard of hearing. Mary would say there was no news, and then she would tell him something that I had not heard about. If he did not understand, she raised her voice. Both of them were absent-minded.

When my mother was not there, Mary kept the window-shades, even in the front, drawn clear down to the sills, day and night. She called them blinds. The furniture migrated to different places: backed up against walls, piled up in corners under covers. It was a laundry light, Mary's, some relation to that which came through the north windows, at ground level, above the square dark stone tubs in the basement. She was never entirely separated from the washing, or what she called the house-cleaning, or putting things away even if they had not been got out. She wore clothes that were faded until they looked dusty, all verging on the same color. On her they appeared to belong to somebody older. I came to believe that they were my grandmother's clothes, which had been lent to Mary. When I saw a Salvation Army uniform I thought that Mary might well be inside it when the woman turned around: that would be how Mary would dress up. For everyday—which was how I saw her—she wrapped her head in a duster, even out in the street, as my mother said. That too was a custom she had inherited. One of my father's sisters, Alma, said it made Mary look like a mop. But Alma also wore a duster, and what she said was not to be repeated. Down in the basement, in her duster, in the steam, Mary worked the wringer, not hearing a thing, in a trance. "She doesn't hear," someone would explain, right next to her, and Mary would nod and look out the window at the yard, where it was winter, the height of the water in the tubs. My mother worried that Mary would get her hand caught in the wringer, and she did once: it was said that she didn't hear it coming.

Some meaning of the word "naphtha" was inexplicably hers, and echoed the smell of her damp apron that reached below her knees, and of the duster on her head, and of her hands, long shapeless and rough, running from gray to orange. With those hands she tugged my clothes onto me and fastened them up, right or wrong, or pulled them off. Whatever she touched was the wrong size. When I was left with her and she gave me a bath, from the moment it was announced, it felt like a mistake that nobody within hearing could do anything about. The water was sure to be either too hot or too cold, and she could not hear what was said about it, nor hear it running when it should have stopped. The sound kept on. She looked crosser than when she was washing other things. The heavy hands gripped and rubbed and remained strangers. Washcloth into ears. Years later when it was my sister's turn she said Mary hurt. I had felt that, and had never got used to it, and yet the words startled me and did not sound right. I knew, as one knows a fact, that Mary had never been a child. She had always been exactly the same. Naturally she could not be told anything. There were things that were true in themselves that were not true when it came to her.

When she bathed me, the hands descended directly out of her deaf place, to scrub, and what they scrubbed happened to be part of me. She had neck skin on her arms. There was not always a body inside her dress and gray cardigan. Maybe there was nothing there at all. Ivory celluloid, swathed in that same skin. When I was in the tub she did not know me, though she still knew things about me which I could not even guess. She kept them secret. She was used to holding pins in her mouth, clothespins or ordinary pins, which nobody should do. When she put them down she lost them. There was a danger of her glasses falling off into the tub and breaking, if she were bumped. For that reason I too should hold put. And she dripped. It was an effort for her to approach that other skin, naked though only a child's. She hung on. It might fly out of her hand and be dashed against the wall: fish, bird, frog, her own flesh and blood. When I heard of accidents in bathtubs, blood flowing in the water, I thought of Mary, and yet I was not afraid of her, though there was something about her of the large insect which one is taught is benign. She cracked her gum, whence the word gumption. She hummed a note with no resonance, to listen to and lean against, and she sucked her teeth, for a distraction. The knees of her stockings were constantly wet. She had a green sponge rubber kneeling pad worn rough and thin in the middle—the breadboard becoming green bread at last. All she would have had to do would have been to turn the pad to the side, to be scrubbing the floor, the walls, anything else, as she did more often than there was any call for. They were all sloshed at in the same way, vehement and hurried, for fear somebody might come, and dirt still be there. She got soap-water over everything. My mother said that sometimes Mary was not much help. Mary could hear my mother less well than she could hear my father.

She was noisy, a clatterer in the kitchen. My mother preferred her not to do the dishes. Mary's own bones and joints got in her way. If she set down the plate for the dog, she was liable to break it. They said she was too heavy for light work and too light for heavy work. But she could do things that were forbidden. She was an incomprehensible verse from a familiar hymn. All around her lay the age of the kidnappers. She had a crystal set, in her room. Many times her mouth said Lindbergh. Among her possessions was a picture of him as a young man, everything in it the color of his flying suit. The year that he flew the Atlantic I was born. What did that mean? Never take candy from strangers.

Mary never seemed to have heard that the kidnappers came once and offered me candy. A lady in a white hat walked close to the gate and spoke to me, and held out white tablets stamped with the heads of thistles, while a man stood a little way off, watching. I looked hard at the tablets, through the pickets of the gate, and said nothing, and those strangers went away. My father had been stern when I had told about it, long afterwards, and had asked whether there had been a car. I tried to remember. There must have been a car. I seemed to have done something wrong. Would I know the lady, or the man, if I saw them? I was to come to my father immediately if it happened again. Did anyone really believe it? Had it happened at all?

Mary could not be counted on to bear in mind from day to day everything that was not allowed: the list was too long, and she was too forgetful. If she felt that she had slipped up she might contribute some makeshift injunction of her own; it always retained the faltering accent of the hurried guess, and was obeyed out of general obedience, without particular belief. Apparently she had not been warned that indelible pencils are poisonous. There were many things like that which she did not seem to know, and it was interesting that she survived at all. As for me, it was unthinkable that I would ever go into her room, next to the bathroom. I was forbidden even to stand outside it, partly because it was at the head of the stairs, which I might fall down. Smells of string, paper, mothballs, varnish, and Mary, drifted out if the door was left open for a moment, as when my mother and Mary were putting things away in there. We had no attic, as my mother explained. I imagined that everything I glimpsed, inside there, vanished when the door shut. Another landscape began then, with another sky. Mary's, and secret.

But she invited me in there, one day, herself. She took it into her head. There was no one else in the house. She was minding me. Rules sometimes came adrift. She led me in and stood there, facing me, and I stood there. She was entertaining me. I listened to her breathe. The room was smaller than it looked from outside, and smelled more. The shades were all the way down—as you could see from out in the street, which made my mother shake her head—and the light was the brown of old paper. Furniture, and bundles wrapped in newspaper, were piled around the walls, in shades of tan. Some of the things in there were hers, I had heard my mother say, and some of them belonged to us, but I could see no way of telling them apart. I could not even be sure in every case which were things, and which were just the covers of things. Aunty Mary showed me a stone-gray picture of a thin man in his underwear, with one bare foot in front of him and one fist swung forward. She held it down for me to see good. That man, she told me, was Bernarr MacFadden, and he was walking very fast, which he taught people how to do, and she was one of them. I thought of how fast she walked, and now I knew why. Behind her on a shelf stood a huge glass jar, like the ones in the drugstore, half full of something red, the one bright color in the room. She turned around and took the lid off and fished out a few red things the size of newborn fingernails, shaped like hearts. She explained that they were the

shape of hearts, just like real ones, but were candy. And she
held them out to me. I was almost certain that I should not
take any. She was not a stranger, but she was not one of my
parents, either, and candy was very seldom allowed, even
at home. She told me to go ahead. She said go on, they're
cinnamon. Go on, they won't do no harm, they're cinnamon.
I took one. It was exciting. Go on, take more, she said, there's
nothing to them. I took another one. I closed my hand over
them. Go on, eat one, she said, eat it right now. I had been
thinking of saving them. She took one out of the jar and
popped it into her mouth, to show me. Then she stuck her
tongue out with the cinnamon heart melting on it, wet and
shiny, and the middle of her tongue was bright red. All at
once her face jumped apart like water, behind her glasses:
she was laughing. I put one of the hearts in my mouth and it
burned. I told her, but she said never mind that, they was
good. Wasn't they? And I nodded, and let it melt and burn,
as she said to, while I watched her, but nothing else happened.
As I went along the hall I opened my hand and saw that the
other heart had made the palm bright red, like her tongue,
and I put it away. I still imagined the other sky, inside her
room, but I thought it must be invisible if anyone was in
there.

Even at that time she was evoked by things she had forgotten—random scraps said to be redolent of her, and perhaps
never true. Maybe she said that thing about God's country
once, and as a joke, or told it about somebody else. Her
cooking—which she practiced only when my mother was
away—was like that: something that was talked about, to
describe her, and came to stand for her like an initial. Mostly
she cooked pork, it was said. And potatoes. The day she read
that macaroni was a change from potatoes she thought that
might be an idea, and gave it a try, and it was. The fact that
she had said so became another of her initials. The food she
got ready was alluded to, long afterwards, as a recurrent disaster, patiently appreciated. By implication it was generally

burned, chipped, ruined, dropped, thrown out and rescued, smoking, smelling of the wash—but in fact it may have been nothing so definite, in its time. Give a dog a bad name. Her shopping was in the same line. She bought things heaven knew where, not in the stores where my mother went, but in places she found on her own, pushing me in front of her in the go-cart. She stomped all over town, walking fast, and produced one real event that passed into history: she got lost. She gripped the bar of the go-cart and stormed ahead, ramming the shopping cart and me farther and farther into the unknown, crossing street after wrong street in her black cloche hat and long family skirt, her purse clamped under her arm, while it deliberately got later. Thinking, "Lindbergh." But also thinking, "Supper."

For years it was explained that she came from somewhere else, and was strange to the town.

And yet people whom my parents never recognized knew her. A Polish woman, for instance, whom she used to bump into on the corner, as she said. The first time on a lovely day, with my sister tucked up in the big baby carriage in the yard in back of the house, shrieking. Teething, possibly, but she used to shriek to herself at length, for no reason that was ever discovered. And Mary, coming back from somewhere, saw the woman standing listening, in wonder, and when she got up to her they both stood, and the woman turned and said, "My god how that priest's baby can yell." She was a fat woman, Mary always remembered to say. And after that they nodded, or even spoke, if they saw each other in stores. My parents said that Mary was making a few friends. Grocers inquired after her when she had been gone for some time, and that was worth mentioning.

When I heard that ritual phrase about her being a stranger to town, I tried to imagine how the town must appear to her. Which was difficult, because whatever else I was, apparently I was not a stranger there, myself—though I knew less about the place than Mary did. I realized, though, that for her, Central Avenue, for example, was not a single street (she never learned the names of the streets, but neither did I, for that matter) but a whole region, over that way. I envisaged her striding along through that ill-defined area, faster than usual, without the go-cart, in a yellow light. The curbs were higher than when I was along. I recognized very little, though it was somewhere I was supposed to know, as in "*you* remember Central Avenue." I knew how changeable that region was. Often, in thinking about it, I lined the blocks with more open carpenter shops (I knew only one), barber shops (I knew one, with a face of the sun smoking a cigar—a wrong thing to do—on the wall), cigar stores (I knew one, with a block out front where there had once been an Indian), than turned out to be there when I saw the places the next time. Between Mary and the shadowy people she passed—backs going both ways—there was a silence, like that around a magnet I had been shown on my father's desk, but had not been given to hold. People stared at Mary. I watched them. Doubtless what was more curious about her than any external feature was her curiosity itself, a current that twitched and drove her, apparently aimlessly, and planted her with her feet apart and her mouth open, where nobody else thought of looking. She said she wanted to see. That restlessness of hers was something she shared with others of my father's family, but the fumbling inquiry that nagged her all her days had been born dead or pinched out or walled up in most of the others, and they never recognized it except in the way she embarrassed them. To the Greeks a stumbling-block.

All around her the world was supposedly saying "Pay no attention," and she didn't, but in her own way. Certain things got to be more than she could take, though. The heat. She perspired awful. I realized that she wore dusters under clothes. She despised Mrs. Callen, the gentle, waddling inhabitant, for some time, of the front room in the basement. Mrs. Callen was not a relative. She was no relation at all. She rented that room, although the fact was never put plainly but in hushed, reluctant admissions, hastily. Mrs. Callen must not hear it, though there was nothing shameful in it. It was nobody's business. At a proper distance she was called Callie. One door of her room opened into the laundry, in back, which also contained her kitchen. Her eating and preparing to eat, and Mary's deaf sloshing, overlapped more often than my mother said was at all needful. Mary acknowledged the sight of Mrs. Callen by clucking her tongue. "F - a - t," she would mutter, and chew nothing in her mouth. Callie found out where to get cabbages for a nickel, and Mary sniffed, and wiped her nose with the back of one hand after the other. "How are you, Mrs. Callen?" my father would ask, and she would say "I'm just plain hungry." It grew into another name for her. She said she dreamed constantly of a seven-layer cake, even in the afternoons. She broke down and bought one, not fresh, half-price, from a cheap baker, occasionally when she was out anyway. She said her shoes were wet by the time she got home, from her mouth watering. And she sat down right there with her hat on, and ate the whole thing. "See her coming, look at her bag," Mary said. "Just something to put in her g - u - t." Callie wore green dresses cut low in front, and the skin below her neck was turkey red. She pinned up her rusty hair with tortoise shell combs. She had an old radio, faint and crackly, and she held me up so I could put my ear to it—though I was not supposed to do that—and in the smell of her body I listened.

She had moved there while it was still the old brown house, in the age before it was painted. Then my father had conjured out of his congregation an eager jack-of-all-trades, a small dark wiry spark-plug of a man, who called himself Eggie. Eggie drove a delivery truck, part of the time, for Delmonte's White Rose Tea, only because his voluminous Italian wife's name was Rose. Rose was shy, and bigger than he was. He explained with admiration, rolling his eyes, that she was a lot of woman. He had gold teeth. He arrived with his ladders, pots, brushes, and buckets in a hearse which he had picked up, called a hoise, as in hoist. (Hoist was the noun; the verb was highst.) Thirty dollars he had paid for the hoise, and had put in the plywood sides himself: he did his own body-woik. He had with him his helper, Dumb Genie, big, broad, and freckled. What they called skyhooks were clamped to the edges of the roof, and the scaffolds squealed up and down on pulleys, and the summer began to smell of paint. My father helped with the painting when he had time, even though he was the minister, and day by day the house turned green, with buff trim; three coats, at a bargain. I was big enough to hold a paint brush, and was allowed to, from time to time, and to wear a new painter's cap, like a bucket, but the hat held little magic for me because I was an Indian. Before the hoise, Eggie told me, they had had a Plymouth that came over on the Mayflower. They drove it around with only one headlight and a big rock in the back. Up in Massachusetts, there, they ran out of gas and got caught for speeding both, and the cop said either they fix that other headlight or they get rid of that rock, so they dump the rock since they were broke. So it's called Plymouth Rock. Genie, on a scaffold, stepped into a bucket of buff trim and kicked it high up in the air and all down the three floors of the side of the house along New York Avenue. It bounced off the roof of the bay window on the way to the sidewalk, where no one happened to be passing. God alone saved Genie from going the same way. People tramped through the long, thick puddle, stamped, muttered, tracked it up and down the street. The yellow cloud shape dried, shriveled, gathered dirt in the wrinkles, developed knowledge of its own, and would stay there forever. By a trash fire in the back yard I heard Genie say, "Shit," and I repeated the new word, and saw their faces change. They told me, with lowered voices, never to say that word, woid, never let nobody hear me, don't never let my father hear me say that. Don't want to be like dumb Genie.

I sat at the top of the front steps and whispered the magic syllable over and over into the ear of Tippie, our toy fox terrier, trying to surprise its secret.

Every day that summer was the hottest on record, and they had carried an old pale green, chafed, wicker settee out under the kitchen window, against the north wall of the house, and given it a coat of the darker green. The wall behind it was of painted brick, up as far as the second story, and there was more shade there than anywhere else. Whoever was minding us, when it was not too hot to be out, could sit there, and most days Callie would come out in the afternoon and take the air for a while on the settee, wearing a broad black straw hat, which changed her into somebody else—I thought a god-mother would probably look like that—and black glass beads. With her left hand she held a big black umbrella over her head, and with her right hand she fanned herself: she had a wide palm fan like the ones in the hymn racks in church. My mother said it only made you hotter. Her fanning kept the settee creaking and the umbrella swaying. Callie turned red-der out in the air, and she sighed and nodded off—like the cat, she said, though we had none. The leaning of the umbrella woke her up. The heat was bad enough, but that umbrella drove Mary beyond endurance. The kitchen window was right above the settee, and Mary kept leaning out and looking and clucking her tongue. Beside the window was the squeak-ing pulley for the clothesline out to the garage that had once been a barn. Mary hung out everything that could be hung out to drip—wash-rags or anything else—while Callie just sat there. If Mary could find something that needed shaking, she shook it out of the window: dustmops, dusters, rugs—after which she hung them on the line. Finally she emptied a bucket of water onto the quavering black dome below.

Heaven knows what my parents said to Callie. She went off to see relatives in Bayonne for a spell, and came back just in time for Mary's departure, all in the same heat wave. While Callie was away, the front room was painted—redecorated—

for a surprise, and she said she was surprised. My mother had gone over to New York herself, to get Mary's Pullman reservation, for the eighth of July—my mother's birthday. I was in bed, with measles and a temperature. On the day itself, while Mary was getting her things finally together, packing the blue suit she and my mother had bought on a spring foray to Wanamaker's, the old wooden icebox was lugged out and replaced by a new electric refrigerator. I was given some of the accompanying literature in bed: a brightly illustrated fable for the children of the lucky household, about a knight in armor who lived up in the white tower on top of the refrigerator, and came down at night to rout the demons of decay and disease who were about to pounce on the terrified food. It was educational. My mother took Mary to the night train to Pittsburgh, and saw her off. She said that it was only Mary's physical self that left, at that time: mentally, Mary had been in Pennsylvania for some weeks past.

We too went to Pennsylvania, on visits, but I did not see Mary again for more than twenty years. The rest of the family did not have much to do with her. My father called on her, sometimes, when he went back home on visits. I heard that she had moved, had not been well, was better, had moved back—scraps of information as bodiless as the sizes of clothes. When I was old enough, I went to see her myself.

She was living in Kittaning, on the Allegheny River northeast of Pittsburgh. Other relatives had lived there; some still did. My father's mother had taken her eight children to the town when my father was ten or eleven, and he had got his first job there, in a dry goods store. My parents had gone back to that part of the country at the time of the Korean War, and my father had two small country churches a few miles from the one in which he had started in the ministry. He went into Kittaning regularly, and occasionally dropped in on Mary. My mother was in the town every week day, working in the Child Welfare office, in the courthouse, under the glance of a politician quietly known as Cesspool, and she saw

Mary more regularly than my father did, and was better informed about Mary's interests. I had been abroad for seven years, and the patterns in the bricks in the streets and sidewalks rose to me, through the echoing smell of soft-coal smoke, out of trips to see the family in the age when Mary had lived, and even traveled, with us. The awnings on the front porches, and the pallid, withered, washed and ironed persons out on the rockers, in their shade, looked the same. The railroad track ran along the sidewalk, level with it. Everything was familiar, but I could not find the street I was looking for. I inquired, at last, of a dim rocking figure whose glasses were watching me. "Why it's right there," she said, pointing to the edge of the porch. The alley, looking like a driveway, with no sign. That was Clay Street. It was the first house on the left. Mary was out front, talking to a plump neighbor.

Clearly a neighbor: no purse and no hat, standing out in the alley with pink arms folded, a short woman the shape of a melting bell, in a bright yellow dress. Mary was inside the closed crinkled-wire gate—they were talking over it—and of course she had not changed at all. A duster on her head, an old gray cardigan, a long faded Grandma dress, and scuffed heavy shoes, as it was in the beginning. I never learned what she lived on. She glinted suspiciously in my direction, as I came along the alley. Getting braced to say no we don't want none. When my father approached old acquaintances whom he had not seen for years, and who he thought did not recognize him, he would make some inquiry, perhaps an embarrassing one, alluding to something long past, and then it would be a joke they could both tell afterwards. Mary and her neighbor were as grave as though they were discussing their respective plumbing. They both paused to stare at me, and I went up to the wire gate and told Mary who I was.

She drew back, shying, looking past me at her neighbor for an answer. She looked at me with her mouth open—not an expression of astonishment, in particular, but simply a way of looking that I recognized. She was not the only one in the family who stared with open mouth, but each of them, when they did it, looked like the originator of the gesture. I suspected that she had not heard me, and that I had to tell her again, louder. She shied again, and then she leaned toward me, over the gate, without saying anything, her face blank. It came to me that she thought I was telling her that I was my father. I repeated the name by which she had known me as a child. I asked her whether she didn't remember, because she still gave no sign. "Well," she said at last, "I never did think you'd look like that." She moved her lips as though they were thicker than they were. Then she said, "What did you want?" meaning only that she did not know what to say. It seemed complicated to explain that I just wanted to see her.

This, she told me, was Mrs. Dawd: the neighbor in the yellow dress. Mrs. Dawd was a comfort to her. They went to meetings of the Sunrise Group together. Mary asked me whether I knew the Sunrise people, and told me that I should. They cleared up many things. Mrs. Dawd beamed good will. She had bulb-shaped teeth no bigger than a child's, and a face that appeared to have suffered irregular extraction, and to be slowly caving in. From it came a soft voice, plaintive and distant, yet steady. In fact, Mary and I both felt her absence when she excused herself and turned to go home, along the alley, and we were left with nothing but what related us.

Mary said, "Just a minute and I'll unlock the door," and she marched off along the cement walk beside the house and disappeared leaving me at the gate. Small graying frame house painted white unnumbered years before, the porch almost out to the fence along the alley. Porch furniture huddled face down. Sunny Saturday afternoon at the beginning of September, the only sound coming from a switch engine, along the tracks blocks away. After a while I heard a thumping, a scraping, a prying and racketing of locks, and a chain, and the wooden door inside the screen door on the porch was sucked open, revealing Mary veiled by the screen, who fumbled

72

some more with latches and then flapped to me to go around and come in by the side. There was a glass door there, also locked. A twisted wreck of a youngish man peered up at me out of the panes. One hand reached up to the knob. Mary appeared behind him, and together they let me in to a vestibule smelling of shellac, rubber, and some ghost of burnt sugar. There were doors, varnished and grained, on all sides. Through one of them the cripple took himself, closing it behind him, and Mary, when she had led me through another into a room full of dark sepia, and shut us in, mumbled to me that that was Mr. Brom-something, as though that, at last, and in confidence, took care of everything. For of course, her inflection implied, I knew who Mr. Brom-something was. I had been reared among such assumptions. I tried to remember whether her teeth had always mauled her words so unmercifully, and to guess whether that was all I was ever to know about him. But then she insisted that he was a very fine man, and clean. And he could hear, when she didn't, and he answered the door for her. She dropped her voice as she told about him. He had had an accident in the elevator shaft, in the vicinity of Buffalo. He had been working in the elevator, or going to work in it. He had fallen into the shaft, or the elevator had fallen onto him. Her teeth made a paste of such distinctions, and I did not want to start by asking her, in a raised voice, to stand there and repeat exactly the manner in which catastrophe in the form of an elevator had befallen Mr. Brom-something, so I never knew, to be precise. And so he had come to live there. She rented it to him back there, and people came and seen after him sometimes, and he was getting better but he never would be all right. But good enough, maybe, to get his job back.

She was turning and stacking things on top of other things, in the dim room. The dining room, at one time. The shades were drawn, the walls were lapped with brown sideboards, dressers, tables piled with magazines, bundles, folded laundry, propped ironing boards. On the wall, a painting of Florida on

glass, housing a broken thermometer among the palms and fla-
mingos. A plaque with verses To Dad, on wallpaper the color
of woodstain, splotched with images of browned poinsettias
and peach blossoms. In the time when Mary had lived with
us, my mother had had a dress—a gown, it was—with flowers
of that kind on it. She had been talked into it by a lady in the
church who was described, with repect, as dressy, and who
had hair like the plaster heads in beauty shop windows. Mar-
celles. Organdy, the dress was called. A way of being. The
outside was loose gauze, and the inside was the color named
peach, shiny, with those flowers on it, meant to show through.
Part of the gown could also be worn under a white crocheted
dress that someone else had made for her, as my mother demonstrated in that other dining room. I liked the gauzy one better, and asked why she didn't wear it. She said it was dashing,
and laughed, holding it up on its hanger, and looking at it,
and then holding it up in front of her, and then taking it upstairs to put away. Mary led me into the front room and
raised the blind onto the porch part way, and opened the
front door inside the screen. "We can have some air," she
said, and told me to sit down, pointing to a tubular porch
chair, by the round wooden table in the middle of the room.

Then she trucked off into another front room and rum-
maged around in drawers, and rustled and blew, and finally
came back and sat down in a rocker, as after some unaccus-
tomed exertion, and announced that she had been putting a
new battery in her hearing aid. She sat facing me: the long
aproned empty valley of a lap, the narrow fingernails bitten
to the quick, with deep ditches on either side, on the big
fingers. Even with a new battery, though, she said, it didn't
always work right, she didn't know why. "Say something
now," she said, twisting some minute wired object in her
hand. "Hello Aunty Mary," I answered obediently; strange
child. "Well, that's as good as it'll get," she said. "I can hear
you." But she went on fidgeting with it, and finally shoved it
inside the front of her dress—the place that I had once been

told was where the *boosom* was—with a movement of impatience rather than satisfaction. She said it came and went. She got out a different pair of glasses, too, that looked new, except for their shape, and she put them on, tentatively, still in doubt about buying them, and looked at me through them, and then over the gold tops. She returned to the subject of her hearing aid, and told me the history of its temperament, and where she had bought it, and why, and what they had assured her about it there, and the instructions. At first I thought that the discussion of the hearing aid was the prelude to the visit proper, and then I realized that it was already part of the visit proper, as were the silences. She said she was glad to see me, after one pause, and then she listened—not to me, but to the sound in her hearing aid. She looked at me, and shook her head, and sat back. I had caught her housecleaning the cellar, she told me, to explain something besides the duster on her head, which she patted and tucked, with gestures of unthinkable age. "Oh my," she said, referring to the cellar, and slowly shaking her head. "The dust," she said, clucking her tongue. Neither of us knew what to ask—there was that, shared like the name.

How was my sister and her kids now, she said. They come to see her, once. She guessed she didn't make such a good impression: they didn't come back. She said she had such good friends. Mrs. Dawd, she said. You met Mrs. Dawd. Mrs. Dawd is after the truth, Mary told me, and that means a lot to me, she said. It was Mrs. Dawd that had first taken Mary along to this Sunrise meeting, and that had been a help. I'll say, she said.

As far as I could discover, then and on later visits, that was Mary's life. My mother said she was a Russellite. Saturdays and Sundays, Mary told me, she could get the Jehovah's Witnesses on her earphones, and oh they had a lot to say to her, though less now than at one time. There had not been many silences in that subject before Mary came right out and asked me about my own salvation, picking up a real thread at last.

We lurched off onto the subject of baptism. She stared at me with indulgent suspicion. "I'll tell you," she said, "I'm not one of them that says once a Methodist always a Methodist."

I supposed that she was alluding to her aunt, my grand-mother, Arvilla, who had never been altogether easy in her mind at the thought of my father's lapsing into Presbyterian-ism, even for the sake of an education to the—Presbyterian—ministry. He always pretended to laugh it off, as a joke be-tween them, but Arvilla's smile knew better, and so did he. Mary was above such narrowness.

"A lot of people got their eyes closed," she said. "I was baptized Baptist, over to Mouth Bethel. That's immersion they do to you there. That was *after* I was sprinkled Methodist, you see. Then I was baptized all over again in the Jehovah's Witnesses."

And she was off, expounding to me their doctrine as it drummed inside her duster. The exact number destined to be saved—though she poured contempt, in passing, on the idea of predestination as the Presbyterians held it. When the re-vealed number—a hundred and forty-four thousand—was at last fulfilled, they would turn out, taken all together, to be the Bride of Christ, and would enter into the Kingdom right here on earth. There were not many more to go, now, and the last ones would not even die. They would live on, here, in the Kingdom of Heaven on Earth, for a thousand years, she in-sisted, and she told me to think about that. And at the end of that age, the world would end, and time and everything would be finished, and then the saved would be taken up into heaven; it was right there in scripture, and she could show me. Her preachments washed toward me in low waves that I thought might be running parallel to the fluctuations of her hearing aid. There was a continuity in them, an ardor and color and gleam that were missing from her words about our common condition, yet I tried to lure her back to the waiting life with its shades on windows, varnished days, brown paper, and old childhoods. They would all be there, she said; sometimes she thought of it and could hardly stay put. The thought of seeing them again, and then the world together, with them, for a thousand years.

I asked her who would be there.

Jim, she said. Her father. Fawther. She always had known she would see him again. She could still feel how he would hug her. He was a warm man. But she informed me that my father would not be there, unless he mended—or minded—his ways. The preachers, they thought they knew so much. She had obviously worked on converting him from his patent Presbyterianism to her own successive lights, even by way of confiding in him, on occasion. He had told me she'd bend my ear if she got half a chance. D.D., she said: did I know what that *really* meant, after a preacher's name? Meant Darn Devil, was what it really meant, and Dirty Dog, too, and I could tell him she said so. She'd told him herself, but he really knew it, if he'd been honest, without her having to say it. And that was why he didn't come so much to see her, any more, because the truth hurts. Now Anne, my mother, she wasn't so bad, but he had had too much influence on Anne, too. Couldn't help but be, after so many years. Mary supposed he'd prejudiced me against the truth too, and against Mary.

I tried to draw her back to when she had lived with us; her face remained blank, but then it had always looked that way to me. Oh yes, she remembered the go-cart, and getting lost, she guessed. She did not laugh. The incident had been of no importance to her, and she recalled it with indifference, vaguely. She had been going to get pork somewhere. She'd heard that if you cooked it long enough and slow enough it would come out like chicken. Well, she did, and it had been all right. But not like chicken, though. She thought my father preferred it fried, the usual way, even if it disagreed with him. And she was that way too.

She remembered everything I could think of, but without a spark. What was I expecting, the Resurrection? She nodded, like a patient saying yes they could feel that, but without adding anything of her own. One by one I produced my coins. Talk of beginnings, all beginnings, and all mine. What was that time to her? Ordinary. An unreturning number. A ticket to something she had not attended.

I said that my father had told me she was the one who knew about the family.

"What about them?" she said.

He had called it history, and it amused him, at the same time, to refer to the family as "the clan."

She said, well she supposed she did know some things, probably as much as anybody. But why? What did I want in things like that? None of the rest of them thought anything of all that. They never paid no mind.

I said I didn't even know much about my grandfather, John, her uncle. I had met him only once, when I was a child. Everything about him had been kept out of sight. I knew that my grandfather had not lived with my grandmother for some years before I was born. A few other facts or shadows of facts had been gleaned from the rare hints. Most of them began and led back to the one that had come to eclipse even his name: he Drank. As a child I had assumed that what my elders knew was the same for all of them: if they had knowledge of a given thing or person it would be the same knowledge. It took many years for me to suspect that their differences were reflected in what they saw and how they remembered it, and to understand that even the versions they professed to share were still merely versions. I did not have to be told that it was forbidden to ask my aunts or my grandmother about my grandfather, and I never heard my grandmother speak of him. When eventually I brought up the subject with my aunts, it was always like knocking something over on the tablecloth, and everything was taken care of with the one phrase that should tell me all I needed to know. But now that I knew that Mary's views of things were not synonymous with my aunts' finalities, I hoped that she might afford me some clear glimpse of her own. I clung to the notion that more must be known of John D. than the others made out.

"They say he drank," Mary informed me.

Well even her own father said that. John's brother. She guessed it must have been pretty bad, but then a lot of people liked to point the finger that wasn't above a drink themselves. Even Jim might have had a drink, sometimes, after all. And there was others in the family that was that way, whatever was said. She didn't set so much store by all that as some of them did. And some that maybe never took a drop weren't any prizes, either. Quite a few.

She left the subject ajar. She referred to John as a human being like other human beings whom anyone might know. But Mary said she didn't remember him, too much. Her own father had been different.

There were three brothers, she said to me: Jim, Jake, and John.

For one sentence the story had found for itself the clear, magisterial ring of a classic; its remoteness was that of legend. I had heard the same fact before, but coming from my father or one of his sisters it had remained as indefinite as the brown repeated beings in wallpaper. When Mary said it she was announcing a law of nature. Their father's name was Jacob.

Old Jacob, dead long before she was born. He had a brother named William, about whom I know nothing at all, for certain. It is unlikely, but possible, that my father was named after that William, and I was named after my father. I am not sure which of the brothers—but it was probably William—she said owned a stonemason's establishment, near Stroudsburg. Before the time of *Moby Dick*. Solid, then. Daily fingerprints in stone dust. And he was well set up, too, there, and evidently with quite a few men working for him. Horsehair sofas. The first daguerreotypes, none of them destined to survive. But maybe it was Jake. One or the other of them was worth $14,000, at the time, Mary said. In Stroudsburg.

There was money around then. They was in the hotel business, too. A lot of the family was, one time or other. A tavern, a coach house, one of them you drove in the courtyard and with your horse, right in, and they put your wagon away and you went on in, and stopped. It must have been quite the place. A thing of consequence, in them days.

Mary mumbled, and tacked from one thing to another, and I could not be sure, half the time, who she was talking about, all braided out of their lives into a single current. If I asked her a question, or to repeat, she just said, "What?" and then usually went right on with what she was saying. One of them, I understood, was an educated man. Taught school, kept a tavern, one or both. "Which of them?" I asked. "What?" she said. And then, "Have you ever been to Stroudsburg?" "Yes," I said.

"Well, he just got up and left." That was Jacob, I learned, later. But from the way she wandered into it, I listened to most of the story thinking it was William. He simply disappeared from one day to the next. Nobody knew what become of him. He never wrote to let them know. He didn't tell anybody where he'd be. It was years before any of them from around there heard of him again, and then somebody had come across him. Mary didn't say how. "He'd come out here," she said. "He'd been here for years."

"Who found him?"

"What? Oh, just somebody found him, you know." She paused, looking past me, and rocked.

"He was up at Adrian," she said, by way of explanation.

"Where?"

"What? Adrian. You know. Up the river from Rimerton. Cow Creek Furnace. So that's where he come."

When she paused I was always afraid she had forgotten the subject.

"They say by that time he was pretty well known, out this way," she said, still with him. "And well thought of, too."

"What did he do?"

"What? Do? How do you mean, do? Oh, I don't know. Maybe taught school. Somebody, there was somebody taught school. Maybe had a hotel. Had a place up there on the mountain, that side of the river. Well, they asked him, you know, why he'd just got up like that and left, without a word to anybody. Was he in some kind of trouble or something. To do a thing like that. That's what I heard. But he said no, he just got fed up."

"What age was he then?"

"What?"

"When he left."

"Yes."

"When he left Stroudsburg how old was he?"

"Yes." She stared at me. Then she shrugged. "Oh. He was grown up," she said to me, finally. She knew about it because her father had told her. If she'd got it right. I had been thinking, still, that she had been talking about William, and I was wondering what had become of his stonemason's establishment, how he had managed to shake off its dust, and sell off the tavern or whatever it had been, to do a thing like that. I was trying not to form a picture of him, on the basis of that one recounted act: it could not possibly be just, or like him, and it would eclipse the real shadow, the ignorance of him and his world, which was the truth. But I was wondering who had taken over the quarry works, stone yards, tavern ledgers, stables, and cellars, none of which perhaps ever existed, and what had become of his successors, how long they had had to wait according to the law at that time, and what had become of them in turn. What things had looked permanent to them. And then Mary seemed to think it was Jim, her father, who had found William on the mountain, but no, that never happened. Instead it was Jim who had said to his mother —and that was Hannah—"Mother, why did my father just up and leave like that, was he in some kind of trouble, or something?"

Jim had said, "My father," so it was Jacob he was talking

about. It was Jacob whom Mary had been talking about all the time. Old Jake, as they called him later, referring to his whole life from their own point of view, which was eternally that of his heirs, who remembered him only as children, and he must have been a young man still, when he got fed up and left. So we were Jacob's children, and Hannah's.

"Their mother was a Ruffner."

"Whose mother?"

"Jim's. Ruffner. Some spell it Rufner, though. They were red-headed."

"Where was she from?"

"Who?"

"Jim's mother. Hannah."

"Oh"—Mary shook her head. After a moment she said, "There was land in Rhode Island, in Old Jacob's will."

It came back to her that Jim, her father, had told her how, about the time when he was just starting over at the furnace, he had found a lot of old letters and things written on sheepskin. In there was all about Merwins coming to Stroudsburg on horseback. From Philadelphia, he said, they were coming. Imagine. But oh, those things got lost. He forgot what was done with them, or anything. If he ever had them, he never saw them after that. They must have been up at his mother's. That was away back when he was a boy, before the war.

"What about the Ruffners?"

"Well, I don't know any more than that. I suppose they was German, with a name like that. I knew a Mrs. Ruffner out here, no relation. She was German."

"Then I guess our name's German too," Mary added, charitably. "VINE they tell me is the way they used to spell it, at one time. But I don't know."

Her accent was on the I, not the V or the E, so that it sounded like an adjective.

I told her that I had heard that the family had come originally from Wales.

My father had said that a man with an estate of some kind

on Blue Mountain had got in touch with him: wrote and asked my father to go and see him, up at his place. He spelled his name the same way we did, and he understood how we were related. According to my father, this relative had spent just a mint of money on the family tree. He could trace what the exact relationship was, from the facts he had there, and he knew where most of the other relatives were. He had shown my father the family tree that he had drawn up. It was a big chart, my father said. And though I was not a child when he told me about it, the way he said it made me see it unrolled in a long room like a hall, lined with books of reference to nothing else. My father said he had never cared much for all that kind of thing. But it was quite an estate. I imagined a pale blue room, a bit dark, in a house that looked like a motor lodge. This man had said they came from Wales, and who they were, and when they had come. Rumors with names. Mary had never heard of him.

"Some say English, too," she said. "And I heard French, too, or part French, some way. Descent, anyway. But they were mostly Germans, back around there, a lot of them, then. More than anything. Dutch—that's really German. Most of the time they aren't Dutch at all, it's just the way they say Dutch there. So maybe that's why they figured to spell it that way. To go along with the rest."

She could remember her grandmother. She said that when she was small sometimes they put her in bed with her grandma, she couldn't remember why. In a feather bed. They would put Mary to bed first and tell her to go to sleep, but she'd lie awake in the big strange bed waiting for her grandmother to come to bed. Mary could hear them talking out there. They had a lantern. She said she was not afraid of the dark. She would still be awake when her grandmother came in and whispered, "Are you asleep?" but she knew she was supposed to be asleep, and if she said yes she would simply be told to go to sleep, so she didn't answer, and it was dark. She liked being in that bed. In the dark that big skinny arm would come over her to hold her into the bed, so she couldn't fall out. She liked that.

It was cold, maybe, when they went to see her, Grandma, and she lay there wishing Grandma would hurry up and come and help keep the bed warm, and she fell asleep waiting sometimes, and woke up with this long bony arm over her. She was a homely old thing.

"What do you mean, homely?"

"She was so big and tall, and oh she was so boney. Old thing. I was just as glad when she come. In case I was to be frightened, you know. At home there was my brothers in the bed but they was so much smaller, they didn't know any-thing."

"I thought I was waking up in the wagon, see. And I might fall out."

"Where were they coming from?"

"What?"

"In the wagon. Where were those people coming from?"

"Oh, I never knew. It was just a wagon."

"Where did Hannah come from?"

"Oh, back there."

"Where did she grow up?"

"I don't know that I ever knew. It appears there was some-thing away back about somebody coming in a boat from England. But maybe that was somebody else."

Mary said she had a picture of her grandmother. One of those big old round ones they used to have, in a frame, a gold frame. "You've seen those," she said.

I said I hadn't seen that one, and would like to.

"Well, I'll show it to you," Mary said. I imagined a face at a window, behind a curtain, gray. A shadow on a flat cloud. Mary didn't move. I realized that she'd meant—in that way they all had—that she'd show it to me some other time, and I said, with little hope, that I'd like to see it then.

"Oh, I'll show it to you," she said. "It's put away. I'd have to get it out. It's safe in there, in back of a lot of other things. I'd have to find it."

"Would it be so hard to find?"

"Oh, no, I know just where it is. I'd have to get it out, though."

"Couldn't we get it out now?"

"I will, some time. So you can see it. Not today. It's all done up, you know, back of them things. It's great big, and it's all done up, out of the dust. And people break in, you know, and I wouldn't even hear them. And they steal old things. Which is about all I've got. So I keep them put away. Well, I'll get it out for you. You can even have it, if your father don't want it, and I don't think he'd have no use for it. I'll give it to you, some of these days."

Every time I went to see her she said the same thing, but I never saw the picture.

"Their father was shot," you know, she said.

"Whose father?"

"Jim, Jake, and John's."

"Old Jake was shot?"

She nodded.

I must have looked surprised.

"Well," she said, "he was. Shot. Up at Montgomeryville. Across the river there."

Her geography was older than she was. It was still the way she had heard it. Everything went by the rivers—a landscape not yet shriveled by roads.

"How did it happen?" I asked.

"He was murdered," she said.

Apparently he had been running for office, some kind of political office. That was behind it, some way. He had got mixed up in politics. Pawlitics. And this other man had shot him. It was at night, you know. And they never did see who it was. He went out to the store with a pillowcase, to get some coffee. Cawfee. He'd took a pillowcase, to get it in. And they found him laying there. He was shot. In the top of his head. He'd been to the store, and he was coming back. There was coffee in the pillowcase. And there was a comb.

They carried him into a house there. It was dark. He died the next afternoon, about three o'clock. He ran a hotel there, a big hotel on the hill up above Templeton.

Did he know who shot him?

He was unconscious the whole time. Oh, they knew who shot him, afterwards, mind, even if they weren't sure right away. But they never could do anything about it. They all knew, pretty sure. Sure enough. A man with a name something like Zillafro, they used to say. There was a scarf they recognized, that their father had on when he went out that night. Maybe it had been cold, anyway they remembered this scarf he had on when he went out, and afterwards they saw this Zillafro or some name like that wearing it. Well, I suppose he could have just picked it up. Anyway, I guess there'd been a disagreement of some kind. And this man had a gun. But they couldn't prove anything. That was in 1862.

She didn't believe there was ever a picture of Old Jake at any age, or she never saw one. She believed he was buried up there near Montgomeryville, somewhere. So then there were these three boys.

Their mother came to where she couldn't keep them all three. She couldn't make ends meet. So they were farmed out. Two of them anyways. Jim was put out to some folks named Heinz, up at Widnoon. That was the Heinzes. They had a farm, dairy. They made prize butter. They used to get fifty cents a pound for it even at the time. It was so well churned it would keep for a year, mind, and everybody wanted it.

Then John the Rimers took. Over to Rimer. Some call it Rimerton, and they have for years, but it don't make no difference. It's the same place.

She asked me whether I had ever been there, and when I said I had she went on to describe it to me as though I'd told her I'd never seen it.

Down along the river with the one main thoroughfare, just dirt, and the railroad line running along next to it. Pennsylvania Railroad, down from Erie. The frame church up on the hill over the tracks. There was a big rock across the river with the name Rimer painted on it in white letters about so high. I told her it was still there, and she clucked and shook her head. She said it was always there. It said Rimer. Not Rimer*ton*. She always figured it was for the boats.

I said I thought it had been some time since there'd been any boat traffic. I told her that the army had built a dam up above Rimerton, near Cosmos. Beyond the underpass. She said yes, she'd heard that. But there wasn't any dam back then.

She believed the Rimers farmed and had a store.

And Jake, he was the youngest, so his mother kept him home with her, up at Montgomeryville.

Jim always wanted to be a doctor, Mary said. Did I know that? Just the way she always wanted to be a nurse. But we didn't either of us work out, she said. She might have been speaking of someone else. Jim was with the Heinzes until he was sixteen. They'd had a little boy died about the time he come there, or a while before. So Jim was there till he was sixteen or so, and then his mother couldn't take care of things without him any more, she couldn't make out, so he had to make some money to support her. And she told him he could make a dollar a day over at the furnace. That was good wages for that time. So he had to go and do it.

"Which furnace was that?"

"What?"

"Where he went to work. Mahoning Furnace? Redbank Furnace?"

"Oh, I don't know as he—"

She trailed off. Hannah with the boys to bring up had set her to thinking of herself, a generation later, with her younger brothers, in a wooden house like an echo. And John's wife, Arvilla, my own grandmother, had brought up her children, for the most part, on her own. I hesitated, feeling ashamed not to know, but then I asked Mary what had happened to her mother. Sarah. Mary wasn't hearing me. She started to tell me about herself when she was eleven or twelve, and her brothers were small and they were asleep. They were too small to understand.

She said maybe Jim wouldn't get home until late. Sometimes he'd work the night shift, and she wouldn't sleep. She just couldn't sleep. She got so worried about Hell. She said she never could abide the thought of Hell, once she learned about Hell after you was dead. Her brothers would be asleep, and she'd lie awake and then she'd get up even if it was cold, she couldn't stay there, and she'd get up in her bare feet and walk the floor boards, and my but maybe they'd be cold, and she would oh she would sob and cry.

I wondered whether Mary had learned about Hell after her mother died, and she was trying to find out something about death. Or whether she had heard about it before that, and how, and what had made it open in front of her. Dreams of desertion. Jim come home one night, Mary said, and found her up like that, just in her nightgown, and she was crying. I kept thinking that I had heard somewhere that she was big-boned from a child.

He was a kind man, she said. He used to tell me that me and him was different. He said we could talk, him and me, we could talk, you know, to each other, about things. He took an interest. Oh a lot of those things, he took an interest in too, which none of the others did. Old things and all of that. He always did and so did I. But I didn't know he did, up until then. I was small, then. But we could always talk about things, some. But I never had said to him about Hell, not a word. You know, you don't. About that. Dying or none of that. But that time he asked me what was the matter. He put his arms around me. He took me on his knee. Oh, and my teeth was chattering.

Well, he asked me until I told him. All about Hell, and

that I was crying about that, and about dying. I told him that I was crying about Hell, and that was the truth. I said I just couldn't believe it, that there was a real Hell like that. I said was there? All the people just burning and burning for all eternity. You know, Billy, I never could believe that.

And he told me he couldn't either, he said. He told me that of course there wasn't any Hell like that. There wasn't anything of that kind. He never had believed that, whatever anybody had told him. He always knew there wasn't any such a thing, but we didn't need to tell anybody.

"Your father believes in Hell, though," Mary said. "Doesn't he?"

I said I didn't know.

"Well, maybe he doesn't, maybe he does," she said. "He's a preacher, they're supposed to."

So that was how she came to be interested in revelation. Always looking in the Bible. But not the churches: none of them satisfied her, after a while. She said Jim went into the Knights of Pythias, and into the Moose and the Red Men. He was sociable, and liked to talk. But she never could find what she was looking for. She shook her head at the preachers. She said she had tried one thing after another. She got back to instructing me in the doctrine of the Jehovah's Witnesses again, and I tried to induce her to tell me how she had come to join them. But she said she didn't get so much out of them, now, either, as she used to. And lately she'd taken to going to this new Sunrise group with Mrs. Dawd—she felt for some leaflets, proving the scriptures, on the small faded wicker table next to her rocker. They were there with the Bible.

She told me there was an uncle of mine I ought to talk to. He was interested in the truth too, although not so much. But she said he never spoke to my father about that. And when you see him, she said, you don't need to say anything to him about these other people, now, that I've been concerned with. But even they, she admitted, did not altogether satisfy her. There was another group, yet, that had advertised, and she'd read about and liked the sound of, and she had written off to them just to see. But these people here don't need to know about that, she said.

"These new people are an evangelist who has a college," she told me. "And what he knows about, you see, is Who Shall Rule Space. It told about that in the advertisement," she said. "It's all in the scripture. Who Shall Rule Space."

"What I always liked was prophecy," she said. Prawphecy. She had discovered that that was it, what she had always been craving. And that craving itself was a kind of explanation for everything. It was her secret pride. She said she wanted to know what was going to happen. The more she knew, the more she wanted to know. She told me to think what it would be like to meet again. "Well," she said, "I hope you get your eyes opened before too long. Time is running out."

I asked her which of her family were still alive. She spoke of a brother up at Clarion. Some of them came from up around there. Clarion always sounded to me of clarion.

And we got onto how many people in the family had eye trouble. Cataracts and who had them. She had them. "They come over me just like that," she said. "Last year I went over to this eye doctor in Tarentum and he said to me my what good eyes you've got for your age, and this year I get so's I can't see what I'm doing. But I can read just the same."

She said there were some out in Ohio who spelled the name our way, near Akron, in the cemetery there, and there was one she knew of, spelled our way, who fought under Washington. And there was a bricklayer in Florida.

She told me she had a cousin there in town who had had three husbands. The third time she had married a—Mary told me his name as though it were a nationality, a foreign one. This cousin used to get herself up, with her hair and all. Mary waggled her hands on both sides of her head.

"And clothes," Mary said.

The woman would be in her seventies by then. Last Mary knew, she was living with her third husband down town in a three-dollar hotel they had, along the river, but she wasn't sociable. She didn't want to talk to Mary, and Mary had given up going to see her, and might not even know if she was dead. He was a Catholic, and they drank, anyway. One time they were going to build a big house and they took some money and went into Pittsburgh to get the plumbing fixtures but instead of that they got drunk and came back without them and never built at all. Why did I want to know about things like that, she asked.

I told her I didn't know.

She said there was one she had heard about, it sounded as though he had to do with the army, and he had made a book about the family. And she wanted to find out and get a copy. She was surprised I hadn't heard about him.

And Jake, she told me, her uncle, had had a great time, for years, trying to prove that he was related to somebody by our name who had died and left quite a lot of money. The Denton in his name was what was supposed to prove it, but she never understood about that too well.

Jim and Jake had a cousin, too, who was pretty well fixed, named Vince. Vince was a sheriff. People used to come to see him, and he showed them the rope he had hanged the criminals with. He married a daughter of Jay Gould's, Mary said. I told her I had never heard anything about that. Mary nodded and rocked and said this woman had written to her, and invited her down to a big place they had, near Philly. She had even sent Mary a lot of pictures of herself and of the estate. They had those long white fences, and she forgot how many rooms. They had a big greenhouse, she believed. Mary still had the pictures, and she said she would get them out and show me, some time. Oh they had horses, it was a horse place, and they had a big collection of Indian relics, and things of that kind. They had a number of other places besides—they just sent the pictures of that one, and wanted her to come. They said she was to come and stay just as long as suited her. Now, maybe they had wanted her to be a companion, or something like that, or maybe they had just wanted her to come and visit, or to look her over, but she'd never gone. I asked her why not.

"Oh," she said, "that Gould, I guess he wasn't much count. None of those Goulds ever amounted to much."

Each time I saw her it was harder. If I asked her about any of the others, living or dead, she was as likely as not to say, "But I told you that." Meaning that I had not listened, or had not cared enough to remember. After the first reunion, though she always seemed pleased to see me, she was increasingly prone to place me in the distance reserved for the present, and to address me with a flickering mistrust as one of the family. She and my father's sisters each talked about the others being tight. When I last went to see Mary she had been out in the front room sorting her buttons because it was a nice day.

The Skyline

Tʜɪs time I could almost have walked past it, looking for
it, in the bright sunlight of late October. The afternoon
shining everywhere. Yellow in the leaves; the telephone wires
motionless.

What is it, after all, that I thought to recognize?

Over and over again we are told, and then discover, that
when you go back it is all smaller. But each time there appears
to have been a mistake. There is nothing to measure by, and
whoever might know is not there.

And only five years this time, since I last came here, looking. No trace of that visit except this one. There is the place
now, when I was still thinking it was a little farther—perhaps
the width of one house, or half a house, farther. I suppose I
had expected the shrinking to—what? Stop?

And this is all there is. The narrow lot between the long
side of the apartment house and the one story industrial structure whose purpose no one could ever explain to me, long
ago, so that I have never known. It was described as "some
kind of warehouse," and it appears to have changed least of
anything here: a building never quite in use, always between
uses. Both buildings were here when my father's yellow brick
church stood on the site between them, in the days of street-

cars and rumble seats. I was nine when we moved away, and the church building, with its steeple sometimes called a spire, and its cross full of light bulbs, like a sign advertising something else, was sold a few years later, and torn down not long after that.

I cannot see how that stolid yellow facade with its rose window dull as a box, seen from the outside, its twin front doors approached by a pair of cement walks and two flights of cement steps, and another walk, around to the side, to iron stairs down to the basement, could ever have fitted into this patch overgrown with the few species that return here, specifically here, remembering, whatever has happened to the place. I look to see whether sections have not been sold off, on one side or the other, but no, that is not possible: the lot takes up the whole space between those neighboring buildings. But then, only the site has grown smaller. The church itself never shrank at all. It vanished.

Like the size it assumed once in my father's eyes, when he first saw it, a year or so before I was born. A man of thirty, and it looked real enough to him, at some point, to be an object of ambition. What had he heard, from whom, that brought him to look up at it, here? Right here. Who met him, chosen by the elders? They stepped in off the street, talking. A few fragments of the cement walk lead into the tall autumn weeds. He stood there, some place in the air, and preached. And the congregation sat in rows, above the place where the bushes have grown thick and the hardy asters are blooming, and listened. Above some section of what is now weeds they conferred, and found that a majority of them approved. Who urged? Who was persuaded? They elected to extend the call, as my father would say, to the younger man. Younger, I learned, did not mean younger than somebody else, nor than something else. Just younger. He was younger then. As I never saw him.

After his first congregations—small rural pastorates in western Pennsylvania, where the roads were still dirt—he saw the

church on Palisade Avenue as a step up in the world. He
called it, for a time, a challenge. He would have denied that
he found it, ever, frightening—subtly and sleeplessly vertigi-
nous. Beyond where it stood, framed by the surviving buildings, is the famous view: the New York skyline, rising from
the river, gray, keen, elegant, glittering. Massive and silent,
over the water. Larger and closer than I had remembered.

I do not know whether my mother was with him, on that
visit, nor what part she had in the decision to accept the call,
when it came. In the mail. She believed in the duties of a minister's wife, and she never spared herself. As I understand the
chronology, they moved to Union City—in the new Buick—
only a few weeks before I was born. I was brought here, the
first time, in my mother's womb. The First Presbyterian
Church of Union City, New Jersey—though there was no
second. They were informed that the neighborhood had
changed considerably, before they came. So many foreigners
moving in. Mostly Italians. People had moved away. Many
members of the congregation had a long way to come now,
on Sundays. That was part of the challenge.

Another was the condition of the building itself. My father
pointed out run-down details with a sectarian satisfaction,
clucking his tongue, shaking his head, poking the evidence
with a slow, thick finger. Square yellow brick columns topped
with cement flanked the twin entrances from the sidewalk.
Cracks in the cement. The walks themselves needing attention. The patch of front yard neglected, between the walks,
where my father already planned to install a glassed-in bulletin board facing the street: a flat box with a Gothic roof, the
wood painted black every year. His pride. An innovation that
he would bring to his congregation, right from the start. Besides announcements of church events he would fill it with
posters, referred to half seriously as "signs of the times."
Changed once a week, but recurring. One more frequently
than the rest: the top section of a globe, with a huge figure
of Christ looming over it, arms outstretched, bright yellow

radiating from him into the space around him and down onto the dark topography of the curve below him, the unidentifiable dream continents. "I Am The Light Of The World," the poster said. The principal color was blue, which faded faster than the rest. I was disappointed, one day when I had been allowed to be present as my father opened a mailing tube and I learned that the posters came in series, in the mail, including, perhaps, the phrase "signs of the times" and, I think, a new copy each time of "I Am The Light Of The World." The colors were fresh and dark once more—a source of pleasure and encouragement to my father, in his shirt sleeves, as he unrolled it and held it flat. He said, to no one, that it was a lovely thing.

For a reason I do not know, it is the steps to the left-hand door that they climb at the beginning, my father brisk and charged with inexpressible office, my mother moving more slowly on her small feet—the pace of a small, quiet stranger being led. In those days she dressed in long cotton jerseys reaching well below the waist. Tans and pinks. And light shawls, all to disguise the pregnancy. She carried a folded white handkerchief, and looked up, with a distant smile. Both of my parents were short. The wide-brimmed gray fedoras that my father wore then made him look still more so. He had a way of shooting out his chin repeatedly, to pull the skin of his throat up through his shirt collar, and then giving his hat-brim an abrupt tug (origin, I believed, of the term "snap-brim") before stepping, with a bounce, into the street he was about to cross. The sound of his feet on the church steps was a deliberate announcement, and with another bounce, and a long stride, he swung the door open as a gesture, removing his hat with the other hand and waving her past him. Of course the doors too would need some work. The hinges were hoarse, the brass was green and mottled, the varnish was like thawing ice. But the heavy doors themselves, which were noticed only in passing—what power, what unguessed reserves, unbroken antiquity, silent presence they embodied! It made no difference to the doors whether they were locked or stood open. The smell of the wood, on the outside, was an unknown name. And on the inside it was the unfading echo of the marine interior darkness. On both sides the resinous taste was forbidden, bitter, heady.

Green carpet, musty cloud, met them in the shadows inside the door. The light muffled, filtered, refracted through small panes of leaded glass in double doors to the side, which led into the room between the entrances that was used for elders' and trustees' meetings, advanced Sunday School classes, and mid–week prayer meetings, and for kissing the bride after weddings. In kindergarten and first grade I wondered whether I could have three brides at once, since I liked them all, and kiss them in that room with nobody seeing. But that would be hard, because the room was full of yellowish light from a row of stained-glass windows facing the street, and, besides the glazed doors at either end, it had a row of clear glass windows into the main church, where people came and went and could see everything: the upright piano and its stool, the ranks of chairs, the bulletins piled on the tables. I realized that I would have to do the kissing somewhere else, and if possible without a wedding.

Inside the front doors, where the trees have grown up, steep dark wooden stairs, intricately made, went down to the basement. And up, on the left side to the organ loft, and on the right to the room under the steeple, where the rope hung that rang the bell on Sunday mornings. Only those authorized to do so were allowed to go up into either sanctum, and their comings and goings to the loft and the steeple were invisible. I knew those dignitaries at other times, in other places—even in other parts of the church. But the organist appeared (though I was told not to turn around and look to see if he was there) or the top of his head bobbed up behind the music rack of the organ, and the bell rang, proving the presence of the bell-ringer in the room under the steeple, without my having been able to catch a glimpse of either of them emerg-

ing from somewhere and climbing the stairs. At the beginning
I could not understand how the organist got up there, and
when I asked I was told to hush. It seemed to be a secret that
he came and went at all, and I wondered whether we were
supposed to believe that he was up there all the time. Once
in the middle of a week I—I myself—was allowed up to the
organ loft with my father. He, distracted and vexed, looking
for something. Tiers of plain choir benches, under the rose
window. Stacks of old hymnals with the bindings falling off.
Choir music, folded flags, everything deep in gray dust. The
closed organ, like a rounded crate, standing in the middle.
Don't touch anything—very emphatically. My father bending
down, peering into boxes, dusting his fingers, puffing. Just
stand right there and don't touch anything. Seeing the familiar
church from that new height, it felt as though the organ loft
were floating like a cloud, or as though I had suddenly grown
out of the top of my head and were flying over the pews
below. My father didn't seem to find what he was looking
for up there. When I asked him he didn't hear, leading the
way down the dusty stairs.

The green-carpeted floor of the church auditorium sloped
down to the brass rail and green velvet curtain in front of the
communion table (nothing so "Roman" as an altar). Four
aisles, and they were steep enough so that when four ushers
had taken up the collection—better to say "the offering"—on
Sundays, and had assembled in the back of the church under
the polished balcony of the organ loft, and my father in his
black gown had raised his arms and we had all stood up, and
the ushers marched down front with the collection, to the
rail, their pace accelerated and their tread grew heavier, thundered, as they reached the bottom and drew up short, to bow
their heads over the wooden plates full of change and bills and
folded envelopes, and wait for the benediction. While it was
being pronounced the windows and the room still echoed.
And then the organ took over, and "Praise God from Whom
all blessings flow / Praise Him all creatures here below. . . ."

In the middle of it my mother's voice, not round but resolute, from up under the short veil of her hat.

In the pause before the sermon, during that low wave of rustling and settling that whispered through the pews and was gone, she produced from her purse two small pads of paper and two pencils and handed them, fragrant from her gloves, to my sister on one side of her, and to me on the other. So that we could draw pictures during the sermon, and keep ourselves quiet. Hold them down on your knees, not up to show. And don't use the eraser, or make a noise tearing the pages or turning them. Some of the congregation—she told her friends, in reference to the practice—some of the older members in particular, might not altogether approve. The young minister's wife, with ideas of her own. But others agreed that it was a very sensible solution: it was too much to expect the children to sit still and listen to the whole sermon, which was over their heads. "What was over our heads?" I asked, occasionally. But there it stayed, as I was content that it should. I was glad to be allowed to draw. My father pretended not to know that we drew during his sermons. My mother said to just not say anything about it. Each time it came to his notice he acted surprised to learn it, shook his head, but continued to let it pass. I listened to the sermons anyway, parts of them. What were called the illustrations. They were stories. The King of England sending a battleship to rescue one of his subjects. The child Teddy Roosevelt afraid to go to church because of The Zeal. The Zeal of Thy house hath eaten me up—he had heard that in a psalm. Which produced a murmur of knowing amusement that was over my head as well, but made me realize that grown-ups did not consider The Zeal to be frightening, though my father suggested that perhaps they should be more frightened of it than they were. Thinking it over, and looking around carefully, during prayers, I concluded that our church probably had no Zeal at all. It was something from a long time ago, like a dragon. Where would a Zeal live, in my father's church? I tried to imagine one, hiding up in a big crack in the wall between the tall windows, or disguising itself as a huge stain on the stain-colored wallpaper, but I could never get it real enough to frighten me, on Sunday mornings. I knew that nothing so historic was likely to appear there.

On the other hand, those stains, shaped like great animals, shadows, clouds—I realized eventually that they were individual manifestations of The Damp that my father frowned and glowered about so often at supper. At such times the church was referred to as "The Plant." It was The House of the Lord even so. "Couldn't the Lord stop the stains?" I asked. "Never mind," I was told, and the subject was washed over. A palimpsest. The congregation failed to raise enough money to repair the plant adequately. Faithful members of the church, when they were talking with my father, shook their heads about the others—half-hearted and unreliable—and sighed. The church, they agreed, could only be what the spirit of its members made it. Nodding of hats. As for me, I never could really see the stains on the wall as symptoms of the failing spirit of the congregation. The stains were themselves. They were always themselves. When they changed I leaped in my body. They were *appearing*. Their lives were unknown to everybody. I had no doubt of their power. To me they represented a different plane from the one on which adults of the congregation droned and agreed, so that direct conflict between the stains and the church officers was hard to imagine. But if the conflict was real, as it was repeatedly said to be—a ceaseless struggle with The Damp—I was certain of the outcome. The stains were patient and silent. They might be hidden, but they would survive and return, and with no effort on their part they would prevail in the long run. I felt respect for them; awe. But I was never afraid of the malevolence which my father and the church officers clearly attributed to them. I regarded them as remote, august spirits, who might even be friends.

They loomed most powerfully, and were discussed most

often (though it was some years before I observed it) in the autumn and winter, when I had colds one after the other, and sat through the prayers with my nose stuffed up, and was supposed to try to wait until the hymns before blowing it, if I possibly could. Our pew was near the front, and I was not allowed to turn around and stare at anything, but during prayers, when our heads, supposedly, were bowed, I could tilt my face up to the side and roll my eyes to watch them, until my mother noticed. And on the way in and out I could look up at them, though I did not want it to be obvious that I was paying attention to them. In summer they withdrew into themselves and I would wonder where they were, and miss them. The sun came through the long yellow windows on the south, over the side aisle, at that season, and tapering bands of sunlight moved across the pews, the heads, the fluttering print dresses, the cotton suits, the fans (my mother said fanning yourself only made you hotter, and though there were cardboard fans in the hymnal racks, we were not permitted to remove them) and over the green carpet between the front pew and the low green velvet curtain hanging from brass rings on its brass rod. The sunlight whitened them all. I watched it change position in the course of the sermon, and between the beginning and end of a prayer. I saw it climb a brass post, the leg of the communion table. I saw it move. That bit of floor up in front of the church by the rail—how empty it remained, through the sermon! My father's voice flew over it, but the sunlight on the green pattern was untouched. There was the spot where I had been held up when I was a few weeks old, and baptized, one Sunday morning in autumn, by a friend of my father's named Andy. Andy Richards. Referred to as though he were a close friend of mine, though I think I never saw him after that day. But later I had such a clear image of being held up in an arm, and the green of the carpet, that I believed I really remembered that moment. I was told that it was impossible for me to have remembered something from that age, and the sunlight on the carpet—when in fact the baptism took place in the autumn—also makes it unlikely that the image is an actual memory, but it remains clear, and whether it comes from a dream or from suggestions or from a glimpse of the occasion itself I cannot now be sure. But the place—that was the place. I was told that I did not cry, as babies often do during that ceremony, but looked around and, at the touch of the water, laughed.

On the same spot, near the baptismal font, sometimes on Sunday mornings in summer a folding chair stood empty, and when the service was drawing breath a guest performer would be announced. Then there would be a rustling of bulletins, in search of the name there. A melancholy old man in a gray shirt sat down in the chair once, gray hair plastered straight across his forehead, and without looking at anybody, in total silence, he opened a chewed wooden violin case and took out a saw and a violin bow, set the saw handle carefully between his high-buttoned black shoes with turned-up toes, pulled his pants tight around his legs, and still without looking at anybody began to draw the bow over the back of the saw, teasing tremulous water sounds out of the blade. Hairs of the bow broke and waved back and forth in a light of their own. He stopped after a while and started again, without a word. "Come Thou Almighty King." The notes wavered and emerged slowly, rising to a surface and evaporating from it. Several times he stopped, tore off the hairs, and started again, with sequences of notes that I did not recognize and followed blindly. Then he got up and bowed, put back the saw and bow, and took them past us up the aisle. Nobody seemed to know him. In whispers someone asked whether he was Italian, and someone said he was a carpenter. Another time a lady in velvet played a harp there, and my father, who habitually said that he loved music but couldn't carry a tune in a bucket, and who whistled the first six notes of "The Old Rugged Cross," and nothing further, over and over, all his life, to my mother's hopeless irritation, announced that we were fortu-

nate to have been able to hear her, and everyone said afterwards what a beautiful instrument the harp was, and how
long it took to learn to play it. Once a tall girl sat there and
played a clarinet, accompanied by soft notes on the organ. I
never saw any of those people again.

There in front of the rail my tool box was brought, for a
bride to kneel on during her wedding at night. I was told
about it afterwards—a laughing secret. I didn't see the wedding itself because it took place after my sister's and my bedtime, and because we were then considered too young to go
to weddings. An evening wedding in any case (but it was
really *night*, I thought) was heralded by a special wave of
whispers and consultations in lowered voices. It was more
than a rarity. No one could remember whether there had ever
been one at the church. My father had probably never per-
formed one. It was spoken of as something modern, and a bit
fast. Everyone involved seemed to feel that they were doing
something racy, and to be slightly surprised to find themselves
getting away with it. But Mandy, the bride—they kept telling
each other—had very definite ideas. She was a character. She
kept people waiting. My father said she was a clip. The stages
in the making of her wedding gown provided news, on the
sidewalk after church, for weeks before the event. There
were several rehearsals of the ceremony, but it was not until
the night itself, after I was in bed and supposed to be asleep,
that my father came up to the house with two of the ushers
and fetched the tool box. Mandy had decided that she wanted
it to be a kneeling wedding, which was another daring notion
in a Presbyterian service. People liked her, and said afterwards
that it had been a beautiful idea, but you could tell that they
would not have wanted it to become a custom.

No one was supposed to know that it had really been my
tool box, under the cushion she was kneeling on, unless my
parents told them. I couldn't see why the use of the tool box
shouldn't be mentioned in the ordinary way, but that was one
of the many unexplained and perhaps inexplicable injunc-

tions. The fact that they had used it, that it had occurred to someone (my father in his ministerial role) as the fitting centerpiece and support for a grown-up ceremony at the church, gave me a feeling of importance—mine, but remote. Not to be claimed, grasped, or acknowledged, and yet closer and more real than my sense of the box itself, which was mine in name only. It didn't look like a tool box, people said, admiringly, when my father showed it to them. You'd never know it was a tool box, they said. I didn't know what a tool box was expected to look like, and I would have preferred for it to look like one, even though they said it was better this way. There were real tools in it, which added to their surprise —and why should they be surprised, even though the tools were not used? The ushers never thought to take the tools out, and heard them clink as they carried the box down Fourth Street under the poplar trees and the street lights to the church, that night. The sound, and the memory of it, made them laugh. I knew each of those tools, its feel, its smell, and its name which I had been taught when the box was given to me at Christmas—my fourth Christmas, I think. Santa Claus had brought it, but it was my father who made the presentation, guiding everyone's attention to it with the promise of something momentous, and raised eyebrows and forefinger. Though it might be a little too old for me, yet. I would learn to appreciate it as I grew older. The box was not wrapped, but simply concealed under some paper and other presents, and tied shut with a wide, dark red ribbon in a bow, which was untied as I watched, and the ribbon folded and put away. My father's revelation of the box was preceded by a cloud of cautions: "Just a minute. Are you sure your hands are clean? Now be careful." What I saw was—a box. Or a chest. "It's a beautiful thing," my father said, shaking his head and clucking his tongue. It looked like a piece of furniture. Polished dark wood, which we were told was mahogany, with a scalloped edge around the lid—a yard long and a foot wide— and with antiqued bronze-finish handles on either end, though they were never to be used to lift it by, because they might not be strong enough. I must be careful not to scratch it, which meant not coming too near it. I was told that I might open it now, since someone else was with me, but as I started to, my father said, "Wait. Just a minute, now," and took hold of the heavy lid. "You'll have to be careful not to drop it," he told me.

A rich, forbidding smell rose from the dark interior. I realized later that it was compounded of the wood stains—one for the hard wood of the box, and another, that left an oily surface, for the softer wood of the small drawer and the runners it rested on—and from shellac and machine oil protecting the new steel of tools. I recognized it as the word of the box—magic, suggestive, enticing, treacherous, and oppressive. I was told that I must never open the box unless my father was present. And the tools were not to be used now, of course, but later, when I was older and had learned how. I would only scratch the box with them and cut myself and damage the tools, which were very fine, if I tried to use them right away. But one by one they were taken out and given to me to hold. Each time I was told to be careful, and taught the name. Hammer: blond, bright, cold. Be careful not to drop it on your toe. Other people, watching, echoed that wisdom. A plane, painted gray, with a red wheel on it. Full of potential damages. My father demonstrated how the blade came out, and put it back, and showed me how a carpenter planed wood, in the air. A tape measure, a screwdriver, a used stone chisel, a brace and bit. A square, the blue of whose blade impressed me, and its responsibility for squareness, pure squareness: its official possession of a universal form, which was all it was and all that it did—as a tool.

The flashiest of them all, the most solemnly prohibited, and the one that my father most admired and praised, was a hatchet, all of one piece of steel, as he showed me. He allowed me to hold it for a moment and then took it back to point out the notch for drawing nails, the round hammerhead, the handle made of rings of leather which I would never have thought were leather, the thinness of the blade, the way it rang when my father flicked it with a finger. He told stories about the sharpening of hatchets, and he put it away carefully at the bottom of the box, where I was never to touch it until I grew up. (My father explained that the collection of tools was far from complete, and that others might be added later on, now that I had a real box for them. As long as I behaved myself.) But the tool that appeared to me as the hope and eye of the whole assembly, the indication that the existence of these particular objects extended beyond their circumstances, the one with which I felt immediate friendship and a shared joke, was the small wooden level (I was not told, then, that it was called a "spirit level"—simply a "level"). Block of deceptively light wood, easily damaged, and on the top, under the brass plate, the glass tube, breakable, in which the bubble moved back and forth in its iridescent green fluid. That was the tool I believed in.

My mother stood aside, through all this, and watched. Unconvinced, but perhaps not aware of that; certainly not sure of it. Removed.

When I was told, in time, of Mandy's wedding, I imagined watching it from the organ loft. Everyone agreed that the box had looked beautiful, surrounded by flowers and covered with a satin cushion. Later, reading of Pandora's box, I supposed it looked like the tool box.

But the more secular church events, the suppers and socials, as well as the Sunday School services and the children's Sunday School classes, took place in the basement. One surprising thing about the site is the way the basement hollow too has vanished, and all signs of where it was. A building can be removed, but a hole? They must have filled it in with rubble, and then roots groped through it in the dark again, as though for the first time. A few small pieces of crushed mortar look recent—added much later than the demolition, when the growth was already there and the lot had long since been "waste." The basement was probably not very deep after all. There were windows on all sides—far up the walls, it is true, but perhaps not quite as high as I remember them from the viewpoint of a child. They looked out into underground recesses with iron grilles across the tops. On the north side, toward the apartment building, they let in a poor, dirty light, but on the side to the west, facing the street, the light was clear and promising. On the south, toward the factory-warehouse, a flight of iron steps led down from outside, under a frosted glass room, to a side door, and when there was some event in the basement, and the church, above, was not being used, that door was the main entrance. I remember it chiefly in winter, perhaps because on winter Sundays, when the turn-out was small, especially during the increasingly frequent ailments of the furnace and boiler, services were held in the basement, which was easier and cheaper to heat, although the sounds of the boiler and radiators hissing and clanking sometimes racketed dramatically above my father's voice. Once, down there, during winter, I blew my nose during a prayer, because suddenly I had to, and a fat woman gave a little shriek—she thought the boiler was bursting. When the actual services were held downstairs the front doors of the church would be locked and after we were seated on folding chairs we could see the feet and legs of late comers descending the black stairs outside the white window. They usually stamped, as though no one could hear them, at the bottom, in the cemented cubical outside the door: when we had services down there it was often raining or snowing or sleeting outside, and after the closing benediction the few who had showed up congratulated each other and themselves on having come, even if they had got there late and had entered, embarrassed, in the middle of a prayer or of the sermon itself.

The basement ceiling was supported by iron pillars, which I found mysterious and admirable. Just like that they held up the whole thing, with no sign of strain. I would lay my hand on them to touch that utter ability. They were always cool, and if I set my ear against them I could hear that they rang. However quiet or far away it was, that note was always there. The iron pillars were a people to themselves. In my earliest recollections they are painted a somber red. The whole basement then was old reds and browns. There was talk of how dark it was, and one year, after a drive for funds for the job, the basement was repainted: the back room toward the street, which was a step higher than the main room; the main room itself; and at least part of the kitchen, beyond, with its big coffee urns and zinc tubs under the grimy windows, and its slatted floor—an area totally forbidden to me, so that my knowledge of it is mostly shadows. The new color was pistachio green, though that was not what it was called. With a stenciled Gothic trellis design on it, repeated around the walls, in chocolate brown. Everyone was proud of the result. And the paint was not dry, the first gathering to celebrate it had not taken place, when the rains, which had been abnormally heavy that season, blocked the sewer and gutter on Palisade Avenue in front of the church, filled the avenue, and the black public water backed up and flooded the basement four feet deep, and the rain kept on falling for days. Roasting dishes and coffee pots, it was said, floated in the kitchen, and the slats of the floor bumped around like rafts. The furnace and boiler were left for dead, for a while. The walls dried out and were repainted, but the floor, they all agreed, would never be the same.

I see it was all turning green even then, though no one thought of it that way, no doubt. The pale mat green of the basement joining the water greens of the church above: carpet greens fading under sunbeams in the aisles, worn gray near the doors, looking newest and oldest in the corners, where the nap (a word I weighed and relished) stayed dark and untrodden, like velvet. And the deep green of the velvet curtains up front by the communion table, above which the brass of the rail, the gold of a cross on the table (my father's daring touch: staunch Presbyterians might think it Romish, he said, but he didn't see that the Catholics should have a monopoly on the cross), gilded vine patterns traced on the wall above the choir stalls, and the dull gilt of the organ pipes, stood out, shone, even when the church was unlit. But apart from their gleaming I can find no memory of any color in that part of the church that was the dim, removed focus of it all, into which the few members of the choir sailed at the beginning of services, in their black gowns, sank down, and melted into the shadow, and in which my father sat during anthems, out of sight, hidden by the wide lectern, from the pew where we were sitting. Out of that darkness, after a moment of silence, or in the middle of what the bulletin announced as an organ meditation, he would suddenly emerge with his arms raised, the sleeves of his gown hanging like those in the poster facing the street, and say dramatically, "Let us pray." During prayers I did not dare to raise my head and look at him for long, but through other parts of the service if I fixed my eyes on him I found that an aura of light came and went around him. It was a trick of the eyes, and I knew it, and knew that it would not be encouraged if I spoke of it, so I never mentioned it, but I learned to make that luminous phantom grow larger, more intense, spread out like rays in water, while my father's voice rose and fell, coming through it from somewhere else. The name for that part of the church was the sanctuary. It was holy, and forbidden to everyone except those taking part in a service. I stood up there once or twice, and filed across, at some Sunday School ceremonial. But then my attention was on the occasion more than on the place. I was aware of the strangeness of being on the platform, how high it felt, as though I were standing on glass, dazzled. Otherwise, that part of the church, as I remember it, is distinct but not defined. The faces of the waiting choir members are dim, or they fade out altogether. My father appears and announces or he subsides from the pulpit in silence after a sermon. I was told that there was something up there in that place, which nobody could see, and that it was always there. It was in the pulpit, and near the communion table and my father's chair. It was not an "it." When the place was empty I would turn my eyes suddenly to look, though I knew I would not surprise what was there.

And the green continued, with the same carpet pattern, in the rooms on either side of the sanctuary. The choir room, on the north side, in the shade of the apartment building, where the light was cool as bare plaster, and the tops of the long, varnished cupboards in which the choir robes hung during the week were piled with boxes and brown paper rolls, and a door opened onto a narrow, steep, spiral staircase, lightless. On it pale green flower vases risen from the dead stood in tiers. It led, I learned, to an unmapped, scarcely known region behind the organ pipes. Up there were other organ pipes—real ones. Those stairs were totally forbidden, and I regarded with awe the few men of the congregation known to have been up there.

And the green carpeted the vestry, on the south side of the sanctuary, into which the sun shone through the same yellow stained glass as that in the main church, but more intimately, since the room was much smaller. Again, in there, were cupboards for robes, but the room was grander and in better order than the choir room, just as there were bands of black velvet on my father's preaching robe and none on the choir robes. The room smelled of large books bound in leather, and the varnish in the sunlight. On the walls were two extremely large photographs, framed, under glass, of battleships, one of them the *Utah*. The brass plate below the picture said that it had twelve Babcock and Wilcox boilers. I have forgotten its maximum speed. If you looked closely you could see sailors, somewhat retouched, up above the smoke, in the round cage towers which were there so that the lookouts could see better and tell the people below where to aim the guns. In this room my father seemed to be continually mumbling important things to himself, leafing through papers. He sometimes said that he was running over his sermon in his mind. And here too a door opened into a narrow staircase, a straight one. I imagined that it was secret. It climbed toward a window outside an upstairs study.

A few times, but very few, my father took me up to that study, which he used, off and on, during the first years in Union City. Two desks, side by side, made one long one standing in the middle of the floor—an arrangement that he repeated later in his life. Filing cabinets, wooden chests of drawers piled with folders, glass-fronted bookcases, shelves of registers and huge tomes, flags leaning in a corner, everything rich with dust. Nothing was to be touched. My father especially admired, praised, and told me particularly not to touch a revolving bookcase full of dust and small wrapped boxes, and a dictionary on the desk beside it, an immense volume whose merit was one with its fragility. On the farther desk the big Underwood typewriter, already old, that accompanied him all his life, bulked under its black shroud. On the walls, photographs, portraits of former pastors of the church, and of unknown ancients; a picture of a beautiful woman standing and raising a flag—a commemoration of some phase of my father's brother Sam's World War career in the marines; class pictures, one of my father's own class at seminary, and others of classes he had never seen and knew nothing about. And that was enough questions, I was told. If I was to be allowed up there I must be completely quiet, or else my father would have to take me home. Did I think I could be quiet? I thought I could. My father turned me to the window just inside the door, looking out across Hoboken and the river. With a window seat, and a velvet cushion on it—green. There, my father said: I could get up there and look out the window and be as quiet as I could be. I could watch the boats coming and going and not say anything. And it was true. They plied upstream, downstream, in a silence I could watch, through the clear afternoon light of autumn, just as it is: the river blue and gray, the black hulls, orange hulls, gray hulls, the bow waves and the wakes. There were more of them then, as I remember. Liners, tugs, barges freighted with whole railroad trains. And ferries, yawning and turning to and from the dark arches in the green arcades of ferry barns on the far side. Smoke rose, utterly out of reach, unaware of being watched. White steam leaped from hooters, and long afterwards the sound arrived. And behind me the typewriter clattered and thumped, and my father muttered to himself. Once he pushed back his chair and took me downstairs into the church and had me sit in a pew—any pew!—prickly with responsibility, to listen to a passage of sermon. For him to go over it, for his own purpose, and to see (he added) whether I was old enough to understand. Since I was the only one in the pews, and had been charged with this extraordinary and wholly unexpected office, I imagined that the rhetorical questions were addressed to me personally, and tried to answer them, which was a bad mistake. After that I became invisible, and a while later was summoned to follow my father upstairs again, to the window seat. He spoke well of how quiet I could be, there, but said he could see that the sermon was still too old for me.

How often I was allowed up there, while he worked, I have no idea. Not many times, certainly, and they have run together. It may indeed have been only once. In our later years in Union City, after I had started school, he used that study less. But both of us came to speak of my going there to watch the river from the window, while he worked, as though it were a regular and cherished custom. Both preferred to think of it that way. He wanted to believe that he was companionable to me. My being there in that study represented a passing moment of expansiveness which he liked to think was the usual, the normal—though necessarily preoccupied—characteristic of his way with me. He hoped to be able to take it for granted. And for me, being there, even having been there, was a mark of his favor, a privilege and—as he himself said—a "surprise." I was told that I loved to watch the river, and it was so; and I was still far from beginning to distinguish the one (being told) from the other (it being so). Being allowed to watch the river was prized even more in retrospect, the feeling about it intensified by the rarity of the permission and the uncertainty of its ever being repeated. At the time and afterwards, that watching was a held breath. Which had its effect on the way it is remembered with a completeness that I could not have foreseen at the time. My father's own separateness is there deepening around him, and his fear of being wherever he imagined he was: the cockiness faltering, the rhetoric hardening over—they were all in that room at that moment. I was aware of them without knowing, and long afterwards I would be able to discover them and see that they had been there the whole time.

He sat at the desk in his shirt sleeves, thumping, pausing, muttering a muted version of the pulpit intonation and enunciation that were over my head. The sounds addressed no one I could imagine, and they arose from a person who was a mystery to me: my father The Minister, impressive and unknowable, as he was meant to be. It was a role concocted from the whole of his life, from ministers and local dignitaries whom his mother, and friends of her generation, had admired back on the Allegheny, in Western Pennsylvania, before the present century, in the village on the river bank, where he had been born. In his mother's mind, in his sisters' minds, in the mind with which he had grown up, the minister was the great man, and there he was. An unquestioning Republican by upbringing, he had arrived within sight of Manhattan on the eve of the great depression.

The whole side of the apartment building catches the sunlight, as it has done for most of three decades. Curtains blow from the windows. People have grown up in those rooms, with no building next door. Trees on the site, of the kind we were told might be locusts, are several times smaller than I am. Doves, mocking birds, even a sparrow hawk, know the tops of them. I never saw those when I was a child. And there through the leaves, emanating its startling silence that is like an echo, is the same glittering city. I can almost see, over there, the place where I have been living for years.

Laurie

I T got to where Edna wouldn't answer when the phone rang. "I just don't answer," she said. "I know." She meant, "I know that's going pretty far, and I don't care. I've been driven to it." And she also meant, "I know who's calling." She said she could tell by the sound of the ring that it was her sister Alma, next door, so near that the shadows of the two roofs made one shadow through most of the day. Her older—or, as she was careful to say, her elder—sister, Alma, who had once peered over the railing of a child's crib and the baby (her brother's daughter) had screamed. Alma calling up again to tell Edna some new story about Laurie, and to insist that Edna should get the police right away. And bring an ambulance and a doctor for Laurie, who was bleeding all over the place. Edna said, "But I just don't hear." And she nodded quickly as though she had got the better of that one, but from her restlessness and the way she could not let go of the subject it was obvious that she had done nothing of the kind. When the phone rang, she said, she stood right where she was, or she sat still in the chair—the blue-painted wicker one out on the front sun porch, or the carved one with the brownish purple velvet cushion, next to the radio in the dining room—until the phone stopped calling her. "She can just ring and ring," Edna said, "until I could—". She blew a little laugh down her nose. "I can tell she's saying, 'I *know* you're in there, and I can keep right on ringing until you answer me.' But I won't. She finally gets tired. And I'm right here all the time. She knows that. She watches when I go out or come in. I don't know what else she does in there, everything piled up the way she's got it. Food lying all around the kitchen. You know she won't answer her own door most of the time. People go up the steps and they ring and ring. And then they knock. And she's in there, all right. They can hear her moving around. And she may be hard of hearing, but she knows they're there. They even see her pull back the edge of the curtain, like that, and look out, and she'll say, 'What do you *want?*' and then close the curtain and never open the door. Maybe then they go around and try the side door. And she'll call out, 'If you don't stop that right now I'll get the police.' And they hear her rattle the chain on the other side of the door." Edna drooped, worn out by the whole situation. It had been a long time since she had knocked on Alma's door.

They were both old enough for people to wonder about their ages and make guesses as to how long they might last— one of the unconfessed habits. Neither of them had had bodies for a long time except in terms of the medicine cabinets in their bathrooms and the sizes of their clothes, or at least of their oxfords, but their footsteps were still heavy. Pieces of china tinkled faintly in the dressers when they walked through their houses. Neither of them heard clearly. Some days worse than others. Edna called Alma "Dutch" as a familiar reference: all the rest of the brothers and sisters called her that among themselves, but to outsiders they pretended that they didn't, really. The name conveyed a judgment of Alma, a distance from her, a washing of the hands, and a certain awe. They explained that "Dutch" meant "stingy"—or at least they had come to believe that it meant stingy, back when they had all been children, miles up the river, across from the big rock under the trees on the far shore, with the name of the village painted on it in white, for boats, which passed up and down in those days, and stopped at the landing. But "Dutch" had just meant "strange" to start with, referring to the Dutch who were Germans, in fact, and were supposed to say things that everyone agreed were always funny, such as "Go the hill up." Maybe the reason the family had arrived at calling Alma "strange" when what they meant was "stingy" was that they were stingy too, and knew it, and wanted to point a finger at Alma, to say that she was stingier than they were: *she* was Stingy. And she was. And "strange" came to mean "stingy" so that they could say so all the time. Edna said that Alma frequently did not answer her telephone, either. Edna could sit in the kitchen and hear the telephone ringing over at Alma's, and tell that nobody was coming to answer it, when she knew that Alma was right there and could hear it if she wanted to. She said she knew that people wondered about Alma.

Edna was the one who had always done what was needed, and then Alma had said "we." They called their mother "Grandma" to children, and "Mumma" to each other and everyone else, unless they had occasion to use her full name, which they did as though it were a title. When Edna and her husband had been living in New Kensington, Mumma had lived with them for so long that it seemed she had always been there, and that all of their lives had been arranged that way from the beginning. They had all come to feel that the world was like that, with Mumma living at Eddie's and Port's, in the front bedroom upstairs, the biggest room in the house, facing out over the railroad tracks. So many years she had seen the river going by, outside the back door, and then the trains racing past, darkening the house with their storm shadows, and then for so long she had not seen the water any more, but more trains than ever, and the viaduct with cars on it. She could still see them when at last she was sick there for so long that it came to seem that that was a lifetime too, in her rocking chair by the one window, bent over with her head on a board tied to the wooden arms so that she could look out at the room or at the sky tipped clear over sideways. Some days Alma would come down the alley in back, and stop by after breakfast on her way to the store, and would stand in the kitchen or sit down for a minute and ask, "Well, how is Mumma today?" And after their mother died at ninety-six, Alma would say, to the few people she stopped to talk to on the street, "Well, *we* was always good to our Mumma, anyway."

People had always been afraid of Alma. Even when she and Edna were children, with all their brothers and their one younger sister, up the tracks along the river, Alma, with her red hair and freckles, had been the terror of the neighborhood. She boasted that she could lick any boy her age in the place, and she was right: she would stand on the front porch and dare them to try to get to the top before she knocked them down and sent them home crying, with bloody faces. Mumma put a stop to that, or at least she tried to, but even Mumma, who kept a tight rein knotted on all of them, and whom nobody talked back to, said that she couldn't think where Alma had got it from—certainly not from Mumma's own side of the family. She had been heard to mumble that Alma was a cross they had to bear, and she repeated that they must all pray. But it did not appear to be the Lord's will for Alma's disposition to sweeten as she got her growth, and later on when the family moved downriver into town Mumma had wondered out loud whether Alma would ever get married and be taken off their hands. She did, though, in the next phase of their lives, when they had moved again, farther downriver, to a bigger town: New Kensington. There Alma was introduced to Ralph at a church occasion, and in His good time God joined them in holy matrimony. Ralph was bony and round-shouldered, with a long, sharp, aquiline nose thin as a drum-head, and he talked through it, just as Alma talked through hers. When she said, "Ralph," it sounded like a cat on a back fence, and when he said, "Alma," it sounded like another, but much quieter, as though he hoped she would not hear him.

He had what all of them—Mumma, Edna, and the rest of the family—agreed was a good job, down at the big Alcoa Aluminum plant. They said he was a foreman. When the family spoke of his position it seemed that Ralph must be the vice president, except that he kept getting moved up. He never betrayed the slightest hankering for a change, but kept the same job all his working life because you couldn't do no better than that, and he would describe the pension growing and waiting for him when he retired.

Ralph's wide-brimmed greenish-tan hat which, like the rest of his clothes, always looked as though he had just worn it home from the haberdasher's, was virtually as necessary to him as the large, gold-rimmed, pink-tinted glasses that had clasped his nose bone until they were part of his face and his voice. His hat was a detachable and variable part of his head. It was the way he turned and nodded and talked. If you had seen his hat alone on a hatrack, you could have told it was Ralph's. He wore his hat when he sat out on the porch swing of his house, and often he wore it indoors, and when he took it off the ghost of it remained on his head, which appeared to be naked and not at home, the thin hair missing the warm hat-band and the dark close cover, and you could see that being out from under the hat was a momentary condition, an interlude of suspended credulity.

He and Alma bought a big tan-painted frame house on the hill several blocks above Mumma's, with a long flight of wooden steps and a pipe railing up the bank out front, and they got a rat terrier like Mumma's and Edna's, which they named Sally. When Sally died they got another Sally. Alma became pregnant, but the baby, a girl, died. Or, as the family put it, she lost it, and could have no more children, which some said was a mercy. The details remained a mystery. But for the rest of her life the loss was cited in efforts to explain why Alma was the way she was. The tan house looked out

over downtown New Kensington, to the bluffs across the
river, but she kept the windows locked, the blinds down to
the sills, the curtains drawn shut, the inside doors locked and
bolted and the outer glass doors locked and latched. She
would have done that wherever they might have lived.

Ralph's salary grew steadily with the years, and in time
they moved down from the old wooden house to a new red
brick one with a wide paved front porch and deep awnings,
only a street up from Mumma's—the alley ran between the
two streets—but in a section that was said to be more residential. And he and Alma acquired a new Studebaker the color
of Ralph's hat, and kept it locked in the brick garage that
opened onto the alley in back. The car was of Ralph's choos-
ing. By then he confided, in a low voice, sitting on one of the
glazed chintz cushions stamped with orange flowers, on the
new tin glider out among the echoes of the porch, that he let
Alma have her way about everything else, but he reserved
his freedom with respect to two things: the choice of his
clothes and of the car. It was a used statement, spoken with
no one in mind. His clothes: the hat, the suit without a
wrinkle, the polished thin expensive shoes, and the fine-knit
socks with thin clocks up the sides. Most of the outer garments appeared to be shades of his hat. Partly because he was
bone-thin and stooped he seemed huddled in them. Even in his
shirt and suspenders. Even in his undershirt. In his suit as in his
gabardine topcoat, when he stood up it seemed that he could
be hung on a hanger and put away without getting out of
them. And although they looked new the clothes resembled
him. And so did the Studebaker, with its narrow vertical radiator grille. You could see why he had chosen each of the garments, and the car. He kept the Studebaker under a sheet in
the immaculate hushed garage, where the sunbeams came in
through the clean windows and moved across the blank floor,
warming the smells of Simoniz and oil and gray velvet car
upholstery. He took off the sheet and backed the car out only
on special occasions. As he grew older he changed the model

once or twice, at long intervals, and he drove less and less. Eventually, when the neighbors acquired televisions, he and Alma bought one too, and Alma sat on the edge of her easy chair watching the wrestlers through her cataracts, smacking her lips and slapping her knee under the long faded dress, calling out "Kill him! Kill him!" while Ralph sat back in the shade of his hat and said nothing.

Edna had married too, back at the same time as Alma. Her husband was a tall, loose-limbed, gentle, shambling figure with dark skin and black wiry hair which he kept cropped short like a brush. Port knew everybody he saw, and he got along with everybody. He had a high, hoarse, laughing voice. He never learned to drive. He walked everywhere as though he were coming home. He swung along the bright, windy railroad tracks the same way he did on the sidewalk, with his head tipped a little to one side. Edna was somewhat sideways and lop-sided too. It was one of the things they had in common, and it grew more pronounced with the years. They bought a small house, with a sun porch in front, and a stained glass window, on Stanton Avenue, facing the Pennsylvania Railroad tracks. When Port got home their rat terrier named Patty would yap on the cellar stairs and her nails would pelt like a storm of rice until he let her out. Then he would settle out on the sun porch, by the white-painted wicker table where the Zenith, in the form of an old veneer model of a country church, stood on the big doily that Mumma had crocheted, and he would bend his ear to the Gothic grille to follow the distant ball game through the static. If it was a warm day he would sit there in his undershirt even though Edna would come to the slightly raised window behind the radio, or to the door of the porch, and say, "Port, now you put your shirt on before somebody sees you." He paid no attention, except to look, for a moment, like someone who is getting away with something. When Edna was out of sight in the back of the house he might take out his false teeth too, and lay them down carefully on the doily, but if she came out and caught him at that he would wad them back into their place again, raising his eyebrows and looking up at the canary cage.

Whereas Ralph's clothes were a careful fit, Port's were apt to look too long and loose for him, tall though he was—like hand-me-downs. Sometimes Edna or he picked up shirts and underwear for him at sales, several at a time, if they were going at two or three for something. If his size wasn't to be found in the sale they got him the size larger. That would be better than having things too small. And since they weren't needed right away, Edna wrapped them in newspaper and put them on a shelf for later on.

Nobody talked much about Port's job, as though there was not much to be said about it. It was a job, that was all. He worked down at the post office, which they always re-ferred to as the new post office. He unloaded and sorted mail bags. That was what he did. There was no promise that he would stay there forever if a real opportunity presented itself some day, but the job was handy, and it was the government, so it was as steady as anything could be. They did not forget the depression. And there were supposed to be employee benefits. He and Edna never had a child. He taught the rat terrier to jump through the hoop of his arms.

Mumma got the house next door to them, which was shaded by a toby tree, so that the rooms were dark and cool. Mumma too had her rat terrier in the cellar, and an old canary named Dicky, who sang, it was said, when she talked to him, if he was feeling well. Usually he was not feeling well, and had not been feeling well for some time, because he was moulting. Mumma's black ormolu clock with its gold lions and Roman numerals chimed in front of the mirror on the mantelpiece, and the house filled with silence and the past. When a train roared by as the clock was striking, the silence after it had gone was deep and long, and people who had been talking stood and stared. Mumma had a white china poodle with a black head and orange glass eyes, that was very old and was hers like her shadow or her name. Then one year Alma or somebody out shopping found some new china dogs, small but nice, and inexpensive, at the five and ten, and that year at Christmas everybody got them as presents. Alma had a police dog with a chip out of one front foot. Edna had a ginger-colored bulldog, very life-like. Mumma had a fox terrier, but it looked new and unsettled near the poodle, even though it had its own doily to stand on. Mumma took many of her meals with Port and Edna, and even when she ate alone Edna usually took something over to her. They all treated the two buildings like rooms of the same house, so it seemed natural, when Mumma could no longer get around easily, for her to move over from her own place to theirs, once and for all.

Despite his long limbs and his easy gait there had always been a lurking frailty about Port, though it was not a thing that anyone noticed until afterwards. Lifting mail bags involved the danger of hernia, and occasionally in the evenings he complained of the ache in his back, but such things were treated as the wear and tear inevitably incurred in earning one's bread. Then one day Port fell backwards off the top of a mail truck and was carried home with a serious injury to his back, and he was left lying flat for months, in pain that was severe most of the time, and never absent. He and Edna began their experience of the extent and the limitations of the employee benefits accruing from his job with the government. The doctors spoke calmly and knowledgeably, but they made no promises, and nothing they prescribed had much lasting effect. They agreed that the damage would take a long time to heal, and that Port's back might never recover completely, or be free of pain. At last Port was permitted to get up and ease himself around the house. Edna had to help him dress. And after more months he was allowed, as much for moral as for physical reasons, to go back to work—doing things that required no lifting, of course. But even that was too much. The severe pain returned, and Port had to keep taking days and weeks off, lying flat, a prey to depression. Eventually it became impossible for him to walk down to the post office at all, even with the stiff and groping step that had become his, and he lay at home, helpless, growing weaker, his resistance to disease of any kind ebbing away, until finally, still in middle age, he died.

Then Mumma died, and Alma's and Edna's younger brother, Bill, the one who had been to college and become a preacher, moved back from Philadelphia with his wife, and became the pastor of a small church up at Elderton, in the country. Their children had grown up and left home, but even so the tiny, dilapidated frame house by the highway which the congregation had been using as a manse was not what the new pastor and his wife felt was adequate. It was neither what they were used to nor what they had in mind The manse was sold, and the minister, whose endowment policies were maturing by then, bought forty acres a few miles outside the village, with a view of the surrounding ridges on all sides. He sold the woods off one whole slope for timber, and built a stone house on the hilltop. He brought Edna up for visits from time to time. Usually it was just for the afternoon, and she walked around idly with her black purse clamped tightly beneath her arm, and looked at the distance, sat in a chair and said "Mm–hm" to herself, over and over, had some early supper, usually cold cuts, at the table by the picture window, and Bill drove her back to New Kensington afterwards. A few times when Bill was away and his wife was up there alone, Edna came and stayed until he got back. And once or twice when Bill and his wife went on a trip together, Edna was glad enough to come up and live there alone while they were gone, feeding the dog and cats, watering the petunias when she remembered to. The nearest neighbor was a mile away, and Edna of course could not drive, but friends from the church stopped off to see her when they were passing, and took her into the village to do her shopping. She double-locked every door behind her so obsessively that she locked herself out and was saved only by the chance visit of a neighbor who had a spare key. By that time she had sold the house in New Kensington where Port and Mumma had died, and was living in two rooms in a converted attic in the house of a high-school art teacher. While she was staying up on the hilltop in the stone house she made some inquiries of the people she got to know, and after Bill and his wife came back she announced her intention of buying a house in Elderton and moving there. It was not what the pastor's wife would have suggested, and she wondered whether Edna would be happy, but she said it was not really her business, and dropped the subject.

Edna bought a small house on the only street, you might say, in the village. Elderton is one of many local settlements that once were crossroads. The houses lined the four roads for some distance from the intersection, and then there were no more, and that was that. Several of the buildings dated back to the early years of the nineteenth century, and even before that, and the walls of some of them were made of logs inside the clapboard which had been put on much later—recently enough so that there were photographs of houses before the refurbishment (showing second-story porches) and during (showing men with billowing moustaches, and derby hats, posing with hammers) and afterwards (the facades gleaming with fresh paint, and bedight with new gingerbread trim above the banisters.) But most of the extant houses had been built around the time of the Civil War: square, solid, brick or frame, on foundations of great dark, dressed stones. Big trees lined the streets, with flagstoned walks under them, stencilled by fallen leaves. In the thirties and forties, as cars multiplied and their speed increased and came to be regarded as a necessity, the state diverted one of the routes through Elderton and made a by-pass alongside the village: a concrete highway that sliced across the gently curving main street at either end. The new artery paralleled the old shaded avenue, exposing the backs of the houses along one side of it, disclosing their outbuildings and odds and ends running down into the hollow. Where there had been a view of fields and woods, and of line after line of hills, there was a highway, and the light above a concrete slab.

The old gray house that Edna bought was at one end of the main street just before it rejoined the bone-yellow by-pass. Down across from the stop sign where the street ended stood the house that once had been the church manse. And going the other way, up the street past a few front yards, was her brother's church. Edna stuffed her veteran veneer furniture from New Kensington into one more wooden structure. She piled up the clothes waiting to be mended, and some of the old bedding, in a leaning stack next to the table radio, and the magazines and newspapers under the painted wicker tables and on the chapped cushion covers of the porch glider, arranged some cans on the kitchen shelves, and there she was: in that village not far from the one where she had been born, but in this one now she knew nobody at all, not a soul, except for her brother and his wife, some miles out of town, on the hill. Having no friends, she made none. And though she had no car she did not much like to be driven anywhere, either, unless she knew the people very well who offered to drive her. She made a few inquiries to find out who to go to in the village to have her hair done, and she made appointments for that, and walked to the house. Having her hair done was very important to her. It was a proof that she knew what was right, a kind of church-going. Her hair was thin and had turned gray when she was young. She wore it short, curled flat to her head, with a hair net over it. When it had just been rinsed and set the scalp showed through, pink, although her face and neck were more nearly the color of her hair. Apart from having her hair done regularly she was interested in certain religious tracts that came in the mail, and revealed by means of scripture quotations the imminence of the end of the world and of the Day of Judgment. And in very little besides. She had never cared much about food, one way or another. She just fixed something when the time came. She was seldom out on the sun porch in front of the house, because people could look in. Her downstairs rooms were small and dark. What did she do there? Her brother and his wife took her out to their house to supper once or twice a week. Her brother dropped in to see her on his way home from meetings at the church. She seemed all right. Her new life scarcely differed from the old one.

Edna was one thing, as Bill's wife would say. But then one Sunday when Ralph and Alma came up on a visit they got an idea that it would be nice to move up there too, and live in the country. Ralph had retired from his years at the aluminum plant, and had his pension at last. There happened to be a realtor's sign on the small vacant lot next to Edna's house, on the side nearer the church, and Ralph and Edna called the number on the sign, and went to the office and bought the piece without wasting any time, and started plans for building. Edna shook her head and declared repeatedly that she didn't know what to say. As for Bill's wife, she said that when she heard the news she thought she would have a fit. The house became what they called a reality almost as quickly as the decision itself. A cement building covered with yellow aluminum siding. It presented a picture window to the street, next to the striped aluminum awning over the brick front steps. The indication that Ralph and Alma had moved in was the curtain drawn tight across the pane. Ralph cut the grass out front, in his hat. Except for food shopping, a block or two away, and going to church, they never went anywhere, and they never spoke much to anybody.

Everything at Edna's looked old and dark and frayed, like the seats of a run-down movie house. Some of Alma's things looked the same way, but some looked almost new, like merchandise at a five and ten during a sale, or the displays in a second-hand store, in a pink light. Alma's cataracts thickened, but still she sat in front of the television and slapped her knee. Then Ralph began to get pains in the head. A tumor was found, and operated on, but the pains grew worse, and gave him no peace. Alma seemed unable to do anything for him or to grasp the situation except as one more proof of the malevolence of things, from which she had suffered all her life. Gradually Ralph became incapable of taking care of himself, and when he became helpless Alma could not be counted on to get him a glass of water when he called for one, though he went on calling. She vacillated between ignoring the situation, and a resentful panic when the fact was forced upon her. After years of bullying, she became as invalid in her way as he was in his, and wandered around the rooms as though she did not know them. Edna came over and took care of Ralph; she washed him, and helped him down the hall, and cooked for both of them. It went on that way for some time, until he died.

And that left Edna and Alma, alone, next door to each other, after all those years. Edna went on keeping an eye on Alma to make sure she ate. If she didn't go over for a few days, she would notice that Alma seemed to have eaten almost nothing, to judge by the look of the kitchen, except package bread, and potatoes boiled days before. Dutch had never been much of a cook. Ralph used to stand at the stove, under his hat, and fry himself a couple of eggs, half the time, when he got hungry. Edna took things she had cooked over to Alma's, but after a day or two she would find that Dutch had not eaten them at all. The dishes were left on the kitchen floor. When Edna mentioned it, Alma said, "I believe you're trying to poison me." And after that, if Edna took something over to her, Dutch threw it out. Their brother Bill would take Dutch up to the house on the hill, for the afternoon, and she would stand in the middle of the kitchen or the living room with her black patent leather purse clamped under her arm, looking around at nothing in particular for a long time. Once she filled the watering can at the kitchen sink, and took it out and watered the cat sleeping on the wood pile. When she sat down she would perch on the edge of the rocker, smiling like a cat, herself, and rock back and forth, paying attention to nobody, and saying through her nose, "Mm—hmm, mm—hmm." Just as Edna did, but Alma filled the syllables with a nasal vehemence and determination that were hard to interrupt. Bill's wife tried cooking for Dutch, too, but Dutch had always nursed a suspicion of her, and when the dishes were brought to her door she said, "I know you just want to poison me," and would not let them into the house. Her mouth had been puckered for years, as though it closed with a drawstring, and it grew more and more withered. The hair that had once been a dark red remained dark but lost its color. It looked as though she never washed it. Her round face sagged, and her freckles faded into the surrounding pallor.

Occasionally she might surprise a visitor with a mood in which she came out with what sounded like confidences. Nobody, she said, knew about the pump that she had had installed, far below the surface, out under the sidewalk. She might have been referring to the oil pump that had been put in for the furnace, but she called it a water pump. She said it was connected to the cellar by a tunnel that was a secret passageway, and you wouldn't find it unless she told you where to look. The pump, she insisted, was hers, and it was worth more than she was going to tell. It was nobody's business. But it was worth thousands, and nobody need think they were going to get it from her, unless she pleased. Even if she sold the house, maybe, some day, she might not say anything about the pump. She'd just hang onto that, and leave it to anybody she wanted to, when the time came. There were people who would steal it, she said, if they knew it was there. And the thought gave her comfort.

Then, as another instance of the malice and indifference that surrounded her, she might mention Laurie, and as often as not she would do so in terms at once so vague and so matter-of-fact that the person she was talking to might suppose that Dutch was referring to some child who lived nearby, or to one whom she remembered out of her past. And might go on supposing that for some time, partly because her talk wandered so, and she referred as a matter of course to events and people unknown to her hearers. But the details she described would grow more lurid as she went on, and it would become clear that what Dutch was describing was not remote, and not over. She would let it be known that Laurie lived upstairs. Dutch's house had only one floor.

Even before Ralph had taken sick she had talked about Laurie, but with less urgency, and so disjointedly that the reference merged with the rest of her strangenesses, and for a while no one gave them much heed. Ralph, as his friends put it, humored her, and by that time perhaps he scarcely took in what she said to him, and if he heard something odd in her talk he forgot it at once. Or he may have managed to go on thinking, as others came to do, that Dutch was rambling on about the baby girl to whom she had given birth decades before, and who had died. But from the way Dutch talked, it became apparent that in her mind Laurie was a little girl of about ten. While Ralph was dying Alma talked of how Laurie bled. She wanted people who had come to see Ralph to pay attention to Laurie.

And after Ralph died the references to Laurie grew more persistent and more violent. The blood came through the ceiling. She could hear Laurie upstairs, calling and crying and running. Laurie was mauled by a big dog right in back of the house, and Dutch said she had run out and saved the child's life, and picked her up and brought her in, and Edna should call the police. A man attacked Laurie with a hatchet, out on the back walk, and struck her between the legs, and Laurie lay there bleeding all over the walk. Edna should do something right away. Get an ambulance and the police. Edna said, "Where is the little girl now?"

Alma snapped, "I *told* you."

Edna could look out and survey the whole of Dutch's back walk without having to draw the white curtains, and she saw no sign of blood or of a little girl. "I don't see her," she said.

"I had to bring her in here," Dutch answered. "I put her to bed upstairs. Bid, you do as I say, right now."

"Bid" was what their Mumma had called Edna when she was a child. Short for "Biddy Chick"—and the name had stayed in the family. Dutch used the syllable like a projectile. But Bid talked back, and told Dutch to call the police herself if she wanted them. After that, when Edna did her wash and hung out the sheets on the back line she would no more than have got back into the house and shut the kitchen door behind her before Dutch's side door opened and Dutch stomped out and across the walk to spit on the sheets.

And from then on Alma fought with just about everybody. When someone called her on the telephone, if she was in a relatively civil frame of mind she would open the conversation by asking, "What do you want?" Then, without waiting for an answer or finding out who was calling, she might launch into a savage castigation of all those who were bothering her, spying on her, lying about her, stealing or plotting to steal from her, and a detailed statement of what she planned to do about them, and to them. In another mood she would simply pick up the receiver and say, "Now you stop this or I'll call the police," and hang up. She even accused her brother Bill, the preacher, of having stolen the broken wrist watch and the worn topcoat of Ralph's that she had given him herself after Ralph died. Many of Ralph's clothes she had kept, and just put them away.

The closets of Dutch's house, and of Bid's, were wadded to the ceilings with things salted in moth balls and wrapped up in brown paper. Woolens and fur pieces and winter clothes. Winter bedding, much of it home made. Quilts. New shirts and underwear bought in sales, by twos and threes. Wedding dresses. Overcoats for both sexes. Clothing that had belonged to their grandparents and to forbears no longer remembered. Carpets. Curtains. Towels and sheets from white sales in a previous generation, never unwrapped. Tablecloths never unfolded. Apparel from someone's childhood. Clothes for Alma's baby who died. Everything swaddled first in news-paper and string, with brown paper and new string outside that, half the time with nothing written on the bundle to identify the contents. Both Bid and Dutch went periodically to one of the closets in their houses, dragged a chair up to its door, to climb up on, and took out all the bundles, undid them to remind themselves of what was inside, and then put in a few fresh moth balls and packed everything back up again and crammed the bundles onto the shelves as before. Month by month, year by year, they did that, remembering less and less often to write on the brown paper what was inside, so that if they took it into their heads that they wanted something they had put away, they had to rely on remember-ing exactly where they had seen it last, or wait until it turned up again, or suspect that they had been robbed. The whole routine represented a large part of what they called their housework. It demanded a great deal of time and energy, but it reassured them.

Edna got tired of living where she was, as much because of having Dutch living next door, telephoning and spitting on the sheets, as anything else. And finally she sold her house and moved her things once more, back into the same two-room apartment in New Kensington, in the house of her friend the high-school art teacher. She had to find a new hairdresser, and several of her few friends had died. She wor-ried about thieves and about falling on the stairs, the curbs, the icy sidewalks, the front steps—but Dutch receded from her thoughts.

And Dutch stayed on, alone in the yellow house, for an-other year or so, and then she too moved back into town, to a small apartment on the second floor of a two-story brick building that stood by itself, under big trees, on a side street. Even before she moved, one of her few remaining regular visitors, a niece, a married woman in her middle years, with grown children, and problems of her own, who lived on the other side of the river, had taken to bringing in groceries for her, and the original kindness developed into a steady round of shopping for Dutch, as Dutch herself grew less able to get out, and less to be trusted if she did manage to step outside the front door. After Dutch moved, the same niece continued to shop for her, as a matter of course.

Dutch's brother, the preacher, still dropped by to visit her every week or so, but once she had moved, her niece was almost the only person who saw her frequently and regularly. The niece became the main source of information about her aunt, to whom she referred, respectfully, as Aunt Alma, as she had done ever since childhood.

"Don't you pay more than twenty-five cents for a loaf of bread," Alma would tell her niece almost every week. Prices had risen steeply since the shopping days Alma had in mind, and at least half the time the niece had paid for the groceries herself, but Alma insisted that anything above a quarter for a loaf of bread was a proof that the store was cheating her.

"You take that right back," she would say to her niece, when she had managed to read the price through her thick cloudy lenses. And her niece would have to go back out with the bag of groceries Alma had refused, and take off the labels and keep the things in her own refrigerator for a day or so, and then mix them in with some more shopping and drive back to Alma's with them all over again. She had to call up first, before she went to see her aunt, to say that she had some groceries, and ask whether it would be all right to bring them by. Sometimes, when she asked, Alma would say, "What day of the week is it there?"

"It's Tuesday, Aunt Alma."

"Well, it's my Sunday, and Sunday's not for shopping, and you can't come today."

If her niece telephoned an hour or so later, Alma might have forgotten, and it would be possible to deliver the groceries after all.

By the time Alma asked about Sundays she had moved into town to the apartment, where many of the boxes remained packed for the rest of her life, although Alma's brother and her niece came and helped to move her in and to put a bit of order into the place. Alma did not want them getting into her things too much. Getting nosey. Just keep their hands to themselves. An electric wall clock lay face up on a wooden kitchen chair, and that turned out to be its place—never plugged in. Her television took up one corner, and on top of it stood a shrubbery of old framed photographs of relatives at all ages. She moved the pictures back and forth, brought some out to the front and deliberately eclipsed others behind them, according to the shifts of her favor and the latest turn of the story she made up about what each of those people in the frames was doing just then. She was concerned about how long it had been since each of them had been to church. She confused the names on some of the pictures. Got them mixed up. Some of those people were dead, but she was not interested in that. Some of them, she said, were rude to her. Some lied to her. Some was cute.

Once Alma fell down and could not get up, and she lay there for hours, for more than a day, before her niece found her and began to say that something else would have to be done. Once Alma broke her arm in the bathroom and had to have a cast, a particularly large and cumbersome one. She wore it for a long time because she was old and slow to mend. While she had it on she became still more dependent on her niece, who bore up under the charge because she felt she had to; she was sorry for her aunt, and nobody else came forward to take care of her. And she knew that anything could happen. She came and did the housecleaning but was not allowed to touch many of the things in the apartment, and when she had spent two hours cleaning the bathroom she was afraid to use the toilet, herself.

After Alma broke her arm she had trouble with her hair. It never got washed. It was all nested up on top of her head, with pencils stuck through the nest to hold it together. It got matted. Alma complained that it hurt. Her niece offered to wash it. She found that the hair was caked solid, glued with what turned out to be an egg and a melted crayon. When her niece tried to untangle it Alma whined and snapped that she was being hurt. "Don't you harm my hair," she said. And, "Don't you cut my hair," when she saw the scissors. But her niece managed to persuade Alma that she would be more comfortable if her hair were trimmed, and in the end had to cut the whole mat away, and then wash the rest as well as she could.

After Alma had moved into the apartment it seemed that Laurie no longer lived in her house, but somewhere in the neighborhood. Alma worried about Laurie at a distance. At Christmas time she mailed a card to Little Laurie, sending it to her own address. She took to making up small parcels for Laurie, wrapped in old paper and ribbon, and leaving them on the stairs of her apartment. She asked whether her niece had seen Laurie, but her niece had the sense never to lie. Alma began to fuss about what might happen to Laurie: accidents in the street, rape, neglect, cold, hunger. One day she confronted her niece with an old paper bag filled with some of the parcels from the stairs, to be given to Laurie.

"I don't know where she is, Aunt Alma. I don't know how to find her."

Alma told her to go along to the corner and wait there by the post office until Laurie came by on her way home from school. There was no post office at the corner. Alma seemed to imagine that she was still living out in the country town.

"I won't recognize her."

"Yes you *will*," Alma said, and pushed the bag at her niece, and her niece toward the door.

And her niece went down the steps with the rubbed bag, and walked along the street to the corner, in case her aunt was watching from behind the curtains. She stood at the corner for a few minutes. She even caught herself looking along the next block and realized that she was wondering whether there was a post office there that she had never noticed. She laughed at herself, and stood holding the bag up like a baby, smelling the autumn, the damp leaves on the paving stones under the trees. She wondered how she would manage to get power of attorney from Alma, so that she would be able to cope with paying her aunt's bills. She hoped nobody would come by and recognize her and ask what she was doing, standing there on that street corner, on a back street, no shops nearby, just peoples' houses. And holding an old, torn, crumpled paper bag. It would make her feel uncomfortable if she had to explain that she was waiting for a little girl who did not exist, in order to give her the bag. She jogged it up and down gently, and then she turned and walked slowly back, and quietly opened the door of her car and got in, and sat there, wondering what to do. She knew this would happen again. And when she went back up with the bag, Alma would say she had gone to the wrong place, or had not really waited, and was lying. Or she would say that Laurie must be sick, or must have had an accident. And it would go on from there. In a few days the bag would be pushed into her hands again, and she would be ordered out to wait for Laurie. She wondered what was in the bag. With her upbringing she felt ashamed at being curious. But she thought she had better look, for there was no telling what Alma might have put in there. She opened the top and peered in. She could smell moth balls. The first parcel she undid had a small Bible in it. The next one contained old greeting cards: birthdays, Christmases, get-well cards that had been sent to Ralph when he was dying. There was a box full of ribbons tied in bows. An envelope with one dollar in it. A scarf, and a sweater out of one of the brown paper bundles of winter clothes.

Hotel

In a top floor apartment thousands of miles from here, put away out of the light, there is a small collection of yellow postcards, textured like linen in another generation, each of them turning up the same picture, in black and yellow, of a particular hotel in Pittsburgh, and I think of them as mine. Judging from the autos by the curb, the photograph must have been taken shortly after I was born. As far as I know, I have never stayed in that building. There are no x's marking windows on any of the cards; nothing is written on any of the backs where it says "Message" and "Address." The cards are indistinguishable from each other, as though they were new, which in a sense they are. One could say that they have not been used, except that my keeping them has been a use, as I see, and one that has grown without my being aware of it, or trying to imagine its beginning or its end.

For seven years, at least, whenever I have found the cards again—usually as I have been packing to leave, or have just come back and have been looking for something else—they have surfaced apparently unchanged. But each time another interval has ended; I have gone and returned. At the sight of the cards it seems to me that I have done neither, yet my hands holding them again have altered; I am wearing different clothes and supposing some later thing. And I have put them away once more, imagining that I am saving them for another use still to come.

I do not remember now just how I acquired them, and yet I can recall some of the pleasure of it. I know I must have discovered them at about the time of the last, or what I took to be the last, of a series of meetings and partings at the building in the center of the photograph: crossings that marked a sequence which I had come to think of as having a peculiar, as yet indecipherable, significance for me. Coincidental, like the later recurrences of those cards blank on the other side.

It may be that I picked them up first, in surprise, from the dark varnished counter in the lobby of the building in the picture, at some time during the weeks following my father's death. I had occasion to go into that building from time to time, during that indeterminate period, that season, in which many daily occurrences—bare of habit, and taking place in my parents' city, which had never been mine—reached me as moments unaccountably remembered, drifting in lighted water, voices in public rooms. A small flood of objects claiming to evoke and preserve fragments of incidents, and around them a whole past that I could not recognize, came into my keeping then, in ways that I immediately forgot.

But by the year my father died I would not have recognized the lobby. Size, shape, light, color, detail—it retained no clear resemblance to what I recalled at the thought of it, no familiar signal of descent from the long, high, sumptuous, green-and-red carpeted, sunbeamed hall, part throne room and part railroad depot, through which I believed I had walked, more than three decades before, as a child. After so long, I had wondered, when I heard the name, and the wonder recurred when I stood again in front of the many-layered facade and it looked unknowable, but there it was. I had kept learning, for years, how much had gone. I had come to believe that the lapse of known faces was definitive. Hearing the name—that echo—and finding myself standing in front of the structure it referred to, were like being remembered, myself, by someone whose face had changed. The glass doors—heavy, glittering panes set in oak—surely they had not been there in that other age. But it had always been summer then, and they would have been held open.

And going in, passing in, conscious of re-entering a place that had been momentous to me, however briefly, in the far past, and once inside seeing nothing, after all, that I seemed to know, I was aware of a single cool, passing breath, certainly, but then the unfamiliarity that met my eyes wherever I turned appeared to be the most natural phenomenon possible, the very thing that I would have expected, altogether consistent with my growing up. The true and characteristic resemblance.

It occurred to me even so—but I was reluctant to ask about it—that the lobby by that time might have been redecorated, buried, perhaps more than once. It was conceivable that the dining room had been radically expanded, or had been built there as a completely new growth, in the execution of an updated business policy. And that the present entrance, through which I had just passed, might not be the way into the old main lobby at all, but to an annex. Or that if it really were the main entrance now, it had been moved as part of a young-blood plan to attract later and different strangers. I realized then that no one in the room would have known anything of the room's history, if I had been so literal as to raise the matter, and that in any case I would not have known what to ask. Except whether it was the same, and I already had the answers to that.

But it seems just as likely that I first came upon the cards in one of my father's overflowing caches of paper clips, gummed labels, key chains, emery boards, typewriter erasers, shards of art gum, dry pens advertising funeral parlors in Kittanning, innards of mechanical pencils, keys, amber rolls of scotch tape, miniature paper rulers measuring the names of defunct banks in Weehawken, magnifying glasses, buttons, white plastic letter openers in the shape of files of elephants crossing bridges, hotel stationery, post cards showing airplanes motionless in blue, and vistas of broad empty dining rooms—relics, these last, of the restless, vague, distracted trips of the final two decades of his life, when the endowment policies were maturing. (At the age when I first remember seeing that lobby, he had already spoken to me in praise of endowment policies.) Weeks, months, after he had come back from one of those perennially odd, often impromptu sorties to Cuba, Brazil, the Holy Land, or Hong Kong, he might be found in mid-afternoon, supposedly en route to somewhere or from somewhere in the vicinity; he would be sitting in the living room, without apparent intent, in the green soft chair that had been part of the *good* or (more rarely) *parlor* furniture for thirty years, with his gabardine topcoat buttoned, and his hat on, staring across the room at an upper corner. The stare, like the shuffled post-cards, had something to do with his travels and their random nature, but the connection, in both cases, consistently eluded words.

The past itself, the past of others, of places, of his family, most of his own past, seemed to hold no more than a wan, flickering interest for him, apart from a thin collection of dependable references treasured as proofs and names of feelings that he wanted to believe still existed and were his. All his life he used the word "souvenir" as a joke, yet all his life he had been an idle gatherer and string-saver, a harborer of whatever was going free. Periodically, by way of unconsidered justification, he would say of some used trouvaille of his that somebody—often some little child—would be glad to have it, with the implication that he was saving it until he found that person; and sometimes, unpredictably, he did. His worn sympathy for the figure of Ruth, in the Old Testament, never allowed those to whom he spoke of her to forget that she had been a gleaner in the fields. He lingered over the pronunciation of the word "gleaner" with his own illumination. He explained its meaning, for those born too late to have beheld the laudable practice at first hand. My sister was named Ruth.

When, in the years just after the second World War, during a leave from the Presbyterian ministry, he had worked for a large charitable organization concerned with child welfare, one of the activities for which he became known was the setting up and conducting of regional drives to collect used clothing. In those campaigns, as they were called, he was said to have worked as one inspired: his teams collected quantities that broke records. But certain of his superiors criticized his spending so much of his time in the actual collection centers, examining the garments and helping to sort them. More frequently as he grew older he would emerge from his study when other members of the family, and visitors, were sitting talking, and offer someone—child or not—a mechanical pencil, a set of blotters, a comb or a key-ring, out of one of his treasures. He would call it a surprise, and it often happened that the person toward whom he held the thing stared at it with widening unrecognition, and partook of his bewilderment without realizing it. A favorite grandchild said of him, in wonder, that he would give you anything he didn't want. After he died, I—first with my mother, and then alone—entered the sanctuary in his absence, which was his presence as well. When his desk drawers were pulled open and the lidless spilling boxes of relics were laid bare to anyone, there was still some of the power and smell of idols loitering there, which he had fed into them for years as a reserve of hope. And if I discovered the cards there, I must have drawn them out of that context at once, in a sudden satisfied access of legitimacy, feeling that I had come upon something of my own.

And yet he had known that building—both of my parents had—much better than I could claim to, more intimately and exactly, more practically, and for much longer. They had it in mind like a street, well before that picture was developed, and long before I was conceived. They must have taken it for granted, as one of the unremarkable details of the ordinary world, something natural, before they were married, before they ever met, in the years when they were growing up near to, but unseen by, each other. No doubt each of them knew the name before knowing what it referred to; I could hear something of that in the sound of it as it came down to me from them. The hotel was a point of allusion and importance, a local personage around whom odds and ends of information and experience continually crystalized. My parents never told me what occasions of their own lives, if any, may have been associated with it, and I have no way of guessing what it represented to either of them except some bone of the general past, that past which showed many of the same features to them both, yet appeared to each of them so differently. Certainly they never saw that structure, in all those years, as significant.

Partly because of that, because of its local, contemporary familiarity to them, I cannot be sure that the first time I remember coming to the place was really the first time I saw it. But it was new to me, that time. When I heard where we were going, it was a shape about to appear at last out of its name. My parents alluded to it on the way, with a certainty that both contained and excluded me, as they did in mentioning friends or relatives whom I could not recall ever having met. They were not concerned with explaining, and it was true that the name already seemed old to me too, something that was recurring from a shadowy former age. I was nine. The journey to the hotel was charged with anticipation. It was a bright, hot summer day. We were all dressed for Sunday, which made the streets seem farther away. We would have been dressed like that whether it was Sunday or not. My mother's cousin Margie was living at the hotel.

My mother had been left an orphan when she was a small child. An Orphan. I knew the fact as I knew our telephone number, but when she said it to someone (in such a way as to make it plain that the subject was one she did not care to pursue) the word always seemed to me famous and empty:

public, self-conscious, odd. She set it forth without coloring, certainly, but with a renewed deliberateness. The shock that it conveyed each time was still most profoundly her own. She said she had no family. Not even any first cousins, or none that she knew of. Only what she referred to without names or intimacy as distant relatives. Few emerged from that category as people. Aunt Betty, in Ridgewood: a cousin. My mother's great uncle Hess and his daughter Minerva, somewhere in southern Ohio. Her cousin Florence, and Aunt Julia, in Cincinnati. And, in a place of particular honor, her cousin —really her mother's first cousin, Margie.

Almost all that I know about my Aunt Margie I heard from my mother, and a great deal even of what I remember of her is my mother's projection. Margie, for my mother, was one of the last peaks of Atlantis. She represented family not only in the sense of blood tie and continuity, but in that of shared assumptions, attitudes, conduct, gesture. Margie was perhaps twenty years—a whole generation—older than my mother, but I cannot be sure. It is possible that I do not have a record anywhere of when she was born, or where. She was, as my mother said of her with evident approval, extremely reserved. It was one of the first elements of Margie's imposing character that my mother mentioned in telling about her, and when she spoke of it my mother was invoking something in Margie that she recognized and depended on in herself. Though she would have made no such claim, it is possible that she felt this reserve of Margie's to be a distinction that ran in the—all but vanished—family. Margie's existence confirmed her own.

Anyway, a lady's age was nobody's business. To maintain as much was to keep faith with a lost world that was still, for my mother, a private source of strength, judgment and some abiding dream of safety, and this may have been true of Margie as well. I was told from the start that Margie was a beautiful woman and always had been ("her bone structure and her carriage") and in time I realized that both she and my mother had been beautiful, but common physical vanity was not the guiding principle that consistently led my mother to refuse, lightly but in earnest, to tell anyone the year of her own birth. The secret—the eccentricity—became a piece of family patter. When the census taker came around, in 1940, and laid out his papers on the dining room table, she sent me out before she would divulge what she referred to with a laugh—as though they laid bare an unavoidable impropriety— as her vital statistics. She smiled at her own obstinacy, and called it a woman's privilege, but I was no longer a child when I knew that she was two years younger than my father, and the plain fact seemed to have given up a ghost. I think it likely that Margie cherished the same form of reticence as a kind of birthright.

My mother, all her life, hated being photographed. I do not know that Margie shared the aversion, though it is hard to imagine her posing obediently for her picture. If she had done so for a snapshot, the likeness would have had the mien of a daguerrotype; but I have never seen a photograph of her. Both she and my mother left succinct instructions for the disposal of their bodies after death. Both arranged to be cremated. Margie requested that her body, until time for its cremation, should be laid out and covered with a sheet. "Nobody," the words say, "to see my face."

They corresponded—and called it that. As long as Margie lived they wrote to each other regularly, almost every week. If my mother had not heard from Margie for ten days or more, she would mention it to my father, often at a meal, expressing concern. Sometimes he would not be listening. It would not have occurred to any of them, in those years, to telephone to each other. Because of the expense, certainly. My father and some of the trustees of his church, who had held their offices since long before he came as their minister, were engaged in a feud, and they repeatedly delayed payment of his small salary. My mother rehearsed, in moments of exasperation, how little she had to get by on for food shopping, every week. We knew it had been years since she had had any new clothes. A long distance call, clear across the state, would have seemed a sinful waste, like taking a taxi. (I remember being driven in a taxi only once, when I was a child. My mother, my sister, and I came home all the way across Scranton. It cost thirty-five cents, and I do not know now and did not know then the real reason for the unexampled indulgence. It was late on a cold afternoon and snow was beginning to fall, but none of that in itself would have brought about the decision, and I imagine that it represented, in someone who kept neat accounts of every penny she spent, a passing crisis, a sudden rebellion.) Emergencies were announced by telegram. Still, the mention of the expense would have been merely an explanation, a rationalization of a way of living in which long distance telephone calls had no place. As letters did, sometimes coming unexpectedly from old friends who had been silent for years. My mother left letters open for my father to read, or she read out passages to him. She kept lists—continually revised—of birthdays and anniversaries, and sent cards with letters tucked into them. But the regulars were few. The letter knife on my mother's secretary-desk, a page-cutter from the age of uncut books, bore a motto embossed on its blade: "Books, like friends, should be few and well chosen." And the correspondence with Margie had a life of its own. It is hard to imagine what they wrote about at such length and with such regularity. Their lives were not obviously rich in event, and neither of them was given to analysis, description, speculation, or fancy. There was not even much to gossip about. My mother relentlessly reviewed the church activities and recounted the children's latest. She and Margie read some of the same books and magazines and doubtless commented on those. They exchanged news of their handful of mutual acquaintances. But the rest remains a mystery, which doubtless is how both of them wanted it to be left. It would have been in character for them to destroy each other's letters, or most of them, after they had read them a few times and answered them. When my mother died there were not many letters from anyone among her possessions, and from all those decades of hearing from Margie, only the final pencilled notes and instructions, and the news of her death, of kidney cancer, in St. Petersburg, Florida, where she had spent her last years.

My mother was alone when Margie died, in May 1946, just after the end of the second World War. My father had enlisted as a chaplain in the army and was stationed in England with the 112th Field Hospital unit. When he announced to the church that he intended to join the Chaplains' Corps, and during the first months after he put on the uniform and left for training, it was generally agreed that the absence was temporary, that the church would wait and he would come back to it. But probably nobody except the very old and the very young really believed that. How could the church wait? And he had not long been in uniform, and was still coming home regularly on furloughs, when we moved from the old frame twelve-room manse across from the church on Washburn Street, in the part of West Scranton grandly but incongruously referred to as Hyde Park. The manse was sold. I was away at school when the move took place to the other side of town, into an apartment on Madison Avenue, a block from the YWCA, where my mother had taken a job. After the wooden steps, the porches, the echoes, the rattling windows, the attic and cellar, and the high rooms each with its air and time, I came home on weekends to the smell of the respectable small apartment building, pink stucco trowelled into galactic patterns in the halls, imitation red brick linoleum on the stairs, metal casement windows with frosted panes, and the well known furniture crammed into four rooms, or five—and it seemed natural, a proof of growing up, a move into the real world, and without questioning or liking it, I was proud of it. Back from college at holidays, I came up the stairs with a suitcase of dirty clothes, wearing a teal blue overcoat I had earned the money to buy at Samter's, and imagining that I was a man.

That apartment was never thought of as permanent. My parents clearly planned to have a house again, after the war. The closets of those small rooms were piled with packed rows of bundles, and the storage space in the basement was stuffed. Eventually we moved to a much larger, lighter apartment on the other side of Madison Avenue, where there were rooms for each of us, and places for all the surviving furniture. That move too happened while I was away, and I was led in as a stranger to find the known objects already in their new places, apparently intact but perceptibly removed. The new apartment was at the top of a broad resounding wooden stairwell. There was a large screened front porch over the street, which was never used because my mother said it could not be kept clean. Inside that was the living room, with the good furniture from the almost never used front room at the manse. My mother would set her hat, with its short veil, on the back of the sofa, temporarily, when she came in, before bearing it to its place in its closet. My sister came home many weekends, taking the Luzerne Valley Line to the station a few blocks away, or getting a ride with friends, but through the week my mother returned after work to an empty apartment. She made close friends at the Y, who obviously were fond of her company, but often she came up and made lunch by herself, in her own kitchen. She said nothing about being lonely. Her secretary-desk was in the front room, as it had been at the manse, and it was there that she opened her mail—standing, sometimes with her hat still on—and answered Margie's lawyer when the news came that Margie had died.

Whatever grief she felt then, whatever loss by impoverishment, diminishment, disorientation, she kept to herself. After her childhood, death neither surprised nor frightened her, and it would have been unlike her—she would have thought it excessive and dramatic—to recognize in Margie's death the seal at the end of a phase in her life and ours, which it was. She had not been wholly unprepared for the news: Margie had been what they called well along, and her health had been failing. There had been an operation. On May 10, Margie had sent the first note about her illness, from the hospital in St. Petersburg. When the correspondence had been in full health, she and my mother had made each other presents of stationery, and partly because of the resemblance of paper and envelopes, their handwriting looked more similar to me, when I was a child, than it really was. But Margie's last notes were crowded, edge to edge, across small pieces of cheap paper, and her handwriting had stiffened and regressed.

"Dear Ann,
    Just what I am in for I don't know. Have felt very ill for some weeks and now to-day I have landed in Mound Park Hospital. Have had Xray and tests and they do not seem to know what to think about the trouble in the lower right side with such great pain.
    Did so hate to come to a hospital but just could not do anything else for myself. Seems very good so far. Two of us in a nice room. The fun has not started yet—hope it will not be to bad. Wish me luck. Hope all are well.

                              Love to all
                              Margie"

Five days later she had written again. My father also was undergoing tests at that moment, in the army hospital at Camp Lee, Virginia, and Margie's letter began,

". . . So sorry for Bill, know what he is going through. They have not found *anything* so far. Do they put me through!!! Xrays by the 4 or 5s but they have not told much yet. Too much gas to be clear. So nice for you and Bill to have a little trip and I do hope he feels better soon. The pain is just about the same but they have not helped it any at all. Hope they will soon. If I cannot write will get some one to drop you a line if there is any thing to tell . . ."

Three days later, another note:

"Dear Ann,

One week and one day in Mound Park. *Well* we do not know what is coming. My first week hospital bill was $114.53 and that not Dr. or Xray I had before I came in and still they seem to know nothing. To-day they have done nothing—I needed one day to catch up without added pain. This is a good hospital and they say the best Drs—it does seem so strange to find nothing . . ."

And on the 20th she had written to a neighbor who had stayed close to her:

". . . If his services are needed, please have Mr. Baynard.

I have been thinking about cremation and that is my wish. Make arrangements as inexpensive as possible. The hospital was so much, total was awful.

Cordially yours
Margaret J Cubbage"

The neighbor had written to my mother that same day to say that an operation was scheduled for the following morning, and that the surgeon said they really did not know what they would find. Margie had died five days later. The immediate cause of her death was surgical shock following the removal of her right kidney.

For my mother, Margie's death, like her life, had been a link—a last one—with those first lives and deaths that my mother had been born to, but she had no way of saying so, nor any apparent wish to. Except through her puzzlement and vexation at Margie's will, when its terms were made known to her. Margie had willed all of her material possessions, "All of my worldly effects, real, personal and mixed . . . unto my cousin, Billy S. Merwin . . ."—me.

I was startled, as my mother was. I came home from college

to learn that the final word about the will had been received from Margie's lawyer and that my mother had taken care of the necessary paper work, with her characteristic dispatch. There was nothing for me to do. I was referred to throughout the correspondence as Billy.

The rest of Margie's effects had arrived from Florida, too. They were all contained in one large black and black-green folding steamer trunk, unmistakably a veteran of another generation, a life and a world before mine. I seemed to know it. It was the cousin of trunks that had stood in the attic of the manse, filled with relics that meant things unspoken and unsayable to my parents, who alone were allowed even to go near them, and to open the wailing lids and gaze down into the pools and stand waiting for something, before beginning to peel back the surfaces one by one that were separated from each other only by tissue paper: sharkskin vest, black lace gown trimmed with jet beads, more jet beads, more beads, linen, high boots handed down from someone to be worn once on a night coon-hunt when my parents were young and laughed more, not so long before.

Margie's trunk did not look mournful to me, whatever I may have expected. Some old, male, benign, button-booted, ruddy-faced friend of hers who wore Panama hats and striped shirts with white collars. Oshkosh Trunk Company it said, on a brass plate on top—a picture of an Indian in leggings, the trade mark, on top of the words. The name too sounded like a family allusion of unremembered origin, a warranty out of some tempered and scarcely current domestic faith. The shipping tags, raw and new, were still dangling from the latches, and there were keys. My mother had already opened the trunk and knew what was in it, besides the clothes, which she had taken out. I did not want those, she told me.

We were standing facing the trunk in the room that was called the little dining room, off the kitchen and the back porch with its gray stilts. The glass-fronted china closet, from the dining room suite, glittered, reflecting the pale curtains.

The drop-leaf table was folded back, as it often was, and in its place the ironing board was set up. Margie's clothes were piled neatly on the dining room chairs, against the wall. Some were already carefully sorted and stacked in brown paper shopping bags. My mother said of the clothes that she was going to get rid of them all, meaning that she was planning to give them to some organization. She was right when she repeated, regularly, that none of us stopped to consider what she might feel. I was not doing so, at that moment, and probably I did not know how to. I was pre-eminently occupied with sex, and my mother knew it, and knew who it was all about just then, and she forbore to comment. Margie's will, and her trunk standing on several thicknesses of newspaper in the middle of the dusty green imitation Oriental dining room carpet, seemed remote, temporary, improbable. It was not easy, perhaps not possible, for me to give them and the details surounding them what my mother called my full attention. And I was already more advanced than I knew in the habit of not hearing everything my mother said. She knew that too, and she said more than once that she could not conceive what Margie had been thinking of, leaving her clothes to me. Her underclothes. Those folded pieces of loose-knit faded pink jersey that certainly I would never have seen, and would never have wanted to see, in her lifetime. And that she could not understand why Margie had left everything to me in the first place, instead of dividing it equally between my sister and me. My mother had even wondered whether there had been a mistake, but the will was clear. For my part, I found it hard to imagine Margie making her will at all, and thinking of me, or someone who she thought was me. It was hard to believe that the trunk, this grown-up object appearing out of my mother's absent family, representing a past older than either of my parents, was in fact mine and not one more thing being kept for me. The sense of unlikeliness remained when I took two top corners of the trunk in my hands and, to the accompaniment of my mother's saying "Just a minute, now,

Billy," and "Be careful," and of her helping from the side, opened it like a pair of heavy doors.

Margaret J. Cubbage. "Cubbage is an unusual name," my mother would add comfortably, before someone else did. Margie had never married. My mother had heard it said that there had been an engagement, possibly a secret engagement—they used to do such things—to a young man who had gone away and been killed in the World War. It was not something that Margie had ever referred to. Not the kind of thing she ever would have referred to. She said that she had not married because she had never met a man who did not like coffee, and she would not marry a man who did. My father would laugh happily when that saw was repeated, and confess that he himself loved coffee, strong coffee, percolator coffee. It was a problem finding good coffee when you travelled, and he had even considered taking a percolator with him. Margie, if she was present, would almost certainly be standing, tall and straight (did I make it up, or had I been told, to foster awe, that "she had Indian blood on her side"?) and would stare straight at him with her large, very dark, flashing eyes, as though she were looking down, and perhaps nod. She had taught school most of her life, until her retirement. She would have had no trouble maintaining discipline, in any age. My mother said that Margie had been a fine teacher. Her pupils had been fortunate: she taught them to concentrate.

On the left side of the trunk a tan curtain patterned like old wallpaper hung across the interior. On the right side was a stack of drawers covered with striped Pullman green material. Smell of dust and exhausted lavender, old cotton, and the trunk's own faint rank green shadowy odor, akin to the odor of a church on a weekday. The worn sides of the drawers stuck. My mother continued to urge me to be careful. Margie's neighbor, who had written secretly to my mother about Margie's last operation, had packed Margie's things into the trunk, though as she said of Margie "She surely had her affairs in order," and no doubt many of the things had been packed already, when Margie left for the hospital. She may have used the trunk for years, as her chest of drawers, there in Florida where she had no furniture of her own, to speak of. When I was three we had spent one winter in St. Petersburg, for my father's health, but I could not imagine the room where she had lived there, nor where she had died. I could picture her lying, according to her final instructions, on a table, alone in a bare upper room, covered with a sheet, the windows open toward the sea, the woodwork painted white, and curtains blowing—but I knew it probably had not looked at all like that. When I saw her, in my mind, she was walking slowly with a parasol, under the palm trees on the tinted post cards she had sent to my mother.

The drawers yielded up remnants whose coherence was beyond me, like collections of sea shells. Nothing about them was explained, and they themselves explained nothing. My mother had taken out some of the good things. Some plain silver spoons engraved with the name Cubbage. A small box containing a handful of costume jewelry from the end of the last century and the beginning of this one. She told me that some of those pieces should go to my sister, and they did. Empty wallets. An old empty loose-leaf address book. Things seemed to emerge, as the trunk had done, out of the family itself, and out of some long-worn memory of my own. My mother had retired to the kitchen and stayed there, keeping busy. I called out to her as I found some of the things. A silver watch chain with a silver globe hanging from it. Provenance and history unknown. Some alloy coffee spoons with ecclesiastical figures for handles. They were from Venice, my mother said. Margie had been to Europe. She had used that steamer robe on the voyage. It was a good steamer robe. A wall hanging, appliquéd with Egyptian figures. A notebook containing references to Ibsen: jottings on the plays, and passages copied out in full, one of them asserting the need of protecting ourselves from our friends more carefully than from our enemies. "Margie was fond of Ibsen," my mother said. "She was a reader." One by one the objects were doors opening onto nothing. My mother was particularly exercised about the money. She could not imagine what Margie had been thinking of, leaving the whole of that too, to me. And the whole of it, when expenses had been paid—$234 to the hospital, $150 to the funeral home, $70 to the doctor, etc.— came to $1225.65. Margie had had reason to be concerned about hospital bills, and both her attorney and my mother were surprised that there was so little.

> "In regard to source of income," my mother wrote to him, "it is my understanding it was solely her pension, derived from approximately 40 years service. I am somewhat surprised there was no life insurance, in addition to the accident policies. There may be some insurance benefit from the pension fund. It would seem logical that a pension check would have been received to May 25, the date of her death. I am sorry I cannot give you the name of the retirement or pension company from which monthly checks were received."

But there was nothing more.

At one point Margie had said that she would like to have her ashes scattered from an airplane over Florida, but her will, executed a year before she died, stated that she wanted her remains to be placed in the Cubbage family burial plot in Uniondale Cemetery, Pittsburgh (acquired by one William Cubbage, when it was known as Mount Union Cemetery, in 1863). Two days after Margie's death, my mother had written to Margie's neighbor, "The thought of cremation was at first distasteful to me, but when I considered she had requested it for her own good reasons I became reconciled." In due course she took Margie's ashes to the cemetery in Pittsburgh and had them buried there. And she put the money into government bonds in her name and mine. I did not need it, for the time being, she said, and she was right.

I had not missed Margie before—that stern, updrawn figure. Her absence struck me for the first time when there was no one anywhere to thank for having thought of me, by herself, and having made me her sole heir, for whatever unknown reasons. The money should not be frittered away, my mother said, thinking, no doubt, not only of me but also of whoever might urge me to drape them in mink. It should be kept for the day when it would provide something I really wanted. So the clothes went their ways, and the rest of the things that had survived the siftings of Margie's life and death were dispersed, some to be put away once more. What had reminded her of other years and places and people became in turn increasingly distant reminders simply of her—and not even of her but of some figment of her. Mementos. Some were mislaid, or passed into use and were broken or lost. And some stayed with me through more siftings. The money was mentioned less and less often. It became a fact, like something in history: there but not thought of, in a place of its own.

Almost a decade later, after living for five years in Europe, earning little, and that irregularly—but earning it in my own time, tutoring, writing, translating—and with never enough to put anything by, I was in southern France for a few weeks, one July, with a car so old that bets were made about it. That part of the country was still referred to by its inhabitants (and seldom, yet, by the Tourist Bureau) as the Quercy, after a tribe of Gauls whom the Romans called the Cadurcii. It is a region of rivers that flow, for long curving stretches, beneath pale cliffs dropping from upland plateaus. Small, rapid streams such as the Corrèze and the Vézère, flowing through forests, in the northern section. And then broader currents, great shining emanations of the whole terrain—of the caverns underground as well as the hills and pastures and woods under the sky. There are four main rivers: the Dordogne, the Lot, the Tarn, and the Garonne. The Garonne rises in the Spanish Pyrenees, but the sources of the other three are in the highlands of the Massif Central. All four flow westward, and the first three, one by one, join the Garonne, whose estuary enters the Atlantic near Bordeaux.

I was staying in a village on the south shore of the Dordogne, which descends from an extinct volcanic peak, the Puy de Sancy, in the Monts Dore. The pension-hotel had been a castle and an abbey. The walls enveloped an ancient church, with a famous tympanum carved from local marble. Fenelon had lived in the building, and the island just below its windows is called, nowadays, the Isle of Calypso, because it is believed to have been the model for the isle of that name in his novel *Télémaque*.

It was a rainy summer, and the lush woods near the water hung over the road, green, dark, full of green light and bowing green dusk, with openings framing sights of sloping bright pastures shining from inside themselves, red-brown cows with long horns, grazing belly-deep in grass and wild flowers. Walls of ruined stone buildings loomed through the foliage: remains of shepherds' huts, vineyard *cabanes*, pigeon towers, farmhouses, barns. The nearest large city, Limoges, was seventy miles to the north over steep, narrow mountain roads. In the region itself only the few main arteries were paved. Even along the river a dirt and gravel surface wound through water meadows and woods, with holes and washouts in steep places. The hotel put up picnics so that the days were free for exploring.

The old car trundled me through the valley and embodied my own strangeness in that time and country. There were few other cars, and most of them were as old as mine, veterans from the thirties that had spent the war jacked up on blocks in sheep barns and garages in market towns, next to phaetons and carts. When I stopped by fields, under trees, there was no sound of motors anywhere, but only the whisper of the river, rustling of leaves and grass; birds; dogs and cows in the distance. In the afternoons flocks of sheep, and family-sized herds of cows—fours, fives, sixes—took the road in their good time, browsing the rich foliage over the ditches, moved along by children or by old men or women with long sticks. When the rain stopped for over a day there was haying in the meadows: cows with long crocheted face masks to protect them from flies waited, yoked in pairs to two-wheeled blue hay wagons with slanting racks fore and aft, for the load to be built behind them, and they started home as the shadows stretched out across the newly shorn stubble. They had the right of way on the winding roads, which they blocked completely. On the hills the cows leaned into each other, shoulder to shouder. Bunches of hay hung in the trees that bent over the road. Later, when the cows were in their barns being milked, young owls appeared on the shadowy road and stood staring along it, as the nightingales began, late in their season.

The smell of barns drifted even through the market towns that were themselves not much larger than villages, and in the evenings cows swayed through the streets guided by peasants with the same long sticks. Pigs grunted behind arched cellar doors, and were butchered in back alleys, with groups of experts standing around, and the cobbles running blood. The farm dogs appeared to be a random mix, but many of them had one pale and one dark eye. They knew their jobs. They ate soup. The language on the farms was a *patois* descended from a Languedoc tongue older than the French of Tours and Paris. But the word "peasant," with its heritage of poverty and of scorn from other classes that still sap and abuse the peasantry, had been relegated, and replaced, in courteous use, by the phrase "country people." They dominated the fairs as well as the farms. Even in town they sat at table with their berets on and the men held the huge wheels of bread to their chests and cut them with the clasp knives from their pockets, pulling the blades toward them. Bread swelled in the soup, and when they had finished they sluiced out the bowls with wine and drank it off. They were proud of what they called their *polyculture:* they grew everything, from the corn and wheat and giant forage rutabagas for their animals, to their own black wine and their firewood. Their cash crops were milk and walnuts, wool and lambs, plums, tobacco. The year turned through their harvests. It was common for families to have land scattered here and there—plowland and pasture and woods—and several houses, one of which might be used for drying tobacco and storing corn and potatoes and old furniture. They had survived the German occupation without servility or shame. In the Middle Ages the quality that was said to distinguish the Quercynois was *douceur*—something more than gentleness and closer to its literal rendering: sweetness.

Across the river, in a village just raised above the valley plain, a gaunt white-bearded Englishman of seventy, who looked as D. H. Lawrence might have looked if he had attained that age, lived in a long old farmhouse that he had bought after some years of managing an estate elsewhere in France, before the war. He had been involved, in his own way, in the English organic farming and gardening movement, and he cultivated his large vegetable garden and his fruit trees with absorbed devotion, as the fulfilment of a faith. He regarded the region as a last promised land, and revered the old ways of the peasants with their soil and their animals, their food, and each other. At the beginning, he said, he had fixed up his house but he had no furniture to put in it, and he mentioned the matter to his neighbors. Soon afterward the town crier, in the village square, after a roll on the drum, had announced that those who had old furniture they didn't want would do well to bring it out to show to the bearded Englishman; and he had furnished his house that way, for a sum he could afford. Solid pieces carved from walnut and cherry, that had reflected the kitchen fires of generations— some of them fresh from more recent use as rabbit hutches. Now there were two houses in the vicinity that he had agreed to try to sell for their owners.

I went to see them. It seemed far from credible that I could buy—could own—a house in the French countryside, even though the prices then were low. They were very low. Partly, I discovered, because there were empty houses everywhere, in various stages of disrepair, and most of the owners had never thought of selling them and found it hard to believe that anyone from outside the region might want to live in one of those old places. Would I? I was not at all sure, and neither of the ones that the Englishman had to offer presented a temptation. But by the time I had seen them I had begun to play at looking for houses, and I went on playing at it—somebody always knew of another one. It was a pretext for getting to talk with the people and see the villages and the farms and the insides of the buildings. The architecture had changed little, it was said, between the time of the Black Prince and the first World War, and almost nothing had been built since then. Pretending I wanted a house there allowed me to imagine living there, rather than being a tourist, and I had no trouble persuading myself that it was a relatively harmless fantasy. When I was a child I imagined houses, one after the other, in which I lived and had lived in other ages. They were mine, and yet I did not own them. They disappeared, and returned if I remembered them, which seemed as natural as the going and coming of day. Thoreau, in *Walden*, said of his own imagination that it "carried me so far that I even had the refusal of several farms—the refusal was all I wanted." And perhaps it was, finally.

The search, and my own more general curiosity, led up out of the valley onto the plateau above it, the *causse*. The valley life had risen from the deep soil of the river plain and had some of its softness. The soil of the *causse*, in most places, was a thin layer of red clay, hard, and full of chunks of limestone, over a bed of pure limestone that stretched south some thirty miles to the valley of the Lot, and was the roof of a network of caverns, underground rivers, and tunnels, as intricate as the inside of a loaf of bread. The stone was everywhere, and everything was built of it. Freshly turned up by the plow, it was stained by the rusty shades of the soil. The rain washed it pale gray or yellowish white. Broken, it had the bluish stare of cracked bones in a butcher shop. It weathered to darker grays like long-dead branches, or to a lighter golden gray, and lichens, mosses, ivy grew over it. Walls, and the ruins of walls, knee-high, waist-high, shoulder-high, ran everywhere, embraced the smallest field and pasture, pigrun and patch of garden, skirted huge walnut trees, vanished into oak woods. There were so many stones that what appeared to be buildings in some of the fields turned out to be structures of solid dry masonry, reared in order to get the stones out of the plowland. Some of the barnyards were slabs of solid rock, sloping to pools with a little stagnant water in them where ducks waded. The heat shimmered like the leaves, and the middle of the day resounded with cicadas and the tonkle of distant sheep bells, and smelled of box and hay.

A potholed lane passing under the limbs of two rows of old walnut trees led toward empty sky. On the way, off to the left, across fields, I could make out a few dark red and slate-gray roofs of a hamlet. I stopped before I reached it, pulled the car off the lane and left it in deep grass, by a wall. The hamlet lay along the edge of the *causse*, overlooking a vast expanse of valley. Hundreds of feet below was the river, and on a hill out in the plain a castle of red stone. Just in front of me, set back from the lane and its walnut trees and tumbled wall, two long stone barns on the break of the slope, each flanked by a small square tower, eclipsed the valley. Beyond them, toward the village, thickets of brambles half again as high as a door almost hid the roofs of a cluster of farm buildings. Last of all I saw, below the lane, the roof of the one that was the house.

Brambles and ivy had grown far up the dark tiles, some of which had fallen away. The side of the building facing uphill toward the lane was invisible, sunk in a dense tangle of brambles and black bryony. A smaller lane led down past it, and from the set of the roof I could see that the house looked out above the tops of unkempt plum and walnut trees to the broad valley spread out like a reflection, below. A dead stick helped part the brambles, some of the stems as thick as a thumb. I pushed through to the door, weathered darker than the gold-gray stone. Beside it an opening in the wall had been bricked up except for a small square through which I peered and saw pieces of fallen wood, a cracked plaster partition, planks of a flight of stairs to a loft, gaps in the floor, and a corner of window opening, under an arch on the far side, where the light came through a quaking curtain of ivy. Making my way back through the brambles, I looked up. Standing in the long dry grass between the barns and the lane was an old man watching me. Straw hat, round lined face, Gaulish moustache, sloped shoulders in a black jacket faded to shadow color, blue shirt open at the collar, baggy gray trousers, a sash like a bandage, an expression neither hostile nor welcoming. The noon sunlight of the *causse* bleaches the colors from everything, but in my mind he stands out from the surroundings, clear and sharp. He died over a year ago.

He was polite, without giving anything away. He said that he was a neighbor, and that he did not see any harm in looking at the house. He did not volunteer information, but he went on standing there and answered questions while he looked me over. No one had lived in the house for thirty-five years. It had last been used, a while back, for drying tobacco. At one time it had been the village school. That was where he had learned to read and write, in that house. A nun had taught there, a sister. Maybe that was why there were crosses on the ends of the roof, or maybe they were there just because somebody put them there. He had the use of the barns for hay, and for his animals in the winter. The place belonged to a woman who had grown up there and now lived in a small nearby town, with her husband, who was retired.

In the next days, through the haying weather, I came again several times to the wall by the barns, ate lunch under the walnut trees, and floundered through the brambles to the hole in the patch of brickwork. There were birds everywhere:

black-capped and white-throated warblers; redstarts, wrens, robins, and swallows; nuthatches; blue, great, long-tailed and coal tits; green woodpeckers, blackbirds, shrikes; nightingales sang close at hand in the middle of the day. I explored elsewhere. I met people who took me to other houses, most of which were beautiful, and I talked with some of the owners, but the game was still a game. The abandoned farmhouse looking out over the valley was the one that kept coming to mind most often, and I thought I should at least see whether I could talk with the owner, if only in the hope of seeing it from inside.

The neighbors' directions led to another lane off the narrow *causse* road, and a modernized, stuccoed house surrounded by bits of lawn and ornamental garden. I learned at once, from the trim, energetic, gray-haired woman I had come looking for, that she and her husband the Colonel had lived in the colonies throughout his career, and that since his retirement he had been working as an official, selling tickets at one of the famous caverns where tourists descended in an elevator and stepped into boats for a trip along an underground river. She watched through her smile, but she appeared to accept and approve of my interest in the house, to welcome it, though with a slight surprise. And she told me where to get the key, from a retired railroad employee who lived at the crossroads near the hamlet, and picked the plums in the early summer and gathered the walnuts in the autumn.

He was sitting out on the half-moon stones of his doorstep, a few feet off the road: a short man of wonderful rotundity and labored breath, with a black, patent-leather, visored, railroad employee's cap on the back of his head. A strawberry nose presiding over his face. Full round lips sunk behind cheeks that almost swelled his eyes shut, so that it was no distance to smile. The last wet half-inch of a home-rolled cigarette moved from his lower lip to his fingers and back again as though it were lit. He heaved himself up, quaking with good will. He said he was in retirement. He laughed at everything either of us said, wheezed amiably, and said he would be happy to accompany me to the house. He settled into the car, for the half mile ride, with visible satisfaction. He held the big key in his fist like a scepter. He talked, pausing only to pull in another breath; his voice was a deep nasal croak. He wanted me to admire the place he was in charge of. He said he grew his potatoes there.

He wanted me to be impressed also with the fact that he did not have the soul of a peasant but was a genuine petit-bourgeois. That was the faith in which he lived and planned to die. He fetched a sickle to hack at the brambles. I had wondered how he could bend over to pick up the walnuts from the grass. I was surprised to see him puff and grunt, but manage to open something of a path through the heavy growth. He had been using a sickle all his life. His accent and his way with it were so rich that I missed half of what he said, and he was hard of hearing, so that despite his talk I learned less than I wanted to.

The inside of the house would not have been alluring, except that it was the inside of that house. Three rooms, each with a fireplace, though only the central one was old and massive, with a huge beam for a mantel. And each room with large, treacherous holes in the floor. There was a tiny window in the main fireplace. He called that room the kitchen. The cooking had been done on the open fire, and the stone arch had once been the place for washing dishes; there was a stone drain at the foot of the wall. From the window opening I looked out through the ivy, and across to the ridge on the far side of the valley, miles away, and down through the walnut leaves to the river.

Parts of the brick and plaster partitions had fallen. I climbed to the loft and skirted more gaps in the floor, fringed with rotted wood. A gable window, and once more the view of the valley and the river. On the basis of what I had learned in recent conversations with owners, most of the beams appeared to be sound. And the walls—stone, two feet thick—

seemed solid, as my guide assured me they were. Outside once more, he told me what good potatoes he grew there, and—winking—that there was a fine cellar under the whole house, but too overgrown to get into, at the moment. In the autumn he made *eau-de-vie* from the plums, he said, and he promised me a drop.

Several days after that visit I went back to see Mme. the Colonel and the Colonel himself, toward the end of an afternoon, and sat on a modern chair and was served home-made ratafia, thick and gold, and store cookies. Yellow panes in the windows colored the light. Orange flowers glowed on the curtains and upholstery. The Colonel was tall, white-haired, soft-voiced, gentle. We talked of the region. I could hear that what they said of it they had said many times before. Perhaps both of them were used to talking to tourists who came to take the boat ride in the caverns. We touched on the salient facts of our lives, reassuring each other cliché by cliché. They insisted that I have more ratafia, more cookies. I supposed that the Colonel would be prudent and cautious, and that she might be tight-fisted, and I saw that it mattered to me, though I still could not imagine that they would sell the house for any sum that I could hope to offer. I had wondered whether she would be willing to sell it separately from the barns, or even apart from all the other buildings, just as it was, but I decided to leave that proposal for later on. They were pleased that I had liked the house upon closer inspection, as though they had made it ready for me. She spoke of the guardian with a shrug of deprecation and a laugh, and of the neighbors with an automatic scorn. They were backward, she said, and it was due to nothing but their own lack of drive. That was the way they were. I asked her at last whether she would consider selling the place. The Colonel turned to her, to make it clear that the decision was entirely up to her.

She said that the house had come to her from her own mother and that she herself had been born there and had grown up there; her eyes filled. But she said she had thought of selling it, for someone to take care of it. Once she had almost sold it to a lady, and then the lady had changed her mind. That had been some years before. She would not sell it to someone who wanted to resell it and make money on it. But she would consider selling it to someone who wanted it to live in. I assured her that I had neither the wish nor the capacity to speculate, and that if the house were to become mine I would hope to live in it. She nodded, inspecting me again, no doubt trying to imagine me living there. I asked her how much she would sell it for. She said she was not interested in making a big profit on it, and that if she sold it, it would be for the same sum she had agreed on with that lady, the other time. She named a figure that I recognized as exactly the amount, in francs, that Margie had left me. We looked at each other for a moment and then shook hands.

Clear enough. In time I came to know the particular ritual and moral importance of the handshake, on the *causse*. At fairs in the market towns, on cold foggy mornings in late autumn, peasant men in thick corduroys and the wide new-looking berets worn on Sundays and at weddings and funerals, smoke from hand-rolled cigarettes drifting past their creased faces, would clamber over the sides of pens and wade through the gray, heaving, bleating eddies of ewes and lambs—the old *caussenard* breed, with long legs and Roman noses—clutching at a backbone here and there to judge how dense the meat was along the spine. Bids and rejections would fly back and forth, and at some point in the bargaining one of the participants would try to snatch another's hand in the course of some emphatic gesture, while the other, if unwilling to conclude the bargain right there, would avoid the grip and fold his hands safely in each other, behind his back. A clasped hand meant a bargain struck firmly and irrevocably, whether the one whose hand was seized meant it to be so or not.

And once Mme. the Colonel and I had agreed on the main concern, she and her husband were at pains to help the details fall into place as comfortably as possible. Of course I would stay to dinner, to celebrate. They led me on a tour of the cement-lined cellar, from which they emerged laden with jars of homemade patés and preserved goose and mushrooms—the big rich *cèpes* from the chestnut woods—and snails and truffles and bottles of old wine with which to toast every hope awakened by the transfer. The sum she had named was the price for the whole property: the house, the barns, the other outbuildings, the land around them—all of the old farm except its remaining fields and woods and pastures, which were rented out. The conversation moved back and forth from practical plans for concluding the sale, through what I could look forward to in living there, to the vicissitudes of their long career in the colonies. Mme. initiated me into the ways of finding and preparing snails under what she called my own plum trees, and the mysteries of making *eau-de-vie* and ratafia. She recounted the tropical diseases from which she had suffered, and became eloquent in telling of the worms that had multiplied in her body and travelled through it extensively and succumbed at last only to drastic medical treatment; their bodies were still there. They were dead, but they went on moving through her very slowly, year by year, and she would carry them with her to her grave. "You can feel them yourself," she told me, and held out her thin ageing arm. "Right here," she insisted. "Feel."

Even so, the house was still a long way from belonging to me, or seeming to. Or rather, though the sale went through easily, I remained a long way from having a live sense that the house was mine. That was not just because of the inevitable pendulum swing back and away from the excitement of finding it and the original fantasies of being there, or because I had to leave almost as soon as the first papers were signed, and go back to London to earn a living and some money for basic repairs. Almost from the start the house and the commitments it assumed to France, to rural France, to Europe, began to stir up their opposites in me. I had been away from America for five years and I was homesick. I knew that I did

not have enough money to go home and live without for-
feiting the self-employed state, the relative independence of
the years in Europe. Yet I missed the States, or my own images of the States, in a way that clearly surprised many Euro-
pean friends at the time. I wanted to see what my own country and I had become, since I had left. I resisted the tie to
Europe even as I made it and elaborated it. That winter I
arranged to have the roof of the house, and the floors, repaired,
and a rain water cistern and septic tank built. And the following summer I went back and stayed briefly at a hotel in the
valley, visiting the house during the day, to plan the next
stage. But I was not caught up, either by the place or the
work. It was duty, most of it. Something I had let myself in
for. If I had had a chance, during the couple of weeks I was
there, to sell the house for what I had put into it, I would have
done it, with some regret, but also, I think, with relief: a sense
of freedom reclaimed. The next year I did not go there at all.
In the spring I was awarded a small fellowship that took me,
that summer, to Boston.

The neglected house was not the only unfinished thing in
my life that eventually drew me back, reluctantly, and with
all the old reservations and misgivings intact, to Europe. It
had been almost four years since Mme. the Colonel and I had
shaken hands in agreement, when I returned to France,
planning to stay in the house until the frost. I had an exhausted
closed Bedford delivery van painted dull blue with yellow
wheels, a somnolent, sullen hulk that required prolonged
cranking through a hole in the front bumper before it could
be persuaded, suddenly, to lurch into its routine of bangs and
shudders. At its best, on a smooth road, it sounded like a de-
spondent coffee grinder. It was loaded to the sinking point,
and I had been driving since daybreak when I made the turn
at the crossroads once again in the first twilight, and with a
joy that startled me, recognized at the western end of the lines
of walnut trees the piece of empty sky. I eased the behemoth
through the long grass inside the walls along the lane, and

down the slope to the space—cleared of brambles—in front of the door, and let myself in with the long iron key.

House scent of lime and wood aged in shadow. There was no glass in the windows. The floors were covered with rubble from the partition that had been taken down to transform two of the rooms into a single large one with two fireplaces. Swallows had nested above a green tin hanging lamp shade, converting it into an atoll of white droppings. Bats whispered in the beams. I unlashed a rusted cot from the roof of the truck and made my bed between the front door and the big fireplace, in the middle of the main room. The hum of the day on the road drained away. The breeze through the windows smelled of rain and leaves and evening. As the light went, the blackbirds called, and then the first long notes of the nightingales began.

I lay in the dark, listening to the cowbells in the pastures, owls, the flight of bats like a flapping of tongues, the creaks of the old building accustomed to communing with itself. It was the first night, for me, under that roof. I was alone in the cool darkness of the upland, afloat among the farms and woods. The good of lying there in the night air and the night smells and night sounds of the *causse* and in the immeasurable antiquity of the place, was something I had not even imagined.

The fluttering of the unseen bats receded as they left through one of the empty window frames. Already I was displacing them. I had driven hundreds of miles to that particular patch of old splintered floor covered with dust and rubble. Every decision of mine and of my parents had been leading toward that half ruined, half finished structure, its shadows, its darkness, its smells of must and wood and night, the clear sounds of those bells, the notes of those nightingales in that season. At the back of my eyes the road kept appearing and then fading out like an early film that broke for longer and longer intervals, while the ivy and the elder leaves rustled against the stones of the walls about which I knew what amounted to nothing.

I wanted it to stay like that. I did not want to start trying to find furniture, not even if I were to be as lucky as the old Englishman had been with the crier, in his village down across the valley, miles and years away. At the same time that schemes for repairs and conversions and amenities rose and flickered out in my head. I did not want at all to clear the floor and put panes in the windows, paint the walls, move object after object in through the door and set each in place in the rooms, to be convenient and comfortable and pleasing. I did not want to surround myself with all that credibility and believe in it. I wanted to be there without any of what I had come with the intent of putting there. To remain just as I was at that moment in the night of the foreign room that my claim and presence had only begun to mark and alter.

I woke suddenly with a feeling of oppression and fright. In my dream I had been lying there, right where I was, and a gray, greenish light like a luminous shadow had revealed to me, as though by moonlight or lightning, the inside of the heavy front door, a few feet away. An iron bolt ran across it into the masonry. I do not remember whether or not I had locked the door before going to bed. In the dream I could see that it was tightly bolted. But as I watched, fingers, and then a hand, a left hand, more a woman's than a man's but not obviously of either sex, and of no determinate color—the color of the light—appeared around the edge of the door, groping along it. The wrist followed, and part of the arm, and the fingers felt their way to the bolt, which began to turn and loosen. I could hear the bolt grate and the door begin to move. Then I woke. The house was dark and the night was still.

In the morning, as the sunlight came through the opening above the door, I heard the grass swish outside, and a light rap on the parched wood. I raised the latch, to be greeted by the old man who had stared at my first visit to the house, those years before, come now to make me welcome to the village, to show me where he had scythed the grass to the entrance when he had heard I was coming, to offer me tools and hospitality, and to begin to teach me, in a language not my own, what a neighbor is. To tell me, first, as something which he had no trouble accepting, that in the house where he had gone to school, I was at home.

The dream at first seemed to conflict with what I believed I felt about the house. I mentioned it to no one at the time, but as I worked on the building and lived there, and came to see it and the land around it representing different things to me, I thought occasionally that I glimpsed one facet or another of what the dream had been telling me. That autumn, for instance, just as the weather turned cold, after months of hard physical work I caught a fever and lay delirious for days before the symptoms declared themselves as those of a virulent and, it was said, dangerous form of hepatitis, by which time the money had run out—and so forth. Not that I imagined the dream's content to be nothing but menace and warning. I came to love the place. But the house, any house, is its own story, and this is not the story of that house. Over the months and years the thought of Margie, and her intent and role in my having it, and being there, surfaced repeatedly like the questioning of the dream. There could be no explanation, naturally.

Whatever image Margie had formed of me that had persuaded her, late in her life, to leave to me alone the remnant of her savings and the single trunkful of worn belongings which she had kept until then, it must have evolved from two sources: my mother's letters, and Margie's short residence with us in the Scranton manse not long after we moved there. I can only guess at the importance my mother accorded her children in those letters, the confidences and the strain of implicit boasting which served to involve Margie in my mother's own anxiety and pride. It is not hard to imagine my mother addressing and deferring to the school teacher in Margie, to the woman, the elder, the sympathetic but remote authority, the lone vindication out of that distant pantheon, her family.

Margie took, as my mother said, such an interest in the children partly because my mother assumed that she must. That interest was an important element in the complicity between them. Indirectly, and without asking for advice, she invoked Margie's judgment. It was a way of eliciting her approval. They discussed the latest issues of Parents' Magazine: the tests and scores evaluating the children's this and that. They laughed over the phenomenon of competitive parents, and the laughing permitted a further superiority.

The one time that Margie had even seen much of me, the only time when we had been together for long, was during the period when she was living with us in the big brown frame building across from the church, on Washburn Street, when I was ten. I do not remember her arriving, but it seems to me that the trunk I was to inherit was with her then, and that as long as she was living with us it stood open like a chest of drawers in the small room at the head of the back stairs which remained Margie's room long after she had gone again and it had been occupied by others and used for sewing and storage. On the front stairs of the house we—my sister and I— were warned and expected to walk quietly just because we were to walk quietly on stairs and not scuff. On the back stairs we were to walk quietly for the usual reasons and also because those stairs were just outside Margie's room. I am not very certain of all the details of the inside of that room while she was living in it, because although the door to it stood open most of the time and I could see in from the top steps, it was an absolutely forbidden place. We were not even supposed to look inside. It was none of our business. A cool light in there, faded yellows and greens, as in the picture of the plump girl sitting on a bench, looking up and listening to a bird in a tree. And there was the radiator that came, for a while, to occupy a place of such importance in the household. The bed—all but a corner of it—was out of sight. Aunt Margie's bed. Margie's bed. One of the first things she had done after she got there was to go straight downtown to Stoher and Fister's, where the good living room suite had been bought, and buy a bed that she approved of. Single, with a high firm mattress and a walnut veneer headboard. It may be that she did not think much of some of the beds in the house, such as the wide, creaking old tin structure that had been my parents' in the Union City manse. Later, when the subject came up, my father said, if he was being critical of her, that she was high hat, and my mother said she was particular. Her bed stayed in her room after Margie left. At first it supported the pretense that she was keeping it there because she might be back, and it would be waiting for her. When that was gone it remained part of the mark she had made.

Before she came to us it was agreed that Aunt Margie was going to teach my sister and me. There was even talk of our staying home and being taught by Aunt Margie instead of going to school. My parents had a friend out in the western part of the state, south of Erie, who had been a school teacher and then later had taught her own children at home. It was possible, supposedly, to get permission to do that. We had been to visit her and her children. Up until then, when I had only heard of her, I believed that she was Mrs. Wiggs of the Cabbage Patch. But she was herself. The water from the faucets in her tiny house tasted of sulfur. Her children were older than my sister and me, and my mother said that they were years ahead of other children their age, scholastically. Studying at home, they had learned to concentrate. Besides, my mother was convinced that the standards of the sooty old brick Gothic school around the block on Hyde Park Avenue were far below those of the New Jersey school system, and of the Union City school in particular, which my sister and I had come from, and where she had been in the habit of chatting with the teachers. I welcomed the idea of being taught by Aunt Margie. I would have been happy to stay home from the new school, which I disliked, and where I was younger than my classmates and felt out of place and vulnerable. I kept asking my parents whether they had obtained permission for us to be taught at home, but I could tell before long that the subject was receding from their minds. If I mentioned it to my father he would answer as though he had forgotten that the possibility had ever arisen before. He told me that it was good for me to mingle with youngsters of my own age. (The pupils of my own age were all in other classes.) On the other hand he insisted that I must stay out of rough games, which meant games altogether. "And don't get overheated at recess," my mother added. On no account, they agreed, was I to get into fights. If I did, my father said, he would hear of it, and I would be punished severely. "Just walk away from them," my mother said. After school we were to come straight home and not stop to play. We had the yard to play in.

We did not stay home from school, but Margie taught us just the same. She supervised our homework. She could tell immediately whether we knew our lessons or not. I had always had trouble with arithmetic, and in Union City my mother had taken to leaving a sheet of paper with four problems, one each of addition, subtraction, multiplication, and division, on the stool beside my bed at night, for me to solve in the morning before coming downstairs. That is the time of day, she would say, when your mind is fresh. Margie sat with us over our schoolwork, and for me she added arithmetic exercises of her own. The time of day did not matter to her. She would sit with us not only after breakfast but also after we came home in the afternoons. I think I liked the arrangement better than my sister did. Inevitably I had picked up some of my mother's admiring regard for Aunt Margie, and for me too she became a private—a secret—authority. I had more confidence in her than in any of the teachers at school. I realize that she was careful not to conflict with what they may have told me, or with their methods of instruction. But when I had finished homework with her I felt certain that I understood it, even the arithmetic.

Besides, awed though I was, and as everyone else was, by her remote, commanding presence, I liked her. Her attention was unwavering and apparently tireless. She never supplied an answer nor part of one. She was relentless and uncompromising but completely patient: she would stay with whatever it was until it was learned. Most of the time her face was impassive, the large noble features composed, attentive, waiting. Except for those eyes, almost black, and burning. I sat down happily at the big heavy desk in the room we called the playroom, when it was time for her to go over the lessons with me. She stood so straight that no doubt she seemed taller than she was, in her high-necked long dresses of dark solid colors—greens and magentas and blues. Her curled white hair was piled around her head; I never saw it any other way. She put on pince-nez for reading. The light, elusive fragrance around her was probably made up only of soap and powder and lavender sachets left among her clothes. It was impersonal, a disguise of anything physical, but it was always there. She sat beside me to my right, on the side away from the window and a little behind me, her back like a dancer's, one hand on the desk. Sometimes when the lessons were over, or if it was Saturday and raining, we would play games that were more like tests, or work on puzzles, at the desk. Often then, and almost always when homework was finished, I would catch a glimpse of her rare, anomalous smile: her face creasing, eyebrows rising, the corners of her mouth lifting like curtains drawn up, showing the startling teeth, and the eyes for an instant closer, dimmed, approving.

And I went for walks with her, usually to the end of Washburn Street, to the cemetery, with the family fox terrier, Tippie. In Aunt Margie's judgment Tippie did not get enough exercise, cooped up on the back porch and allowed out into the yard only when the children were there. Tippie's nails, as Margie pointed out, were proof of it. They were much too long. They curled. They must hurt the poor dog. Margie took her and had them clipped, and undertook to continue the job herself, but she said that Tippie should be exercised enough to keep them worn down naturally. She led

Tippie forth on a leash and strode along the sidewalk wearing
solid shoes with the heels only slightly raised, a long dark
woolen coat with an amber fur collar, and a cloche hat. She
went almost every day, if the weather was right, and if she
went shopping, alone or with my mother, she took Tippie
with her. If my mother went shopping by herself, she never
took the dog. My father seldom walked anywhere. The children were not allowed out of the yard. Tippie, at first, was
not used to taking walks. She was overweight and she
wheezed. Once, years before, in Union City, some shadowy
figure who was staying with us had taken Tippie out shopping along New York Avenue, and on the way back, across
the street from the house, Tippie had suddenly pulled loose
and dashed for home, and had been run over by a car. I can
hear my mother screaming from somewhere, seeing the whole
thing, and can hear Tippie yelping, and I watch, helplessly,
the white-and-black wheel of small dog spinning underneath
the high car, which speeds up, and I can feel the shock and
fear for the dog, and outrage at the car. (Tippie sustained
nothing worse than a bad fright, an hour of the shakes, and
a minor abrasion outlined in car grease along her spine.) But
I cannot see clearly who it was, that day, who had been walking Tippie. It may even have been Margie, though I can
scarcely believe it, if only because it is hard to imagine Tippie
pulling the leash out of her gloved hand, or such a thing
happening at all when Margie was responsible.

Nobody else went to the Washburn Street Cemetery just
to walk around in there, but if Aunt Margie chose to do it,
that was one thing a cemetery was for, whether people realized it or not. Some days she had already been for her walk,
by herself, when my sister and I got home from school. No
doubt she needed an occasional outing by herself. The cemetery, when she walked in it, was her own place. I knew that
when I was there with her. She did not read the tombstones.
They were there like the trees. I did not ask many questions.
I mentioned, at times, what I had been reading or thinking

about, trying to catch and hold her attention. But I do not remember much about our conversations, if that is what they were. I doubt that we talked much. Cemeteries were also places to be quiet, out of respect, starting on the sidewalk before reaching the gate.

I had other reasons for being glad that Aunt Margie was with us. Whether or not I was clearly conscious of it, she was a counterweight to my father. For all her strictness of mien, she was not capricious nor shaming nor hurtful. And I knew, from things that my mother let fall, and from what I remember feeling at the time, that she did not approve of many of my father's arbitrary and special restrictions, nor of his moody punishments of me in particular. His conduct toward his own children, and especially toward his son—me—was so unlike his way of acting toward other children, with whom he was effusively sentimental, that he was questioned about the difference, then and in later years. He always answered that he treated us, and me, that way, only because of love, and that he was afraid I might get hurt. He would never have admitted that Margie's presence in the house had any influence on his own decisions and actions, but I do not believe that he indulged his frustrations and disappointments upon any of us as freely as he was used to doing, before that steady and at times disdainful regard. My sense that she did not accept without question the whole of my father's rule was a relief to me, though inexpressible and perhaps only partly recognized. It revealed to me a breach in what I had come to think was a closed horizon. Up until then, within that tight household, it had seemed that only disreputable outsiders—non church-members, the benighted, the dirty, Catholics, Democrats, foreigners—did not respectfully admire and embrace my father's superior views, the pastor's views, which included his harsh and peculiar ways with me, for my own good. But Aunt Margie was Aunt Margie, and her own authority. When we were left in her charge we were permitted, occasionally, to do things that we and she knew were nor-

mally forbidden. At the cottage at the lake where we went in
the summers, she allowed me to climb trees, though I could
not imagine her even giving thought to such an activity.
Neither her permissions nor her injunctions were tied to half-
fearful invocations of my father in those phrases that I was
used to hearing from others: "You'd better not let your
father find out about that," or "You'd better not get hurt
doing that. You know what your father would be like." I was
told later of cases in which his wrath had been visited upon
me unpredictably and disproportionately, and Margie—as my
mother put it—had "taken my part." In time my mother even
came to suggest that my father's treatment of me had been one
of the decisive reasons for Margie's leaving us and moving
away. My mother believed that Margie had felt helpless to
improve the situation and had come to fear that by staying
with us she would only make things worse, and she could not
simply stand by and say nothing. But my mother regretted
bitterly and increasingly my father's behavior toward me and
her own inability to counter it, and I have no doubt that some
of his resentment of me was directed against her. How much
of that Margie saw, and how much of it my mother was conscious of, I cannot tell now. More than either of them knew,
perhaps.

But there were other grounds for contention between
Margie and my father. She represented my mother's family,
that all-but-vanished cloud of witnesses. My father would
have been more comfortable if they had not existed; he took
no interest in them and did nothing to encourage hers. For
that matter, both of their families were abrasive subjects. My
mother felt that she had been treated as an unwelcome outsider by my father's mother and his sisters, and they had
whispered, not always behind her back, that she was stuck-up.
My mother invested her own family with attributes of gentility and culture that may or may not have graced them.
Certainly, for the most part, they seem to have been better
educated and gentler than most of my father's family. In any

event, much of the perennial discord engendered by reference to their respective families arose from their feelings about social position. The dissension was grafted into their lives. They lived with it. My father affected to laugh it off, as though it were a temperamental quirk of my mother's, a cliché of marriage, something to be expected from women. It was not so imminent a matter, nor so sore, as to prevent members of my father's family, or my mother's cousin Betty, or Aunt Margie, from living with us at times to help look after the children. But it was there to undermine the longer visits. Something, from the beginning of each of them, was sure to confirm and quicken it.

And with Margie the question of church membership became a further and covert vexation. Nobody would admit that it was a problem, because it was not supposed to be one. My father and my mother both declared—if the topic was unavoidable—that Margie was free to do as she thought best, although each of them surely was thinking something different when saying it. Church affairs of any kind were officially over my head, and too grave for me to expect an answer if I were so forward as to ask about them. So I am not sure just what happened, but I think that Margie left her letter of church membership with her former pastor in Pittsburgh, and put off becoming a member of my father's church. After all, no one was sure how long she was going to stay. But my parents regularly explained away and dismissed this form of reservation on her part, natural though it may have been. I seem to remember, also, passing explanations of her going, occasionally, to listen to other preachers besides my father. Her role in his congregation never was defined. She never committed herself to it.

What he felt, I suppose, as her challenge, and his way of handling it, were aired daily in one deathless theme: the heating, or rather the failure to heat, the manse. She had him there, and he had her. It was an old building. When my father had accepted the call to the Washburn Street church, the appropriate officers of the congregation had led my parents through the manse room by room, and later had had it painted and papered throughout for them. By the time we moved there the special woven grass on a pale green ground, which my parents had chosen, lined the lower part of the front hall; the oatmeal stamped into sheaves and flowers covered the front living room walls. And a new marvel—a surprise—dominated the dining room: a wallpaper like a mural or a backdrop, depicting one scene all the way around the walls, in the style current in picture puzzles and on the tops of chocolate boxes: a lake with huge bushes of pink roses hanging over it, swans drifting on their reflections, and broad flights of marble steps with marble urns and banisters, leading down to the water. Everything appeared to be life size. It was called The Garden of The Muses pattern. My mother was not ever sure that she liked it, altogether. At least not as much as, say, I did. She said we couldn't hang pictures in the dining room. They would fall into the lake. She was more interested in how she was going to keep thirty-six windows clean, and wash and stretch the downstairs curtains. And my father was concerned about how he would ever manage to heat what he soon referred to as that great barn of a place.

The former ministers and their families, some of whose names were scratched in the cement by the side steps to the porch, must have shivered. Coal would have been cheaper in other years, no doubt, and of course the furnace and boiler had been newer. But the house had not been built to be centrally heated. When we moved in there were fireplaces in all the main rooms downstairs except the kitchen and laundry room, and in several of the upstairs bedrooms. We arrived at the end of summer, and on the first chill evenings of autumn, and in the cold mornings, fires of scrap lumber and boxes were lighted in the arched black marble fireplace in the dining room, under the lake with the swans and rose bushes, and there my sister and I dressed before breakfast, and undressed for bed, by firelight. We complained about the cold, but hoped that the arrangement would never change. There were cracks in the floor that could swallow a pencil, and wind rose out of them. The doors and windows rattled in their frames. My father became obsessed with drafts. He would inch softly through the front hall, or up the stairs, as though trying to surprise a thief, and suddenly freeze like a gun dog, raise one hand and call, to anyone, "Come *here*. Just *feel* THIS!" And, radiant with vindication, he would hold one's hand in the right place to catch the cold stream. One by one, to my grief, every fireplace was closed up, plastered and papered over. My parents said they were dirty, besides letting in the cold. Windows and doors were draft-proofed, at least in theory. The furnace was overhauled and a new boiler was put in. The dirt floor of the cellar was covered with cement—which buckled into spectacular craters and broke into shards during its first winter. The summer after that, my father managed to acquire, from a furniture dealer and undertaker in the church (the two callings still went together) a hill of mattress cartons and a load of unwanted wallpaper. And another member of the congregation, an ageing handyman with a hump on his shoulder and a drop on the end of his nose, lugged them all up to the sweltering attic. There I was able to admire his cutting up of the cartons and his nailing of them to the rafters. And afterwards I watched him boil up flour and water paste on the big coal range in the laundry room, and put up the wallpaper with his brushes. It all took him a long time, several months, and through the entire enterprise he whistled one or two phrases, over and over, between his long dingy front teeth. The phrase that he seemed more partial to I never could identify at all. The other, which he also hummed, in certain moods, comprised the first seven notes of "In the Good Old Summertime," so tunelessly rendered that for a long time I could not tell what it was. But it sounded familiar, so I asked him the name of it. He was hard of hearing, and off on some plane of his own. He seemed to find the question somewhat impertinent, so he pretended not to have understood it. My father could never recognize a tune anyway. My mother shook her head when I asked her what song that was. The implication was that the song was not something for me to concern myself about. It might be improper. In any case I should not ask. Suddenly, one day, I recognized it, like an old friend in weird clothes. When the last roll of paper was up, the attic was said to be insulated.

Even after that, the winter temperatures indoors were unpredictable, and the furnace continued to drive my father to paroxysms of exasperation. He managed to joke about it. It was a magazine-feed furnace. He fed it. He supplied it with magazines—of coal. He christened it Bertha. Big Bertha. He rattled and clanked, and fished out clinkers the size of skulls, and he stoked her, and banked her, and put her to bed. Only to wake in the freezing house and fumble down the stairs in his burst slippers and old gray bathrobe to find out that Bertha had gone out, and that he had to start all over again, in the early morning hours, to try to light her, with the sounds of the struggle clanging through the pipes and radiators of the whole house. To the end of his days he was haunted by drafts. He would detect them in buildings that were no concern of his, and wheel as though catching a pickpocket.

The coal trucks eased down the alley beside the house, and the galvanized chutes were lowered over the green picket fence and the rambler rose, and were lengthened across the narrow bit of flower garden and the brick walk, to the dustgray cellar windows below ground level, and ton after ton of wet coal slid down them, each shovel load distinct as a loud breath, into the vast heap in the cellar.

The mines have closed since those days, but at the time Scranton still boasted, a little anxiously, of being the anthracite capital of the world. Good coal was probably cheaper there than anywhere. Yet my father told visitors, especially if they were members of his congregation, that it took a lot of his salary—which was about three thousand dollars a year, when eventually it was paid—just trying to heat this old house. He would inform them in detail exactly how much coal he had burned the previous winter. The quantity always sounded as though it had broken existing records, and the listeners gasped obediently. I believe he said that one winter he had burned over seventy tons. "What kind of coal?" they would ask. Most people evidently burned pea coal, crushed fine in the tall breakers at the edge of town. Pea coal flowed easily in the new automatic-feed furnaces. The big companies claimed to have the best quality. Marvin Colliery. D & H cone-cleaned, washed anthracite. The D & H trucks sported a tall blue wading bird—stork, crane, or heron—on the sides, and the motto "You Scratch My Back and I'll Scratch Yours." But my father, filled with the subject, explained that it was no use stoking Bertha with pea coal. It just dropped through the grates and was lost in ash boxes. He had to use chestnut, although chestnut, unless it was the very best quality, got stuck in the grates and jammed them. His hearers nodded their understanding and shook their heads in sympathy. And he went on to say that with the quantities he had to burn to keep the pressure up in the boiler, he could not always afford the best, even though some of the officers of the big coal companies were members of his congregation. He had to take what he could pay for, and there was often slag in what he bought. So he had to rake out clinkers from the grates, into the dynasty of buckets, baskets, and ash cans that he heaved and lugged and wrestled, almost daily, up the cellar steps, and lined up beside the back gate to the alley. Sometimes the church sexton helped him, but the furnace never did, and the heating of the house became one with the church trustees who withheld his salary and with whatever in his life had mocked his labors and his persistent show of optimism.

And Margie came long before the efforts at insulation were complete. She was there when the first phase was just being

finished—the elementary repairs of the furnace, and the seal-
ing of the more obvious cracks in walls and window frames.
My father could still imply that there were improvements
under way that no one else in the family really understood,
and he could nurse the illusion that he was taking care of the
worst of the problem, that he had it well in hand and deserved
recognition for that. And from the beginning there was one
room in the house that presented no heating problems: his
study. He sealed the windows in there, and he maintained the
winter temperature somewhere in the nineties—there was a
thermometer on the wall, just inside the door. My mother
said that heat like that was bad for him, that it made him tired
and sallow and liable to catch colds when he went out, but
he gave no sign that he heard her. Each of the other rooms
had its own temperament, expressed by its radiator. There
was a lore of loosening valves to draw the steam up. It was
forbidden to remove them, to make it happen faster, and the
retribution for doing so, and getting caught—with a roomful
of steam, wallpaper and furniture varnish drenched and blis-
tered, pipes racketing, and the radiator chooing like a locomotive—was thunderous. Of the twelve rooms in the house,
the one in which the steam rose last, if it ever reached there
at all, was the small back room that was Margie's. Why that
room, rather than another, had been given to her, and why
she was not moved to a different one, I do not know. The
choice may have been hers, and it may have had something
to do with privacy. But she did not like to be cold. In this
case she took it, increasingly, as a personal affront, and she
was right. She too had a thermometer on her wall. She would
stand behind her chair at the dining room table, before a meal,
and draw herself up when my father came in, return his
greeting, and in the pause that followed say, "It was forty-
eight in my room this morning." He would cluck his tongue
and shake his head, and say that the men were trying to
remedy the situation and that he would see what else could
be done about the pressure in the radiators. But Margie's dis-

comfort probably troubled him less each time she mentioned it. He laughed about her way of announcing the temperature, and imitated her—not to her face. Her comments on the heating conveyed her opinion of a growing number of traits in his character, as they had become apparent to her. She was freezing him out, just as he was doing to her. She must have been thinking about Florida for some time before she bought her Pullman ticket for St. Petersburg.

Why had my father ever consented to invite her—because certainly she did not arrive without his expressed approval? He may even have been the one who asked her to come, if the invitation was put forward in conversation. And he and my mother must have talked it over at length, beforehand. Margie had been asked to come and live with us, not just to visit; we all knew that. And my father had known Margie for years. She had stayed with us at other times. It is hard to imagine those two ever getting along warmly together. Margie was unlikely to have been impressed, beyond a respectful allowance for my father's being a minister and my mother's husband. My father was bound to sense her reservation, after a while under the same roof, and to suspect her as my mother's ally and champion. Maybe none of it had assumed much importance, on earlier occasions. Maybe he had managed—maybe they both had managed—to ignore it. Or he had forgotten, or resolved not to let it matter again, not to pay attention to it. Or imagined that this time it would be different. Many of us learn the same things repeatedly. My mother wanted someone to stay with us, at first to help look after the children, and then to help with the housework. Margie was not thought of in either capacity, but my mother coveted her company, her presence. Members of my father's family had been with us, lived with us, from time to time—and sometimes their visits too had raised problems. My father may have felt, and my mother may have urged him to agree, that it was her turn.

Margie may have been invited as early as that day like a

Sunday when we called at her hotel in Pittsburgh, or in a
letter not long afterwards, still redolent of that meeting. It
was a time when my father might have been tempted to be
expansive. In Pittsburgh we were on our way from Union
City to Cincinnati, to the General Assembly of the Presbyterian Church of the United States of America, where my
father was to be moderator. For him, and consequently for
the whole family, the office came as a triumph, the more so
as it followed several disheartening years. In worldly terms,
after the small country churches with which my father began
his ministry, the First Presbyterian Church of Union City,
New Jersey, had appeared to be, as he might have said, a
plum. It came shortly to present large difficulties, financial
and personal, and the depression helped to increase them. And
from the midst of that, to be chosen to be moderator—I was
not sure what a moderator was or did, but it was obviously
something of great importance which promised a leap out of
our ordinary existence. The General Assembly of the Presbyterian Church sounded to me something like Congress, and
my father was going to be head of the whole thing. Almost
like the President. Shopkeepers, the teachers at school, friends
to whom my mother spoke on the street, seemed properly
awed by the importance of the office, but it had to be explained to them. My mother minimized it, modestly, but
agreed that it was an honor.

For some time my father had been telling her that he noticed, or thought he noticed, during Sunday services, delega-
tions from other congregations, who had come to hear the
sermon. If he was right, they were spies of a kind, and their
appearance might result in an invitation to preach at a church
that currently had no pastor, and perhaps eventually in a
call to consider moving his ministry to another congregation.
He had been asked to preach at the Scranton church and had
agreed to do so on the way to Cincinnati, in early summer.
The young moderator-to-be of the General Assembly arrived
with his lovely family.

An elder from the church drove us around town in his new Oldsmobile. He changed his car every two years and recommended the practice. He took us along streets shaded with old trees, past large houses. The street cars swayed and sang differently from the ones in Union City. He showed us the Green Ridge Church, the Elm Park Church, the Scranton family mansion, a coal-breaker, and culm piles. He boasted that there were eighty-one churches in Scranton—a city of between one hundred forty and one hundred forty-four thousand. He said that if he told us the number of years he had lived there he would be telling us his age. He told us. It was over half a century.

We stayed at the Hotel Jermyn. In store windows, on the street outside, there were souvenirs made of polished anthracite. They were so clean that people could handle them wearing white gloves. On the roof of the hotel a pole fifty or maybe a hundred feet high had been set up, with rungs for climbing to the top, where an ordinary round metal dining room tray had been fastened as a platform. A young man and young woman in ballroom dress climbed to the top and danced on the tray, to music from loudspeakers. They were advertising Florsheim Shoes. My father did not approve of dancing, but on this occasion we were allowed to stand on the sidewalk and watch.

The sun streamed through the stained glass windows of the Sunday School rooms, on the corner of Hyde Park Avenue and Washburn Street. Everybody peeked at us during the hymns. The congregation was showing off. It was like Easter. Apparently the visit was a complete success, and even before we left, several officers of the church session told my father privately that he could take their next step for granted: it had already been decided that the church would extend the call to him to come and be their next pastor. The choice was up to him. And it was with that news, on the way to General Assembly, that we stopped, a few days later in the summer, to see Margie at the hotel.

I remember nothing that was said, that afternoon. I was
not expected to join in the grownup conversation, or to follow it, or ask questions. There was bright red in the deep
carpet. We stood for a while near a dark polished door. Black
marble, green cloth, white uniforms, light from empty curtains; a disregarded opulence. Margie's face floats, motionless
there as elsewhere. I imagine I can hear one tone of her voice
—which she never raised—but no words. And my sister is
younger than I am. It may be that no one now remembers
Aunt Margie even as well as I do. I might not remember as
much as I do if she had not made that solitary decision to
leave every material possession to a distant cousin whom she
had last seen nine years before, at the end of his childhood.

In the fifties—in their fifties—my parents moved back to the
western part of the state, and my father's ministry ended as it
had begun, in small country churches only a few miles from
the same ones where he had preached every Sunday as a
young man with his hair cut high above his ears, celluloid
collars, and trousers that did not reach to the tops of his high
shoes. Once again Pittsburgh was their metropolis. In the
sixties the dining room of the hotel in the postcards was used
to entertain writers who were giving public readings at the
Carnegie Library, nearby, and several times my parents and I
had dinner there on such occasions. As the railroads died and
the neglected depot became a makeshift bus station, and air
travel got its grip, several downtown hotels acquired rôles
as terminals for the airlines. Limousines and buses to and from
the airport pulled in there. Often, in those years, I was met
at one of the hotels, when I went home to see my parents.
One of them, usually my mother, would be standing on the
sidewalk or just inside the glass door, waiting, in the irregular
status of those whom the hotel tolerated because of its arrangement with the airlines. My mother knew the doorman,
who was a dispatcher. He would be keeping an eye on her
car, parked just down the block. Then, more and more often
as the drive into town wore on them both, I would get off

there and carry my bags a few blocks to catch another bus up the Allegheny River, and would be met, an hour or so later, at a country service station a couple of miles from the small valley farmhouse which was my parents' home for the last decade of their lives. Or I might speak to the driver and get off a little sooner, at the end of their road, as I did when I went back after my father died in the veterans' hospital near Butler. I climbed down the pulsing steps, that time, into the green and amber June evening, the cool air still sweet in spite of the new Keystone power plant a few miles away, the woods sharp on the hills, sunlight and shadows stretched across the fields, birds singing that I had heard singing before. And Bea, my parents' neighbor on the road, was waiting beside her old car, to take me to the house where other neighbors kept dropping by with gifts of food. My mother counted the cakes, in amazement.

During the weeks after my father's funeral, I made the trip between New York and Pittsburgh a number of times, and when some friend drove me back to Pittsburgh to catch the airline transportation we seldom went all the way downtown, but stopped instead to meet the bus or limousine outside the building that had once been Margie's hotel. Sometimes my mother came along, and more than one of the visits ended there.

In his last years, my father had been what was termed a minister of visitation. He was an associate of a younger pastor, and his work was limited, in principle, to visiting the sick and the elderly in the congregation. Some of the old people he had known for most of his life, and of theirs. He sat with them and listened. He said that he had come to think that it was all that many of them needed, to have somebody listen to them. And he preached at their funerals. When I was there it seemed that there were always one or two funerals a week. I imagined that my father's coat, when he came home from a funeral service, had a particular artificial smell. There were matches and ball-points and combs around the house

bearing the names of funeral parlors—more of them than ever
—and my father spoke as a connoisseur of funeral directors.
I thought for a while that so much of such a practice must be
depressing, but I came instead to understand that for him
that last phase may have been the most valuable part of his
whole ministry. My father and the other pastor at the church
came to like a young undertaker in Vandergrift with whom
they worked frequently. He became a friend of theirs. On
the night that my father died, the hospital some fifty miles
away called after midnight to say that he was failing rapidly
and they did not expect him to live through the night. My
mother got up and dressed to drive there, but felt weak, and
knew that she should not attempt the trip by herself. She was
not sure who to call, at that hour, so she decided to try the
young funeral director, who was often up late, working. He
promised to come immediately and drive her to Butler, but almost as soon as she hung up the receiver the hospital tele-
phoned again to say that it was too late. When the undertaker
arrived he sat up with her until morning.

Afterwards he came to the house regularly to help with
post-funeral details, some of them pretexts to see how she was
managing. At the end of my last visit to my mother, he had
offered, days before I left, to drive me to Pittsburgh. He had
said he had things to do there on the day when I was going.
He invited my mother along, and she decided to come. That
morning we went out under the spruce trees beyond the garden shed my father had built, and stepped over the wet grass
and got into the big silver-gray Cadillac with push buttons
for everything. The undertaker explained to me, as he had
done before, that it was a business car, and had been a bargain.
He had intended to take me to the downtown terminal, or
even to the airport itself but we ran into traffic tie-ups on the
way in. There had been heavy rain for several days, and part
of the freeway was flooded. And the radio predicted more
rain. He finally agreed with my mother that it would be more

prudent to drive, instead, to the nearer terminal: the hotel on the postcards. We took a shortcut and got lost and ran into more traffic, and detours, and the hard rain began. We came to the corner in front of the hotel just as the airport limousine was drawing away from the curb. The light at the corner was red, and the gray Cadillac pulled abreast. The young funeral director hailed the driver. I kissed my mother good-bye. She was wearing a small gray hat with a short veil of the kind I remembered her wearing all my life. The veil felt stiff against my face. I said I would be back, and she nodded. I jumped out into the rain and shut the door, and ran splashing behind the limousine, and threw my bag in. The light had turned green and the Cadillac was pulling away, ahead of us. I could see my mother waving, through the rain-streaked rear window, and I waved back. I never saw her again. We were still in front of that building.

La Pia

A VOICE says, not for the first time, that the race has already been won. The finish line, which may also have been the starting line, must be somewhere at the top of the long square which has been cordoned off all day for the walking race. A white line on an ordinary street, and the contestants crossing it again and again. The bleachers up there in front of the gleaming columns of the expensive hotels are still full of spectators, their faces turning back and forth in the late afternoon light. A few of them are leaving, picking their way along the rows, but the rest are still rapt, watching. The judges must be sitting there below them, behind the barricades, where cafe tables have been set for dignitaries and their families. An hour ago, up there, fat little girls in starched dresses were fidgeting and trying to finish melting sherbets. I cannot see any of them, over the heads of the crowd lining the curb. Waiters stand in doorways behind me, their white sleeves reflecting the gleam of the harbor where the pink hazy sun will set before long. Their hair moves in the breeze that smells of the harbor and of flying puffs of tobacco smoke. The race is not over. The waiters go on watching, ignoring the tables.

The lower end of the square is formed by the avenue that

runs along the sea wall. There it is open, and as the walkers pump themselves around that section of the course they are silhouetted against the glare of the water. The crowd of spectators is thickest up near the bleachers and the bright facades. It thins out along the sides of the square until, down near the harbor end, it is only three, or two, or one deep. Here the watchers sway back and forth in shifting groups, balancing on the curb, drifting over the edge during the gaps between contestants, scrambling back up to get out of the way as more walkers approach. Occasionally a heavy man with his pale coat draped over his shoulders steps down and turns around to address other spectators along the curb, a few words at a time, with gestures, and they glance at him and go on looking past him. His words seem to have nothing to do with the occasion—but where is the occasion? Most of the voices are hushed, though the race has been going on for a long time.

The walkers are the city's mail carriers. The course took them out, first, through carefully chosen sectors of the metropolis, and then led them back for the latter part of the race, the numbered laps around the square. Now and then a ripple of applause rises from somewhere among the spectators, and heads turn toward the bleachers, and a hush falls for a moment. I hear more distinctly—I am reminded of—the slap of the rubber soles of the contestants moving downhill on the far side of the square beyond the tall ornamental shrubbery. They echo, or the sounds are echoes. The walkers come singly, and in clusters with long gaps between them, elbows sculling, and as they turn to cross the lower end of the square I catch the sound of each heavy breath they take. Their shadows flicker through the openings among the spectators on the near side. Each of the walkers is wearing a number, front and back. Their faces show the strain of the race. Their eyes are looking at nothing but the race, as no one else can see it. They are not all young.

And there are favorites. The race has been held for some

years, every September. But this time the city worthies have
directed more attention to it than ever, because of the Trade
Fair. There were posters, and stacks of colored brochures on
slick paper, advertising it, in the train stations on the way
here, over ten days ago. Even then the town was crowded,
and hot. It took several telephone calls before the young man
at the station tourist office could find me a hotel room. I
walked to the address he gave me, following the map on
which he had drawn the route, and found that his call had
arrived at a lucky moment, just as someone was checking
out. The room was still being cleaned: a small, high-ceilinged
cubicle next to the office. One could see, from the mouldings
of the ceiling, that it was a piece cut from what originally
had been a much larger room, a parlor or perhaps a dining
room, one flight of the broad marble staircase above the
street. White jalousies at the windows overlooked the tables
of a restaurant on the sidewalk of the narrow street below.
The portly, pleasant, balding man at the desk helped me
through the formalities while carrying on two other conversations with a family standing in the office, and a third on the
telephone. In all of them he spoke from the harassed, studi-
ously patient, profoundly satisfied state of a hotel manager
when the hotel is full and is likely to remain so for a while.
He referred to The Fair with something like reverence, and
he gave me more brochures—the same as the ones I had been
given at the station, and a handful of them, as though he expected me to pass them out on a street corner. And more of
the brightly illustrated maps of the city that had been prepared for those whom the event was bringing there.

By the time I was installed it was getting dark. Bands of
light shone through the slats in the jalousies, and the shadows
of passers-by floated through them. When I went out into the
street again, bathed after a day's travelling, and freed of the
weight of my luggage, the sidewalks were overflowing with
people, most of whom seemed to be inhabitants of the city
rather than visitors. They hailed each other, and stopped for

animated conversations, blocking the jostling current. I had
dinner at one of the tables below the hotel, and then wandered along the nearby avenues for a while, until the babble
of the crowd had washed the rumble of the long train ride
out of my head, and then I went back and turned in. The
next morning I set out to explore the older quarters of the
city. Signs at the main intersections pointed the way to The
Fair—which was not there yet. It was not what I had come to
see, but I had a look at the pavilions being finished: cranes,
rigging, brightly striped sections tilting upward slowly like
circus tents, men shouting at each other. I watched from the
boulevard, and later from the narrow streets on the hill. I
visited the ancient ruins and the medieval churches. Everywhere the city as it has been is being systematically destroyed.
The old buildings, unless they date from before the fall of the
Byzantine Empire, and are therefore recognizable as monu-
ments, are being abandoned and demolished, and in their
places the dark concrete blocks of a later and grayer empire
are rising.

Walking from one to another of the frescoed churches in
in the city, I made my way, in the afternoon, through the
winding streets up on the hill, where the old neighborhoods,
the cobbles and overhanging upper stories, still survive. And I
found at last, far up the slope, past several areas that have
been razed, and a number of modern villas with porthole windows and garage doors, the small and of late disused monastery church of Agios Nikolaos Orfanos. The fading flaking
walls are arranged in a common Greek monastic form, one
shell inside another. The dusty doors were all standing open.
No one was there. Frescoes on every plastered surface. On
the outside wall of the inner chamber, facing the main door,
scenes of a legend I did not know, or did not recognize. A
saint visiting kings. Three men robed in white appear repeatedly. In one picture they are blindfolded and walking,
and another person has raised a sword to strike them, but the
blade is caught and held, perhaps by the saint of the other

episodes. The dream of a king. The three men are in a boat with a billowing sail. Perhaps it is all the same dream. The story runs onto the other walls. I cannot tell where it begins or ends. And again and again in the frescoes there is a figure lying as though in a small curved boat at sea, or in a pod or a hammock, wrapped like a mummy and surrounded by a cocoon of light, sailing, rocking, dreaming, dead, waiting to be born, or reborn. The center of Kokoschka's *Storm*.

Before I took the train to come here I had been staying for some days by a large lake farther north, between Yugoslav Macedonia and Albania; and standing in front of the frescoes in Agios Nikolaos Orfanos I remembered that as I had been travelling and sleeping on trains through the past days and nights, I had dreamed of lakes and boats. But first there had been a gate through which no one could see who was passing. Then, a night later, a beautiful green and tawny hillside covered with clear streams, above a lake I had loved in my childhood, from which, one year, I had salvaged a sunken boat. Deep woods surrounded the hill, and light came out of it and out of the streams flashing along it like veins running down to the lake. A voice calmly told me that the entire hill was going to be turned into a development where everyone would have to live. Feeling rage and rebellion, I met the architect, who lived in such a development himself, and believed in it, justified it with arguments I had heard repeatedly, talked rapidly and abstractly and smoothly, until he faded. And on the night of my arrival here I had dreamed that I was beside a vast dark lake which also resembled the one I had loved as a child. A number of friends were assembled there together: young men and women. We were all about to emigrate across the lake and leave behind our present citizenship. On the far side, just visible in the misty evening, was a low stone building where there was room for each of us, below the level of the lake. Other friends were already there, and we were happy to think of joining them. The boat, loaded with our belongings, had no center thwart, and I worked at fitting a board across between the gunwales. We were all careful not to let water splash over the side onto the bundles we were taking with us. It was after sunset but the twilight had been the same for a long time and did not change. Low peaceful voices of friends; the gentle rocking of the boat and the slap of the water; the prospect before us.

When I had looked at the frescoes I went out through the courtyard and up to the door of a two story wooden building where the last few monks had lived. The life in the house appeared to have been abruptly ended, a very short time ago. The door from the upstairs porch was open. The kitchen was still a kitchen, with its fireplace and its stove, cupboards and table, though dark and dilapidated and hung with cobwebs. Rubble on the floor. Doors ajar into the other rooms where the shutters on the windows dimmed the light. Rags in corners. A few broken pieces of furniture. On the porch outside, bells hanging under the eave. There was another wooden house like it, across the lane, with wall and gate and courtyard, upstairs porch, kitchen, closed shutters. In the late afternoon light I left them and walked down the lane and the streets of the hill, to the harbor, and a table, here.

Earlier that day I had obtained the permit required by the police for visiting Mount Athos, and I planned to leave for there the next day. I returned this afternoon. A week of walking from monastery to monastery, along mule tracks and foot paths, over the long, craggy, marble peninsula. When I sat here then I had already separated the belongings I had with me and had arranged with the hotel manager to store the greater part of them in his office while I was gone. I did not want to be weighed down by things I would not need, and I hoped they would serve, besides, to stake my claim to the room, which I was careful to reserve for my return, knowing that the city and its hotels would be growing more crowded every day.

Now, incalculably later, everything is still in his office, or it was, a few hours ago. But the room, the reservation—when

he recognized me and I reminded him and showed him the
receipt for the deposit I had paid, the manager looked at me
sadly, apologetically, and craved my understanding and sympathy. I could see, he told me, how difficult things were for
him. There were people sleeping in the dining room, on the
floor. He led me there and showed me the figures wrapped in
sheets. They had been travelling all night, he explained. And
there were others upstairs in the hall. He showed me those
too. And others out on the back roof. The building looked
like a temporary shelter after some natural disaster. It had
not been possible to save the room for me, the manager said,
raising his empty hands in a gesture of helplessness. He was
sorry. He had meant to. He had tried. But there was a couple
with a baby in there now, and they had been there for two
nights and wanted to stay. He promised to find me something.
Employees of the hotel swirled past us clutching piles of
pillows and linen—stray ants at moving time. The manager
paused in his tour for hurried conversations with some of
them, and introduced one of them, ceremoniously, as his
brother, as though the fact of his having a brother somehow
substantiated his explanations. We went back to the office,
where he invited me to sit and wait until he found me somewhere to sleep tonight.

The office was not much bigger than a cupboard, and it was
packed with people waiting, most of them smoking. For some
reason they were all standing, and two chairs by the desk
were empty. The manager beckoned me to one of them and
resumed his own. More people elbowed their way in and
stood like subway passengers at rush hour. Hotel employees
peered over their shoulders from the doorway and shouted
to the manager. He slid out and back several times, the telephone ringing unanswered while he was gone. At last he
waved to me over the heads in the doorway and I extracted
myself from the room and followed him up the stairs.

He told me that it would be impossible—as I had guessed—
for him to give me a room to myself, but that there would be

a bed, later on. On the top floor we walked to the end of a hall and he knocked and turned the handle of the last door on the right, and opened it part way. Inside, a light was on over a basin, and a man in his undershirt was shaving. There were four beds, three of them occupied. One sleeper still had his shoes on. The manager told me that several of the occupants of that room would be checking out in a while, and that I might have the bed farthest from the door, in the evening. He smiled, to convey to me that that was the best he could be expected to do. It seemed likely to me that it was also the best that I would be able to do, even if I wanted to spend the rest of the afternoon looking elsewhere, and I agreed to take it. He told me that I was welcome to leave whatever I wanted to under his desk until the bed was ready. After the day's travelling, I went back to the streets and walked through the quarter of old warehouses and food emporiums, toward the square.

The table here on the sidewalk is hardly the best place from which to watch the race, but I have seen enough by now to be able to recognize some of the contestants as they reappear, and to notice whether they are moving ahead of others, or falling back. I too have favorites among them. I have been watching the harbor, also, and against that blank surface of light I have been remembering moments of the past week and its travels. I am tired, and have been wholly caught up in the journey. I am reluctant to reach the end of it, to come back. Along with the relief I felt when I saw the rest of my baggage behind the manager's desk, there was a flicker of disappointment that the things were still there—a resentment at being, myself, reclaimed. Scenes from the journey rise by themselves and I follow them, looking closely as they dissolve, and passing from one to another, partly for the lingering pleasure of it, as one would leaf through a book of pictures one knew. And partly to impress more deeply particular images and sequences, sad to see that there are gaps already: details that I did not pay enough attention to at the time, and apparently have lost, for now. And partly in the hope that by going over them I may understand something in them that I have not recognized yet.

So I come repeatedly to certain turns of the empty path on the mountain ridges. A descent to a huge chestnut tree, by a gate in a high wall, after sunset. The sound of the wooden clapper like a two-bladed oar, struck with a mallet in the echoing courtyard to summon the monks to services—and the creatures into the Ark before the world-flood. The dim gold and the eyes of hundreds of ikons penetrating the shadows of the churches in the monasteries, appear out of a single firmament. Most deliberately, I keep recollecting parts of the day when I set out from the gate of Megistis Lavra at daybreak to walk around and over the steep end of the peninsula, the south face of the mountain, to the other side.

It was a day associated from the beginning with my mother. There are hermits' caves on the south face, far down the cliff near the sea, and one small isolated group of monks not used to lodging uninvited visitors. But the nearest monastic settlement where I could hope for an evening meal and a bed for the night was at Agia Anna, many miles across the mountain, and I hoped to reach there before dark. My mother's name is Anna. It is now September, and she has been living alone since the day in March when my father entered Deshon Veterans' Hospital near Butler, in western Pennsylvania, where he died, early on the seventh of June.

In the first weeks after his death some of her friends urged her to move away from the small asphalt-shingled farmhouse on the back road to West Lebanon, in which she and my father have lived for the past ten years, and move to an apartment complex somewhere near a town, or in a town; a place with people nearby day and night, and the shopping within walking distance. But she decided to stay on in the old house by herself, at least through the summer. She would rather have her own place, and the quiet and freedom of the country: woods and marshland across the road, the land in back of the house running out to the slope half covered with wheat, and the upper part of the hill dark with overgrown apple orchards, and woods full of deer. The seasons. I doubt that she clings to any landscape, past or present, but she is fond of it there, the glassed-in back porch, the trees and birds outside the windows, the banks covered with ajuga, with which she had lined the windowsill of my father's hospital room, and a clump of which she had planted on his grave. She did not want to leave abruptly, and could not be persuaded that there was any reason to.

She was also considering Bea, her nearest neighbor on the road, a single woman almost her own age. They had done child welfare work together on the Navajo reservation, more than twenty years before, and had remained friends ever since. When Bea retired, my mother helped to arrange for her to have the beautiful big old brick house that is just visible through the spruces and firs, from her own back porch. Both women are too independent to live under the same roof, as some well-meaning souls have suggested they should do. But they see each other virtually every day, and one of them telephones to the other every night before going to bed, just to check. If my mother were to leave, Bea would be that much more alone. They have talked of moving at the same time, somewhere, but for now both of them would rather stay put.

They have their gardens. In May I dug over the vegetable beds for my mother, and planted them up, and we weeded the raspberries and strawberries and asparagus, and fussed over the Japanese beetles. She planned to spend a good bit of the summer out there with her weeder and basket, whatever her friends said. I cannot remember her being sick in bed since I was a small child, but last year when she was all ready to go with a group to Russia on a tour, she had a precautionary physical examination, and the doctor discovered a heart murmur and advised against her going. She was seventy four in July. Friends who have stopped by and found her weeding in the late afternoons have told her that she will keel over, there, some day. She answers that she can't think of a way that she would rather go.

In June we sorted through some of the drawers in my father's study, and she disposed of the pistol that had spent decades in one hiding place or another, in houses my father and she had lived in. Friends dropped by and went away with keepsakes. Before my father's death I had intended to go to Europe for the summer, and one day my mother said to me that she knew I was putting off my plans on her account, and she did not want me to do anything of the kind. She reminded me of her dread, which she had mentioned as long as I had known her, of becoming dependent on others, and she assured me that if the day came when she could not look after things by herself there, she would make some other arrangement. She insisted that if I changed my plans in order to stay and keep an eye on her it would only make her feel that she had become a burden, and it would upset her. She urged me to go ahead with the summer I had planned. We agreed that I would come back in the fall and talk about what she would do then. I left just before the solstice: Pittsburgh, New York, Europe.

Her letters have not reassured me. It has been an abnormally rainy summer there, and she has not been able to get out into the garden much. When it has not been raining, the ground has been too wet and muddy, most of the time, for her to work there. So the weeds have taken over, and when the weather has been dry long enough for her to get out, she has scarcely known where to begin. Slugs, snails, Japanese beetles and other bugs, have profited from the wet weather and the neglect to attack almost everything, so there have been few vegetables, and some of those have been rotten. The children from the nearby farm who for years have been coming to help her, for their spending money—cutting grass, doing jobs that are too heavy for her—have been busy this summer, and between other interests and the weather they have not come often or regularly. And this summer she confesses that even a small effort seems to exhaust her, so that she has to put away her tools and sit down.

She ascribes some of the recent lack of stamina to a bout of flu she caught, not long after I left, which confined her to her bed with a fever, and kept her there for days, and which she has not really managed to throw off all summer. She has had relapses, and has felt tired most of the time. She has mentioned trips to the doctor, and recently her own misgivings at the thought of the impending absence of the young local doctor in whom she has most confidence. He is taking his vacation, and is being replaced for a few weeks by a much older man, some years retired, in whom her friends do not have much faith, and neither does she. But she shrugs it off. He's all we have, she says.

The fatigue still surprises her. She tries to be patient with it. She is aware that my father's last illness, the drive almost every day to the hospital and back—a round trip of ninety miles—the visits themselves, and the deepening realization that he would probably not recover, undermined her strength. She hopes that by being sensible and resting when she knows she is tired, as the young doctor advised her to do, she may get back to feeling herself again. Yet she repeats, as though she were arguing, that she must face the facts. For the past year she has been remarking, with a laugh down her nose, "I'm an old woman," reminding herself, and telling the rest of us something. Which I deny. She keeps naming things that she wants to give me, including some of her savings, and I turn the offers aside and urge her to use what she has for her own pleasure. But the day that she and I went to Vandergrift to the funeral home, to choose my father's casket, as we walked up the half block from the car, under the big trees, she suddenly felt faint. Her legs started to give way. She gripped my arms, and I caught her. She recovered, and refused to be lifted, and once inside the building, sitting down, she said she was much better. The color returned to her face, and her voice sounded normal as we discussed the funeral arrangements. She even laughed. The moment was passed off as something quite ordinary: it was common for people to feel faint at such times. And of course she was tired. She admitted to me later, though, that it was not the first time that had happened, during the past months. When she got home she took off her coat and put on her apron dress and came into the living room to sit down in the easy chair that rocks back. She put her feet up on the cushion, as she has taken to doing, recently. It has become her chair. I have watched her spending more and more time there.

She reads in that chair. Small orderly piles of books wait in their places on the table by her right arm, each with narrow sheets of memo paper from the child welfare organization for which she and my father both worked more than twenty years ago, marking places. On the bookmarks lists of references, page numbers, quotations, questions, words she had looked up in the dictionary on its stand behind the other easy chair, which had become my father's. Books that she has bought; others that I have sent her. The Bible. A history of Russia. Nadezhda Mandelstam's *Hope Against Hope*. Kluckhohn and Leighton's *The Navaho. Bury My Heart At Wounded Knee*. The Viking Portable Emerson and Thoreau. Commentaries on the Gospel According to Mark and on Paul's letters to Timothy, Titus and Philemon. Harper's, The Nation, The New Yorker. As a great self-indulgence, and rarely enough to mention it in letters, she listens to music in that chair. To celebrate my being home she likes to listen to a record or two together—records that she chose herself or that we bought at Horne's in Pittsburgh, or that I have sent her. Elizabeth Schwarzkopf singing Mozart, Janet Baker singing Bach; Vivaldi, Haydn, Schubert. Often now she falls asleep there and wakes a few moments later with a laugh at herself. If it is after supper then, she may get up and go to bed. Though if I tell her to, she is likely to say, "I will," and not move.

We have tried, at those times, to bring up some of what each of us wants to tell the other, and we have managed to speak more frankly than before, but we have not really got very far. In recent years we have been able to say, "I love you," at the end of a visit, or even at the end of a day, and to embrace, and sometimes I have seen her eyes fill, but we both say anything of that kind, to each other, with a drop in the voice, deliberately, shyly, with embarrassment. For some time, as though we had both grown up now, she has been able to talk in a matter-of-fact way of illegitimacy, unmarried mothers, contraception, marital problems, but we can mention almost nothing of our own intimate lives, hers or mine. Once she told me that there was a moment when she might have left my father. I knew that she had been acutely unhappy with him during my own late childhood and early adolescence, but she let me know just one time that there had been someone who wanted her to go away with him, and she had thought she would be happy with him, but she had decided not to do it. She would say nothing more on the subject. I remember her in tears, back when it must have been going on, shaking her head violently and saying, "You'll never know," and I have wondered lately whether that was what she meant, then. She has been so secret, and I have grown up in the habit of being so reticent with her, that it cannot be easy now to find what we want to say to each other. And as I think of how little we have been able to tell each other of our lives so far, I realize how little I know of her, and how hard it is for either of us to follow the same subject for long in talking with each other, and even to pay sustained attention to what the other is saying. She has told me things that I have not heard. Her own urge toward greater candor now returns to the subject of death, her death, as one more thing she feels able to set in order.

Maybe she was never afraid of it. Ever since I was a child I have heard her say that it held no fear for her. All my life she has spoken of her death as rest, a rest to be earned, something she looks forward to. I cannot tell when she began to feel that way, but she knows that the series of deaths that marked and defined her childhood and youth formed and set the feeling, and gave it its bitter sweetness. She has said little about that, but when she has referred to it, it has seemed as though her attitude toward death is the response to those early losses, and it has not changed with time, except to deepen.

First, her father, Hanson Hoadley Jaynes, who died a few days before Christmas, 1900, when she was two, and he was thirty-two. The photographs of him show a thin, clear, gentle face; the large eyes of an open, amiable, intelligent nature. The hairline of his brows is receding, though he must have been scarcely out of his twenties when the pictures were taken. The light, curling hair is parted in the middle. The full handlebar moustache of the nineties, twisted at the ends. My mother scarcely remembers him, of course, and her sense of him has been shaped by the way others around her saw him and spoke of him: kind, responsible, humorous, tender to his wife, loving to his children. The name Hanson came from a Danish ancestor, and there was some feeling of romanticism about it that my mother has never explained. It may have been colored by her notion of the glamor of her maternal grandmother's sister Susan, her Aunt Unie, whom she has described in a note as "a gentlewoman born, devout in her religious beliefs and principles—a fine needlewoman—having prior to leaving Pittsburgh a sewing establishment on Penn Av. near Joseph Horne store and employing five or more seamstresses." After Unie's marriage "somewhat later in life than usual for that period" to Hans Christian Cramer, "a Dane in the business of electrical engineering advanced for that time" the couple had lived in Denmark and Guatemala, as well as Pittsburgh, and Sunbury, Ohio, and the marriage "was very happy" but was cut short by the husband's death at about the same time that Hanson died. The name Hoadley must be English. It was his mother's maiden name. My mother says she thinks a Hoadley was once governor of New York.

The Jayneses were from Ohio, down the river from Marietta. Cheshire, a pretty town, scarcely more than a village. My mother was told that when her own grandfather settled there he announced that he had travelled far and wide and seen nowhere in the world as lovely and pleasant as Cheshire. Apparently there was a certain amount of money in the family; I believe some of it was from pottery or porcelain. And someone manufactured and sold precision scales. But Hanson went to work for the railroad, and he was not the only one in the family who did that. He was a freight agent. My mother still has the collection of passes, in their case, that permitted him to ride most of the railroads in the country, at that time, free—if only on the freight trains, which I imagine meant in the cabooses. The passes survived him tucked snugly in a leather case Compliments of Geo. Adams & Burke Co, Live Stock Commission Merchants, Union Stock Yards Chicago, Union Stock Yards Omaha, "Write For New Inside Book When This One Is Used Up, As Cover Will Outwear Two Or Three Insides." The names on the cards echo their age: The Missouri Pacific; Denver and Rio Grande Railroad Company; Rio Grande Western Railway; The Colorado and Southern; Union Pacific; The Atchison, Topeka & Santa Fe Ry.; Burlington & Missouri River; The Colorado & Northwestern; Chicago, Rock Island and Pacific; Florence & Cripple Creek Railroad; Golden Circle Railroad; Canon City and Cripple Creek Railroad; New York & Texas Steamship Company; The Western Union Telegraph Company (will transmit on its lines on account of this frank Messages signed by H.H. Jaynes); Fort Worth & Denver City Railway; The Colorado Midland Railroad; Denver, Leadville and Gunnison Ry.; Union Pacific Denver and Gulf Ry. Co. Hanson's health was not good, and the railroad sent him out west to an office in Denver, to see if the mountain air would help. He wrote to his wife Bessie from there saying that he felt better and thought she would like it in the West.

They moved to Denver, he and Bessie, and my mother's older brother Morris, born in 1893; Bessie's maiden name had been Morris. There is a sepia print of the three of them taken there, at D. B. Chase's studio, 910 16th Street. Morris is in the middle, a blonde child, perhaps two years old. Grave, with eyes much older than the rest of his face; sad eyes, like his mother's. He is wearing a long white bow almost hidden by a broad lace-trimmed ruff that extends past the shoulders of his jacket. His mouth is serious, generous, patient. When I look at the picture it seems obvious that they knew, singly and together, what lay ahead of them. There are no accounts, as far as I know, of their life in Denver. My mother was born out there, and was told later that she had been wheeled through the Garden of the Gods in her baby carriage.

Bessie and the children went back east on visits, to Ohio, and to Ingram, Pennsylvania, and the trips led to the only words from Hanson to her that still exist. The mountain air had helped his lungs but nothing could effect a cure. Even so, in a letter to Bessie written in late August, 1900, he said he would like to leave Denver that September 10th or 15th "and sojourn in Penn. and Ohio indefinitely, considering health, and possibly locate permanently in Limerick, Temperanceville, or Cheshire." "It is good to know," he told her, "that you are looking so well, but while you always knew that I appreciated your beauty, your manners were so divine that I could frequently comment on it without spoiling you, most beautiful women know it too well, but beauty doesn't cut much figure with me as long as your lovely disposition remains intact. Oh! my dear old sweetheart! don't these beautiful words charm you after so cruel a separation?" He spoke of Dr. H. on whom he had called, the day before, "just for a talk. Have been doing so fine lately that I could not understand why I should feel wheezy and asthmatic during the past 2 or 3 days, as I had gained a pound or two last week thought it might be fatty degeneration of the heart, but Doc gave me some dope and told me to go down where the atmosphere was thicker." He grew weaker, and died four months after the letter was written. They had been married ten years.

Anna Elizabeth and the children went back to the house where her own mother, Anna, lived, in Ingram, near Pittsburgh. Bess's father had been dead for eleven years, but her two brothers, Adin and Bob, were living in the house, Adin working as a house painter and Bob as a city policeman "in an era," my mother says, "when it was more of a profession than a job." The pictures bear out Hanson's words: Bess was a beautiful woman. Delicate features, haunting eyes, a slender, graceful figure. In one snapshot she is holding up my mother in her arms, when my mother is only a few months old, wearing a long, infant's white dress. Bess is smiling. There are few pictures, and most of the others show the young widow and her children in mourning, clothes and faces both.

Bess entrusted the small sum of insurance money that had come to her after her husband's death to her mother's brother Adin ("Addie") Sailor. My mother says he "operated a successful men's tailoring establishment in the Sailor Building on Wood Street, in Pittsburgh." He apparently invested the money unwisely, and lost it all. Left with nothing, Bess took a job as a bookkeeper in the Woman's Exchange in Pittsburgh, "an organization dedicated to helping women . . . in a similar financial situation." A few pages of diary from August and September of 1902, in a firm, clear, rapid hand, provide one of the only glimpses of her life: trips to Cheshire to visit her husband's family and his grave, and to Columbus to stay with other members of his family and hers. Taking pictures of the children. Going with Aunt Unie to the Stock Co. play "Her Majesty"—"first work of the season." On Sept. 5 arranging with Dr. Shields for him to circumcise Morris on Sunday Sept. 7. Morris was then nine. Bathing Morris and Anna and self and retiring early. On Sunday, "up early got room ready for Morris' operation. Nurse came about 10 a.m.—put Morris in bed and read to him Dr. came about 10.45 and by 12 it was over—& Morris got along splendidly I did not stay in room for operation—Morris continued to feel alright—and we all retired early tired out."

Two years later she was dying of cancer. A small envelope with a 2¼" x 4" card in it from J. E. Wishart, Pastor of the United Presbyterian Church of Ingram, Pa., announcing a series of five sermons in June and July on Modern Substitutes For Christianity, beginning on June 8 with "The Insufficiency of Substitutes," and followed on June 22 with "Culture," bears the words "Important Other Side" pencilled in her hand across the face. On the back—her script much smaller, careful, and visibly weak—is her pencilled will. "Morris his Father's watch," balanced by, "Anna My watch." "Morris 1 plain ring. Anna 1 plain ring. Set of cuff buttons each. 1 stud of Father's each. Morris Hoo Hoo button. Anna Topaz ring. Bedding and Table Linen divided as Mama wishes Keeping what else she wants except blue blanket & the green comforts & silk quilt—she to keep rug Anna my machine Morris Chiffonier Aunt Unie something she wants as remembrance Ride [her younger sister] boys same Aug 2 –04 Anna E Jaynes." She died two months later to the day, at sunrise. Those who remembered her spoke of her courage. "Not a murmur or complaint," the obituary says, "escaped her lips." Her mother and brothers, sisters and children, accompanied her body to Cheshire, Ohio, where she was buried beside Hanson at sunset, two days after her death. It was Morris's twelfth birthday.

My mother was six.

She and Morris continued to live with their grandmother, Anna, and their uncles. Before Bess fell sick, my mother believes that she had been hoping to move to Ohio and settle near her Aunt Unie and her father-in-law, Charles Mortimer Jaynes. It is a plan for which my mother still cherishes a certain wistfulness. To her the Jayneses and her Aunt Unie represented unknown horizons, culture, secure gentility. Her regret makes her feel a pang of guilt toward her grandmother, who provided a home for her and her brother "and no doubt imparted to us intangibly thro' her cheerful and generous (almost to a fault) personality in spite of the financial difficulties that plagued her thro' the years."

It must have been a lively household, but cramped and restless. She appears never to have liked or thought much of her uncle Adin, and obviously there was a clash of temperaments from the beginning between her and her mother's sister Marie, whom they called Rida or Ride, and who remained an intimate of the house although she was married and had a home of her own "in a residential section of Wheeling W. Va." Even now my mother cannot mention Ride without her voice revealing dislike and scorn such as she seldom expresses about anyone. Ride, she says, was fast. That went for her clothes, her hair, and her behavior. Ride's husband operated a wholesale produce market in Pittsburgh and judging by the house they lived in my mother considered them quite well-to-do. Shortly after Bess died, Ride was divorced, and her husband was given the custody of the children. Whereupon Ride too moved in with Anna and her own brothers and nephew and niece. In the family, my mother says, they tended to take her side, and blame her husband, Uncle Jack, for the break-up. Except Anna herself, who was fond of her son-in-law and refused to criticize him. It was rumored that he had had what my mother calls "a clandestine romance," and that was what "had triggered the rift." My mother preferred, and prefers, to discredit that talk, "or at least to feel if he did he was justified, to some extent," and she refers again to "the *fact* that he was given custody of the sons." Ride worked as a seamstress at Joseph Horne's, but when she was at home my mother felt that she resented the presence of Morris and of her in the house, though she says Ride was "prone to favor my brother if a choice was needed."

Some of Ride's behavior may have had its roots in the loss of her own children. My mother answered it out of her own loss. She says that she may have been unjust, but that after the deaths of both of her parents, whom she believed "were very much in love always," she "held Ride to account for the fact that she and her husband were given life together and would not accept it."

Even with three members of the family working, there was not much money. They moved from Ingram to Wilkinsburg, where my mother started school. Then to another address in Wilkinsburg. Then to a house on Penn Avenue near East Liberty, where she attended Shakespear School. She has almost never referred to that time, and in the notes she has made she does so with an uncharacteristic violence. She says she "hated and loathed every day spent in the Penn Av. house. It has been torn down *now*. *GOOD*." I doubt that I will ever know why.

To supplement their income her grandmother took in boarders. My mother says she was an excellent cook. And because of the boarders, to have more room they moved again, to a large house on Fifth Avenue in Pittsburgh, and then to another one nearby. And yet my grandmother was improvident, disorganized, possibly untidy. My mother was grateful to her and sorry for her, for her anxieties and the chaos of her life, but there is some remote, dim, unexamined disaffinity and reservation in every reference to her. Still, I am sure she loved her. And she loved her Uncle Bob, the younger of Anna's two sons. He was twenty-four when Bess and the children moved in with Anna, and everyone seems to have liked him. My mother says he was very good-looking. Six feet two in his socks. When he held his arm straight out Anna could stand under his hand, with room to spare. He was easygoing and happy by nature; a pillar of the family. He once kicked a burglar out of the house with one kick—and broke his toe. He had a very pretty Italian Catholic girl friend whom everyone in the house loved, and they were planning to get married. And right then, four years after the death of Bess, Bob too died, quite suddenly. Of blood-poisoning, I believe. Almost at the same time Anna's brother Adin, who had lost Bess's insurance money and most of his own as well, also died. Anna received Bob's insurance money, my mother remembers, which helped for a while, but it did not last long.

The family had shrunk, and they moved from the last of their succession of houses to the first of a series of apartments near the Fifth Avenue High School, from which my mother eventually graduated, taking night classes and working in the daytime. There are snapshots of some of the houses—small frame structures on steep streets—but of the apartments, no pictures of any kind. My mother has never described them. I keep asking her to add to the brief notes about those years that she has let me see. Perhaps this wet summer, confined to the house, she will have written more, on her yellow pad, sitting at the old secretary-desk behind her reading chair—but she has not mentioned doing anything of the kind. When my mother had lived twelve years under Anna's many roofs, her grandmother died, of pneumonia, at the age of sixty-nine. My mother was then nineteen.

The breakup of the household that followed meant at least that she saw no more of Ride—and as a result several members of her family in Ohio, who appear to have felt as she did about her aunt, suddenly re-established contact with her, and there were happy reunions in Ohio, at holidays and summer vacations. And there was Morris. She loved him more than anyone else in her early life, after her mother died. When she talks of him it seems that there was a time when there was only Morris, and that that time never left her. He was not quite five years older than she was, and she tells how she looked up to him, how good he was to her, how patient, how he helped to bring her up. Morris was a serious child and grew up to be a serious young man. Bess had read to him, and he taught himself to read, and loved books all his life. My mother says he usually had one in his pocket, and she describes proudly how he would lose himself in his reading, whatever else may have been going on around him. My mother's abiding respect for anyone's capacity to concentrate is in part a faithful tribute to something she learned, or believes she learned, from Morris; an expression of her admiration for him, as well as a mark of the regard for education that they shared.

For several years, as children, they went visiting, during the summers, in Ohio, in the country near Cheshire. A few brown pictures of them, on a farm, must have been taken there a year or two after their father died. They are outside a barn door, looking tiny, grave, earnest. A tall, bony, graceful man in a white shirt and broad straw hat, a curry comb in one hand—perhaps their father's brother Rowland, or their grandfather Charles—has a colt by the halter. And Morris, standing very straight and facing the camera, in overalls and another straw hat that appears to be too big for him, is holding the reins. My mother, with a wide straw boater held by the brim, is standing beside him, eyes cast down in the bright sunlight. They are distinct from their surroundings as though they were cut away from them, posed there between the invisible photographer and the slatted, whitewashed barn—the world that is no more solid than they are, but appears to be at home around them. They are visitors. Already Morris has the beginnings of the gaunt, hollow-cheeked appearance that grew more pronounced with years, a symptom of the leaking valve of the heart that would cause his death before he was thirty. By the time he is in his twenties the photographs show him looking much older than his years. The large, generous eyes are sunken in their dark-rimmed sockets, and his mouth is that of someone with a fatal illness.

He wanted to go to college, but there was never any prospect of there being enough money for that. When he graduated from high school he took a job as a clerk. For the railroad. One of the things my mother tells of him, always, whether or not she says anything else about him, is that he made her an allowance out of his first salary. My mother was twenty-four, and had been married for less than a year, when he died. He must have had few possessions. I know of almost nothing that was his, except one red and black checked double blanket that was on my bed when I was a child, and still covers a chair where I sit.

How old was he when the first symptoms of his heart deficiency manifested themselves? How long was it before the diagnosis was made? When did he learn the verdict, and how? And when did my mother learn it? How much of their childhood and youth was spent knowing that he could not live very long? Does she remember, or does it seem to be something that was always so?

Doomed early as he was, which may have intensified her feeling for him, Morris, her protector and confederate in the household where she seems never to have felt completely at home, emerges more clearly than anyone else out of my mother's early years. She has disclosed so little that it is hard to piece together the scraps, their chronology and relation. She too would have liked to go on to college after she finished her night classes at high school. She dreamed of studying Greek and mythology and history. She too was beautiful, as her mother had been—and prim and demure as she believed she was supposed to be. She could take dictation and type at extraordinary speeds and with complete accuracy, and remained proud of it. She developed a shorthand of her own, which no one else could read, and although she has taken notes obsessively, daily, for years, of everything that she has considered to be of interest—the children's ailments, what their teachers said, other conversations, trips, readings, letters received, expenditures, sermons, lectures, outings, visits—most of them, unfortunately, have been in that code, in which her secrets are safe. After her grandmother's death she moved into a rooming house with several other young ladies who worked in the same office and attended the same church, and she was living there when my father first came calling.

They met at church, where my father taught a Sunday

School class. Perhaps because Morris's existence seems so exclusively, privately, hermetically my mother's heritage and domain, I have difficulty imagining my father and Morris ever having met, ever having talked with each other, shaken hands, known each other, shared the world. My father in his early twenties—younger than Morris. My father full of energy and purpose. My father the theological student at Grove City College and at Western Seminary, without adequate academic background or interest, but with a gift for extemporaneous public speaking and rhetorical prayer, a zeal fuelled by his own mother for the role of preacher, and a smiling optimistic approach to people and circumstances. He exhorted his Sunday School students never to lose their smiles. My father in high shoes, his pants reaching only to the tops of them, his hair cut very short, far up the sides, and combed straight back on top. He and my mother went on Sunday School outings together, and sat under a big tree beside the river, and hid their faces when someone tried to take their picture. My father's deliberately sunny manner, his ambition and the nature of it—to become a Presbyterian minister—impressed her and appealed to her. She has said that she discovered later that he was not as well educated as she had thought at first. I cannot picture it, but I know that Morris was present at their wedding. I can only wonder, cautiously, about how her grief for Morris's death, a few months later, may have affected her marriage. It is something that I will never be able to ask.

While he was still a divinity student, my father earned a salary as chauffeur for Dr. Shelton, the pastor of one of the large Presbyterian churches in Pittsburgh. Eventually, without graduating, he managed to be ordained and acquire a position as ministerial assistant to the Rev. Stanley Hunter, at North Presbyterian Church on Galveston and North Lincoln Avenues—a step, if an irregular one, toward having a pastorate of his own. It was Dr. Hunter (the origin of my own middle name) who married them in that church, on Wednesday,

Nov. 8, 1922 at 11:30 in the morning. They had been stepping out together for more than two years—to church outings, to lectures. My mother had been fond of going to matinees—theater and opera both. Ethel Barrymore in *Déclassée;* Galli-Curci singing *La Traviata;* Mary Garden singing *Carmen.* On their honeymoon they went to Washington, D.C.—and to the theater, which never interested my father very much.

When they got back they both kept their jobs for a while, until my father was called to his first church, out in the country at Rural Valley, Armstrong County, near where he had been born and had grown up. Years later I learned that while he was still a student, just before the call came, he had been offered a job as a travelling salesman for Wearever Aluminum—he had the samples to prove it, and he had done a bit of selling to show what he could do. My mother had sniffed at the idea, and she came early to disapprove of aluminum for cooking utensils, but when I first learned of the avenue that had not been followed I could not understand why my father had preferred to be a minister. It seemed to me, aged seven or so, that a far more adventurous opportunity had been thrown away, unappreciated.

From the first church they moved on, shortly, to others nearby—Yatesborough, Summerville. Sometimes he would preach at more than one of them on a Sunday, and almost always they were invited home by some member of one of the congregations to Sunday dinner. You served the preacher chicken. That was why chickens ran when they saw the preacher coming.

They had been married for over three years before the first child was born—a boy. My mother always says that he was in every way perfect. But he was injured immediately after birth: some negligence or clumsiness on the part of the doctor or attendant. He was dropped. His skull was damaged and he died of what she calls a rush of blood to the brain, before he was fifteen minutes old. She named him Hanson, and they buried him in the Union Cemetery in Pittsburgh.

His death, just three years after Morris's—he named for her father, and Morris for her mother—seems to have marked the end of youth for my mother, and to have put the seal on many of her expectations. She used to say that she wanted to be buried in the same plot with her firstborn child.

And yet, after Hanson, she had her family. Two children, and her duties as a minister's wife. She did more church work than my father considered necessary. Responsible, efficient, sensible, dependable—entirely. Years of it, of trying to be the best mother possible. She did not brood; is not one for moods, self-pity, melancholy. For decades she seemed never to pause, and yet she has never been what is called nervous. Quick, or—as she says—spry; matter-of-fact; modest but not humble; something of a moral and intellectual snob; practical and courageous and steady. And very determined. Some time after the death and cremation of her cousin Margie, in 1946, she decided that she would prefer to be cremated, herself, when she died. She still said that she would like to have her ashes put in Hanson's grave. Recently she has said she doesn't mind what is done with them, that she will leave that up to the convenience of those who take care of it. She insisted, this last time, on showing me her written instructions, and where they were kept.

Some of her story is fresh to me because I have learned it only since my father died, and I am gradually fitting the new glimpses into what I remember of my mother during my childhood and later. As a child, of course, I did not try to explain her, or think of her as explicable. She was herself. What was so was so, and that was more true of her than of anyone. She was the unquestioned manifestation of the coherence of the world. Her devotion to my sister and me, her solicitude and care for us, were things that both of us took completely for granted. In moments of aggravation she accused us of doing just that, because she did it herself. But beyond the day by day aspect of her existence, which she made over to us consciously, proudly, without fail—though not without moments of resentment—there was always a trackless, twilit, secret country open to no one. Not a dreamland or a cherished mystery into which she retired. It has always been right there with her, like her shadow, whatever she has been doing or saying. It is still there, the real source both of her words and her silence, and Hanson's headstone marks one of its boundaries. To me it seems as though the whole of her life until his death was part of her legendary self, and everything since, whatever else it may have been, has been history.

She has been so capable, reliable, energetic, so reluctant to weigh upon anyone else or relinquish her own decisions, that I have been slow to waken to the change in our positions since my father's illness, and the need for me to begin to take care of her. It has added something to my affection for her, and to my ability to show it, but it is an unfamiliar dance, another growing up, for each of us. The very strangeness of it has helped us with whatever we have managed to convey to each other, since a year ago. She takes more pleasure than ever in going out together, if only to a supermarket. But she does not accept or trust the change without reservation, and she does not seem to regard it as something permanent. As I ponder many of the questions I would like to ask her, I realize that she is no more likely than she ever was to provide answers to them, and since the spring I have been aware that I must ask what I can while there is time. When I was a child, half way to sleep, and was seized by the thought of her death, I lay in the dark crying, wondering how I could make her live longer, and how I would manage to pass the years after her death, until my own. Once at least she came in and found me in tears and asked why. When I told her she said I was not to think about that: it was a long time away, and many things could happen in between, and I would have grown up. It was not something to be afraid of. But lately, when she spoke of the doctor discovering her heart murmur, it struck me that behind her disappointment at having to cancel her trip to Russia, the knowledge gave her a certain satisfaction. It was a confirmation. She appeared to have known for years that her heart was not strong, but had not attached much importance to that, in the world of history. And the fact that it was her heart was evidence of her link with Morris, and with others of her vanished family who had died of ailing hearts. It confirmed that she was heir to her legend. She told me before I left that she did not think her death would be difficult, and that she had a feeling that it was not far off.

She said it on one of the last days I was there. She was sitting in her chair, with her feet up on the big cushion. Her face was calm. Her voice was low and even. She dismissed the subject, except to remind me of something she had already told me: that if she were to die while I was away, she did not want me to waste money coming back for the funeral. If it were to happen that way, she said again, there would be nothing I could do for her anyway. The funeral arrangements had all been taken care of. I would not have to concern myself about any of that. I watch her there when she is asleep, or talking with her eyes closed, her arms on the arms of the chair, hands on the wooden ends of the armrests. Small hands, elegant and trim and smooth. Not the hands of an old woman. Small feet in the gray comfortable shoes she puts on when she comes home. They are old and the gray is cracked. She has always been slightly vain of her feet, and of the fact that they were so narrow, as well as so short, that it was hard for her to find shoes that fit. 5½ quadruple A. I remember her repeating it to salesmen before I first went to school, and their heads shaking with admiration, blankness, or disappointment at not having her size in stock. She is a little vain about her legs, too. They do not seem to have changed in my lifetime, since she was in her thirties. Despite handicaps and barriers made by ourselves and others, it seems that we have approached each other, and have become more frank with each other—but beneath the words, little has really changed between us. When I think of what I want to ask her now, I realize, not for the first time, that the wish to hear, the hankering for information, are almost wholly mine, now, and that as far as she is concerned, perhaps nothing more need be said.

Olive trees, terraced, and above them chestnut groves, high over the sea. Yellow crocuses in the shade. By late morning, that day, the sun was hot, and it was a joy to find figs and large ripe blackberries along the path. The way climbed into the scrub. I heard a bell and looked around and down at the sea, and when I looked back again to where I was, I had wandered aside and lost the faint track. Pushing on in roughly the same direction, I beat a course through arbutus bushes and under chestnut limbs, and found myself in a level, shaded meadow yellow with crocuses and surrounded by ancient chestnut trees. The bell was on the neck of a horse at the far end of the meadow. At the sight of me he made off and disappeared into the woods. I turned back toward the sea, and a little way down the slope came to a one room hermitage, abandoned not long ago. The area outside the door was deep in dry horse dung, and the door itself was open, hanging by one hinge. Inside, the floor boards were still there, but rotting, so that I stepped through, here and there, to the ground a few inches below. The shutters on the windows, the doors to the cupboards in the wall, were still intact. The room was about ten feet by eighteen. The stonework, especially in the fireplace, bespoke skill and care. Two carved limestone corbels, one curve rising above and out of the other, held up the mantel. And the fireplace was built on a single hearthstone rounded at the corners, with a raised lip at the edges, and the fireback rounded, concave, like a deep shell. Sound of the trees, crickets, far away the bell. Below the hermitage I found more berries, a runnel of clear, icy water, and then the path again.

It was not the last time I lost it that day. Early in the afternoon I came to a fork. The way to the left appeared to lead down the cliff. The path to the right looked as though it climbed on over the shoulder of the mountain. I had no map that showed that place. The upper slopes of the mountain were deep in cloud. When I had stopped, not long before, to drink at the cold stream, a monk or muleteer, or monk-muleteer, had passed with a string of mules and horses, and their bells had receded along the path ahead of me before I re-shouldered my pack. Standing at the fork, I heard the bells to my right, some distance above me, and as I peered upward I saw the last of the horses disappear along a narrow ridge, into trees. I turned right. The ascent was so steep that occasionally I needed my hands on the ground in front of me, and I had to pause at shorter and shorter intervals for breath. At first the sun was fierce, but before long the mists began drifting around me and the sweat on my back and face turned chill. The way led into woods and I expected it to start down again toward the western slope, but instead it went on climbing. A congregation of flies followed me, hovering around my head. As I climbed I could hear the bells, in the mist. I scrambled upward for more than two hours, and suddenly, in a pause, I saw, through a rift in the cloud, a bare, utilitarian building, like a base camp or a laboratory or equipment shed. The horses were almost there. The curtain of cloud covered the slope again, and I resumed the climb, doubting the way, wondering whether it led over a pass. It was cold up there, and windy, and I was wet.

The building emerged at last, some hundred yards ahead, and as I approached I could see the horses wandering loose on the bare mountain beyond and above it, where swirling mists hid the summit. Small globe thistles. Black capped warblers. The building was an old *skete*, a house for a small number of monks. I could see that it had been abandoned and was half ruined. Two monks out in back of it were mixing cement, one of them an old man with a long beard, and one who looked like a corsair, with sharp, fierce features, and his head in a kind of turban. The outside of the building was newly cemented over—it looked as though it was not yet dry, because of the humidity of the air—which gave it its bleak, modern appearance. The monks greeted me with some surprise. The path was not the way to Agia Anna. It led only to their *skete*, and from there one could climb to the summit. There was no way from there to Agia Anna except back down the way I had come, and then along the other fork, to the left.

The monks showed me the work they were doing: the repaired walls, the heavy flat stones of the round roof. All the materials, even some of the stones, had arrived there on the backs of the animals grazing the scant vegetation up there in the cloud. The three monks had restored the chapel, with its domed ceiling, and one of them was repainting the frescoes; not much survived of the old ones. The youngest of the monks, brawny and smiling, led me to a spot a few yards beyond the building, and pointed over the edge of the rock. There was a vertical drop. The cliff face melted in cloud below my feet. Cold wind, rising into our faces, snatched at the cloud and tore it, and where it opened I saw that I was looking straight down the other side of the mountain. The blue sea was breaking on huge white rocks, four or five thousand feet directly below me. The monk led me around the building to an opening in the wall on the lowest side. We stepped down to the earthen floor of a large room in which another monk was stirring a large iron pot, over a low fire. The smoke slid up the wall and out through openings in the roof. He was cooking their next meal. They invited me to stay and share it with them, and go down to Agia Anna in the morning, but I knew that I must leave Athos within a few days, and remembered how many places I hoped to visit before going. I thanked the monks. They gave me their blessing, and I set off, back down the mountain.

It was late afternoon as I walked through the woods of tall holly oaks to the west-facing slopes that look down hundreds of feet onto the clustered roofs of Agia Anna. The long, final descent—there seemed to be miles of it—had been cut and built to form a winding marble staircase, the treads polished and scratched by the iron shoes of mules and the heavy hob-nailed soles of monks to a dangerous patina strewn with loose pebbles and gravel. It was easy to slip, and my knees were tired and no longer to be trusted. I went down slowly through the amber light, among the shadows of the holly oaks and then of the olives. At one bend of the path a marble doorway in the hill, to my right, opened into a spring. Lower, a monk riding sidesaddle on a mule passed me, going up. The Athonian greeting is *Evlogite:* "Bless me." The answer is *O Kyrios:* "The Lord."

I came at last to the door in the white outer wall of the *skete* of Agia Anna, and stepped over the high sill into the courtyard. Washed paving stones, the walls giving off the copper light of the late afternoon. At the end of the courtyard a low whitewashed wall, and beyond it, still far below, the sea. The monks were the most welcoming and friendly of any I had met on Athos. Several of them together, and a lay friend, led me to the low wall and showed me the others working, on the terrace just below. They were bringing in the grape harvest in huge purple-stained baskets. Some of the monks were singing as they worked. Kittens were playing, running in and out of lengths of drain pipe. The young monk in charge of visitors brought me the traditional tray of coffee and nougat, ouzo and spring water, and we talked in English. He led me to my room, off a flight of outdoor stairs to the right of the courtyard. It was small, light, airy. The window looked out on the sea and the next peninsula, on the western horizon. Standing there, I tried without success to remember something about St. Anne.

The *skete* is not famous for its frescoes or ikons or architecture, but it is simple and beautiful. It looks as though the monks there love it, and love working on it. It is white, fresh, tended. I had supper with them in a lower room like a cabin on a boat. They were tired but elated by the day's work, and smelled of grapes, and dust, and sweat. We ate potatoes and eggplant and tomatoes and onions and olives and salad and bread, and drank some of their soft amber-colored wine. They said there was not much of it left from last year's harvest. The monks make rosaries and I bought one for my mother. Then I went to bed and slept, and woke with the day already bright.

The young monk who spoke English led me to a breakfast complete with ouzo, and urged me to more of everything, to fortify me for the day's walk. We sat talking, and when I had gathered up my sack we walked together slowly to the main gate and said good-bye as though we had known each other for a long time. It was a clear, still morning. The path along the slope to the New Skete is broad and level, and passes through the shade of olives and holly oaks. At the approach to the New Skete there were overhead arbors with thick, branching, old grape vines. A young monk who spoke English invited me in, plied me with a second breakfast, told me of their gardens, and their ikon painting, and—in his own case—the study of mathematics. Many of the monks there have some subject that they are studying. All the ones I saw were young, cheerful, welcoming, and it was late morning before I found myself again on the craggy west slope of the mountain, in the fiery sunlight. The dewy smell of the earlier hours, the walk under the shady trees, the welcome at the two white *sketes*, suddenly were far behind me.

The cliff fell away abruptly on my left, into a tangle of bushes and trees clinging to the rock face, high above the sea. As I walked I fell to thinking, as I had been doing during the past few days, of the presence of The Virgin on Athos.

Trying to grasp a word in a foreign language. In the legends the whole peninsula is her garden. It was one thing to accept that as local history, tradition, folklore, and another to grope toward what it might mean to those for whom it has been, and still is, the live truth. My childhood in the Presbyterian Church was no help. And I had grown up in the twentieth century, and whatever my opinion of my own era, it was the only one I knew, and it went along with me, even on the footpaths of Athos. But so did that face on the ikons, and what had been seen and painted into it, and returned from it constantly. Where was The Virgin, after all? What was she? How did they speak to her, and what was it in them that spoke? Who were they addressing? Walking along in the noonday sun, leaving the Skete of St. Anne, I wanted to try to speak to that presence, to invoke her attention for my own mother, to tell her that my mother did not have much longer to live, to pray that her death would be—what? Gentle, painless, but above all, a fulfilment. Blessed, whatever that meant. I did not know how to ask, and I became aware that I did not really know what to ask, and that in fact there was probably nothing to ask after all.

A moment came that brought me a sudden assurance so clear and calm, and so unexpected, that I paused and turned away from the sunlight on the sea. I was certain, as though it were a piece of common knowledge, that my mother would not suffer at her death; that the end of her life, when it came, would be merciful, a release. Then, as I walked on, and later in the day, I wondered whether what I believed I knew at that moment and afterwards was the *same* as what she herself believed she knew, and had told me.

Two days later I climbed to the great monastery of Simopetra, on its crag, and arrived while the siesta still reigned. I was shown into a large, breezy, whitewashed room, with blue window frames lining the weathered balcony that was perched above the sheer drop. Beyond the gray, splintered railing, the sea. Around the walls, under yellowing pictures of deceased potentates, seven iron beds with the same plank springs and thin mattresses. In the middle of the room a round table with a central three-footed leg, and a patchwork table-cloth of faded velvets, a long fringe that reached almost to the floor, and the date 1922 embroidered on it. A single chair by the table. A kerosene lamp hanging over the table, from the board ceiling that had been painted gray, perhaps that long ago. Sound of donkeys in the courtyard. Pigeons on the roof. Voice of a monk talking to the donkeys. A loose bit of bed iron slatting in the breeze. Smell of beans from the kitchen, of basil from the courtyard, rue from the cliff under the sun. From the south windows, a full sight of the summit of the mountain, silvery gray, floating in clouds. I was the only guest.

I knew that I would be leaving Athos the next day, and in the somnolent afternoon I wrote to my mother. I had a post card of the monastery and could mark my window. I told her about Agia Anna, the Skete of St. Anne, and the paint-ings, the monasteries, the mountains. I planned to send her what I had written, either from the post office at Daphni, the port of the mountain, or else from a post office later in the day, in the world outside. I thought as I sat there that it might be one of the last times I would write to her before I left Europe on my way back to see her.

I did not know, of course, that by the time the words, and the picture of the monastery, with an arrow pointing to a window on the top floor, entered the white door of the farmhouse in Pennsylvania, my mother would be dead. That she would have had another relapse of the flu that had hung on all summer, and would have gone to the old retired doctor in whom she and her friends had little faith, and that he would have given her a cold shot, and she would have reached home feeling worse, on a thundery rainy afternoon, and looked out at the wet garden from the glassed-in back porch, and tele-phoned to a friend and said that she was feeling tired and was going to have a cup of tea and then go to bed and get some rest. And that the thunderstorms would go on, through the dusk and into the darkness, and Bea would telephone at her own bedtime and get no answer, and be worried, and drive over in the stormy night, and see no lights on, and splash to the door of the back porch and let herself in, and trip over my mother's body on the floor where she had fallen, an hour or two before, as she got up from the table and suddenly felt dizzy, overturning the empty cup.

While the shadows of the walkers flicker past, and I watch the race from behind the spectators, through them, a line and its passage from the *Purgatorio* that have been running in my head all week on the mountain, like a tune, start up again: *e riposato della lunga via.* "And (you have/thou hast) rested from the long way." *Via*, the journey, with its continuing echo or reminder of *vita;* the journey through death that is the way of life, and of the poem. Not in the text, that echo, but summoned by it. The line itself is from the ending of the fifth canto, after the resounding, terrifying, rolling, storm-charged monologue in which Buonconte, missing since the battle of Campaldino, eleven years before the ideal date of the poem's setting, tells of his own end, "wounded in the throat, fleeing on foot and bloodying the plain." And how he called with his last breath on the name of Mary, and an angel snatched his soul, but a devil, in revenge, unleashed storm and flood upon his body. His story has just finished and the full sound and awe of it are reverberating, when the voice of La Pia, diffident, gentle, startling, follows without a break. She must have been close at hand through Buonconte's great speech, because a voice so shy and yet so intimate would not have carried far. She must have been waiting for him to finish, in order to say the few words that are all we know of her. Of the six lines that are hers, in her place outside Purgatory, the first two—a third of the whole—are concerned with the person whom she is addressing: Dante, the pilgrim, the dreamer, the protagonist, the soul. He does not ask for her story; she has to catch his attention. *Deh*, she says. That untranslatable syllable: "oh thou", or "pray". They are not our words. How far from us that form of address is now. We do not know how to use it, how to say it. Yet it is still ours somewhere, because what she is saying is clear, and immediately, inexplicably troubling. *Deh, quando tu sarai tornato al mondo:* "Pray (or, "oh thou") when thou shalt be returned to the world." Something which she herself does not hope ever to do. The line is wistful, the utterance of someone who has suffered loss and grief. There is no reference to herself. The few plain words describing his hope, foretelling its issue, depict the vast gulf between her situation and his, but there is no envy in them, nor in the following line with its image of the rest to which he can look forward— the line that has been running through my head. "Oh thou, when thou shalt be returned to the world/ and (thou hast) rested from the long way . . ." Her words encourage him, congratulate him for the event that she forsees for him, and look forward to a comfort that she does not envisage for herself.

Since everyone in the poem is another reflection of Dante the protagonist, the soul, and of Dante the poet, the image-maker, it is not surprising if La Pia's words wake a distant echo of the opening of a sonnet which Dante had written many years before: *Deh peregrini che pensosi andate.* That same greeting, *Deh.* "Oh you pilgrims who walk deep in thought." In contrast to the formality of the beautiful earlier verse, one hears in the later one a naked directness, and the resonance of experience. In the sonnet Dante, the solitary speaker, the representative and in a sense the sole inhabitant, the body politic, of his *citta dolente*, his sorrowing city (in which he is closer to the situation of the *Inferno* than to that of the *Purgatorio*—the sonnet is a dramatization of despair) speaks of the nameless pilgrims walking deep in their own thought of something, perhaps, which is not present before them. They are outsiders, persons of another condition, strangers to his loss, and his city's loss, of their Beatrice, their blessing and their hope. He is concerned not with them but with his own loss and grief. He expresses surprise that they are not lamenting as they walk through his city. They are outsiders to his universe, where knowledge is awareness of pain and despair, and he attributes their separation from it to ignorance of what to him is the universal sorrow. Their own aspiration and goal is never imagined. Instead he tells them that if they stay he will make them weep. La Pia begins by speaking out of her loss without saying anything about it; she starts by evoking the blessing that lies before him. In her words it is evident that she does not expect him to pause for more than a moment.

And when she has spoken those first lines we still do not know who she is, and Dante the poet, with his peerless sense of the value of every syllable, spends the whole of the next line developing, emphasizing, her reticence, in his own voice, and not telling us. She is identified simply in terms of the order in which she speaks in the situation: the *terzo spirito*, the third spirit—of the canto, and of who knows what else—following the second. Perhaps for the moment it is all of her that he can recognize. She knows more of him and his fate than he himself can claim to know, in his body that still casts a shadow when the sun rises. She stands deeper in his mind than he, the protagonist, knows, and it may be that when she speaks to him he can recall nothing of her, that he has forgotten her.

Her own voice resumes, with her only request: for him to remember her. *Ricorditi di me, che son La Pia:* "Remember (thee of) me, who am La Pia." He does, and we do—but who is she, the shade standing on the nether side of mortal existence, at the foot of the mountain of liberation, to which she has not been admitted? What relation does what we now remember bear to the woman who suffered, and whom Dante at one time, presumably, knew? Who was she in the life from which she has brought to Dante's mind and poem the memory and name that still signify, to her, herself: "who *am* La Pia?" Her next three lines end the canto and all that we know of her. They bring both to completion, and yet they leave both floating, continuing, echoing. The lines are brief, it seems, even for Dante, and condensed as they are they provide something less and more than historical location. Less, because their enigmatic statements no longer serve—and there is no way of knowing whether they ever did—to identify the individual speaker. More, because the allusive, deeply wrought verses have a magnetic power, of a kind that occurs throughout the poem, which draws the listener to the enigma itself, and they have led readers in each generation since they were written to search the records of Dante's age for the single victim who was La Pia, and to find instead instances of unvoiced suffering—unvoiced suffering itself. What did she look like? How old was she? She has been painted, and portrayed in words, but nobody knows who it was who spoke of herself—in Dante's mind—in terms of her own suffering, and asked to be remembered for it, and by it. What violent death had she suffered, that he, and we, are to remember? And why was she there among "the late-repentant?" We have only those lines.

First, the one that haunts *The Wasteland* and supplied Pound with a title for a poem in *Hugh Selwyn Mauberly*: *Sienna mi fe', disfecemi Maremma*, "Siena made me, Maremma unmade me." At once lapidary and ghostly. Geographically specific, and yet—partly because of its formality and its antithetical symmetry, its perfection—oddly remote from the experience it places, and of course from the places themselves. More detached from the speaker than the first gentle lines in which she does not refer to herself. And the rest is her story, which no one now can claim to understand historically, yet which everyone, I imagine, is caught by, hearing in it something unplaceable but distantly familiar:

"he knows it who, first betrothed, had wedded me with his gem." The words knotted out of order, and ending with that *gemma*, her last syllables: the stone, the humanly prized thing out of the earth, the crystal, the focus, the symbol, the gauge, the promise, the enduring impersonal source of radiance.

I have fished the book out of my pocket and gone over the lines and the commentary again, as one does in the hope of hearing through them what is there to be remembered, something more, La Pia. I am thinking of those measureless feminine figures—she is one of them—with which Dante marks the phases of the divine journey, and I am looking out at the empty harbor when I hear someone close at hand say my name. It is Valentinos, who I met a few days ago, on the mountain. He is still covered with the dust and stubble of the week's travels, as I am. A black beret. The long face of an amused owl, the features individually rounded and pink, and further reddened by the sun. Round glasses, above which his eyebrows are generally raised in an expression of pleased, intelligent curiosity. Late thirties, or forty. Sandy hair receding from his high forehead. Short, lively, with one twisted leg shorter than the other, the gnarled right foot in a black, laced, orthopedic shoe. He had not been able to walk much of the way on Athos because of his limp, and he was with a group of young men, a party of nine, from Athens, who all took the fishing boat, most days, from the landing below one monastery to the landing below the next one. Sometimes when the weather was favorable there was more than one boat a day, and it was possible to visit several monasteries, travelling by sea. The young men laughed and pounded each other's shoulders—but not Valentinos'. One of them strummed a guitar and moustache, and sported a wide, stiff-brimmed, ethnic straw hat. Valentinos was older than the others and they addressed him with respect. He had read widely, in the numerous languages he knew: Greek, French, Italian, German, Russian, Turkish, and some English. Since I was travelling on foot, I would set out in the morning before his party caught the fishing boat. Sometimes we would meet at the next monastery on the perimeter of the peninsula, for the mid-day meal, and sometimes again in the evening, so that almost every day there was the pleasure of laughing and greeting again after an interval, and having new travels to recount.

Two days ago we arrived at the same time, in the early afternoon, at the huge nineteenth century Russian monastery of St. Pantaleimon, on the west coast of Athos. At the turn of the century it had housed twelve hundred monks, and had been important to the Russian imperial ambition to acquire a port on the Mediterranean. From the outside the buildings look like sections of a factory compound built a hundred years ago, with Russian ecclesiastical domes on top. There have been disastrous fires, and decades of neglect. A Dutch scholar who had worked there told me that their manuscript library consists of a great mound of papers on the floor in the middle of a big room. Only a few monks live there now, and they are very poor. But one of the cupolas still lodges a monster bell—a Russian monk said that it was the largest bell in the world outside Moscow, where it had been made. The monk fetches keys and leads visitors around the rooms of state and the upstairs church which is large, full of daylight, wood-panelled, a marked contrast to the compact, dim, ancient, plastered and frescoed churches in the courtyards of the Greek monasteries. He points out the large, late paintings: St. George, portraits of the Czars. I went around with Valentinos and his friends. Valentinos translated the Russian mixed with Russian-Greek into French for me, and as we walked out he remarked, smiling benevolently on all that he had just seen, and putting some money into a box on the wall, "Very imposing—and very ugly."

So we have one more meeting, unplanned, beside the harbor —a chance to review the hours since we left Ouranopolis, just outside the Athonian border, early this morning, and to exclaim over the crowds, this evening, in the city. He is not staying the night, so the packed hotels present no problem for him. He is catching a plane to Athens within a couple of hours, and does not have time to sit down and order a drink. He plans to be home tonight. We have already exchanged addresses, and we turn our good wishes again to his autumn in Athens, and my return journey to Pennsylvania to see my mother. We talk about her for a moment. He is shifting his feet, preparing to leave. We begin our valedictory congratulations and our hopes to meet again soon. We are speaking French, standing between the table where I have been sitting, and the backs of the thinning line of spectators. It looks as though the race is over. People are drifting away from the square in clusters of three or four, talking, gesturing, laughing. A woman in a black dress, standing on the street below the curb, is looking up at me, watching me.

She is heavy, middle-aged, her thick hair done up in a loose bun. Her face too is ponderous: large nose, folds under the eyes, fallen cheeks. The dress is the mourning garb of many women of her age in the city, but she wears it with a carelessness that sets her apart from any obvious category, and she is hatless, looking as though she had not dressed specially for the street but had simply stepped out for a moment in her indoor clothes. The dress is in two layers: a black voile over shiny black cotton or satin. Black stockings, thick ankles, long-suffering feet and their black shoes. Valentinos has his back to her, but she catches my eye, and then catches it again and smiles and says something to me. I bend toward her. "Bon jour," she says, louder, rolling the *r* only slightly. I return the greeting, and she says, in French, "I heard you speaking French."

I nod.

"Are you French?"

I tell her that we are not, that my friend is Greek and I am an American. She is curious to know why we are speaking French and how and where we learned it, and I say something about it being a language we both know, and Valentinos says he will have to go and catch his plane. We say our farewells and I walk a few steps with him and then turn back to the table and pay the waiter. The woman is still looking up, watching me. She says she heard us talk about Athos—had we been to Athos? We speak of that, for a moment, and of the Fair. She says she heard me mention my mother, and I nod.

She tells me that she learned French in France, in Grenoble. She studied hard, so that she could come back and work as a governess, to be a help to her husband—in a moment she is telling me her life story, one long account of hope disappointed, of cultural aspirations and commercial enterprise. In spite of her French and her work as governess and secretary to help her husband he had slipped away from her. She is evasive as to what happened to him, whether or not he is dead. She still works as a *gouvernante*. She tells me the names of some of her former employers, and of her present one. And she has brought up her son. He is a young man now, taller than his father, and even better looking. But her son does not care about her, his own mother. He is never at home. He comes back for meals, which she cooks for him, and for clean clothes which she launders for him, and for money which she gives him out of her earnings, but he is never satisfied with anything she does for him, and she is ashamed to say that he has even stolen from her. When she caught him he said it was not theft if he stole from his own mother, and he has done it again, since then. Nothing of hers is safe from him. And in spite of all that he is really a good boy, if only he went around with better friends. She has no one she can talk to about him. She cannot speak openly of such things with her Greek friends and neighbors—I must understand that—and she does not want her employer to find out about the boy's behavior. She might lose her job, and her references for another. But in French, to someone with education, someone from abroad, she can talk. She tells me that her French is growing poorer all the time because she has no chance to practice it here.

She asks me how long I am going to be in the city, and is disappointed when I tell her that I plan to leave tomorrow morning. The sun has gone down in the haze over the harbor. She would have liked to invite me for a meal, she says, at the place where she and her son live, and have him dine with us, if she could persuade him to stay home for one evening. But she knows he would be interested to meet me, she insists. An American. She is sure I would be a good influence on him. I could give him an interest in his studies, in learning languages. At present he will not even try to learn French. She tries to teach him, a word at a time, but he will not repeat them. She tells me that there is room in her apartment, and she asks me where I am staying. I tell her, and I say that my baggage is there, but she answers that I can stay at her apartment if I would like to. I think of the luggage behind the manager's desk, the crowded hotel room, the early train tomorrow morning. I consider going back to the hotel, repacking everything, there in the office, among the legs of those waiting around the desk, while she stands outside somewhere, perhaps. I imagine negotiating with the manager for the deposit, and no doubt losing it, and shouldering all the gear and setting out with her, to listen to her the whole way along the sidewalk to her apartment, and all the rest of the evening. I think of it through the fatigue of the week's walking and the day's long bus ride through the mountains. She continues to talk, and enlarges upon her invitation. I thank her, and tell her of my reservation, at the hotel, and say that I had been about to go back there. She says her son acts as though he does not love her, and that many children nowadays do not love their mothers. She asks me whether I love my mother.

The question stops whatever else I am thinking, and I stare at her swollen features, their expression of a hopeless demand, a deepening isolation. What does she mean by her question?

I say, "Yes," blankly, and the word drops away into space.

And I take my leave of her then, shaking her fat, gray, moist, persistent hand, wishing her well, turning away and stepping into the square from which most of the crowd has gone now, and crossing the area that until a few minutes ago held the circling energy of the contestants.

About the Author

W. S. MERWIN was born in New York City in 1927 and grew up in New Jersey and Pennsylvania. He worked as a tutor in France, Portugal, and Majorca, and has translated from French, Spanish, Latin, and Portuguese. He has published more than a dozen volumes of original poetry and several volumes of prose, including his memoir of life in the south of France, *The Lost Upland*, and a new book of poems, *Travels*. He has been the recipient of a PEN Translation Prize, the Fellowship of the Academy of American Poets, the Bollingen Prize, and the Pulitzer Prize, among many others. He lives in Hawaii and is active in environmental causes.